Current Issues in
U.S. Defense Policy

Center for Defense Information

edited by

David T. Johnson
Barry R. Schneider

Published in cooperation with the
Center for Defense Information

The Praeger Special Studies program—
utilizing the most modern and efficient book
production techniques and a selective
worldwide distribution network—makes
available to the academic, government, and
business communities significant, timely
research in U.S. and international economic, social, and political development.

Current Issues in
U.S. Defense Policy

PRAEGER SPECIAL STUDIES IN INTERNATIONAL POLITICS AND GOVERNMENT

Praeger Publishers   New York   Washington   London

Library of Congress Cataloging in Publication Data

Center for Defense Information.
    Current issues in U.S. defense policy.

    (Praeger special studies in international
politics and government)
    Includes index.
    1. United States—Military policy.   2. United
States—Armed Forces.   3. Weapons systems.
I. Johnson, David Thomas, 1923-   II. Schneider,
Barry R.   III. Title.
UA23.C43   1976   355.03'3073   75-23990
ISBN 0-275-56020-1

PRAEGER PUBLISHERS
111 Fourth Avenue, New York, N.Y. 10003, U.S.A.

Published in the United States of America in 1976
by Praeger Publishers, Inc.

Printed in the United States of America

In 1972, with the help of many others, I established the Center for Defense Information (CDI) as an independent and nonpartisan research and educational agency. Its primary purpose is to provide sound analyses of U.S. military policies, weapon systems, and spending. Based on these analyses, alternative policies are recommended when it appears in the national interest to do so. CDI evaluates U.S. military past performances, current operations, and plans for the future. As the only organization of its kind that does not accept government money, or money from defense contractors, it is perhaps special in its independence.

The center has a staff of analysts with extensive military, government, and research experience. All are in accord that military force is of decreasing utility in settling international differences, and all seek alternatives to the use of military force to achieve national objectives.

Nuclear war would probably spell the end of civilization on earth as we know it. Yet more nations are acquiring nuclear weapons and both the United States and the Soviet Union increase their stockpiles daily. With each passing year, the danger of nuclear war increases.

The United States cannot sustain military policies that do not have broad-based and informed support. It is absolutely essential that a dialogue be established between the public and its government. We are hopeful that these chapters covering the spectrum of important contemporary defense issues will help to fill a vacuum and stimulate greater public awareness of matters that are too often left to government "experts."

The Center for Defense Information has, from its inception, supported a strong national defense, but has opposed excessive spending and unneeded forces or weapons systems. We continue to believe that strong social, political and economic structures are as essential to national security as is military defense, and that their needs must be met if we are to continue to have a strong and vital nation.

Each chapter in this book appears under the name of its senior author or editor. Most of these chapters, however, are products of the joint work of the entire staff of the Center for Defense Information.

Rear Admiral Gene R. La Rocque
U.S. Navy (Retired)
Director
Center for Defense Information

CONTENTS

Page

PREFACE   v
Rear Admiral Gene R. La Rocque

LIST OF TABLES   viii

LIST OF FIGURES AND MAPS   ix

LIST OF ABBREVIATIONS   x

PART I: U.S. FORCES ABROAD

Chapter

1   U.S. POLICY AND THE LESSONS OF VIETNAM   3
    David T. Johnson

2   U.S. FORCES FOR EUROPE AND THE MBFR TALKS   17
    David T. Johnson

3   KOREA AND U.S. STRATEGY FOR NORTHEAST ASIA   42
    Stefan H. Leader

4   JAPAN UNDER U.S. PRESSURE   61
    Dennis F. Verhoff

5   THE INDIAN OCEAN: A NEW NAVAL ARMS RACE   79
    David T. Johnson

6   U.S. ARMS TO THE PERSIAN GULF   99
    Robert Berman

PART II: U.S. WEAPONS PROGRAMS

7   OVERVIEW OF THE MILITARY BUDGET   115
    David T. Johnson

Chapter   Page

8   U.S.-SOVIET STRATEGIC FORCES: SALT AND
THE SEARCH FOR PARITY   129
Stefan H. Leader and Barry R. Schneider

9   NUCLEAR MISSILE SUBMARINES AND NUCLEAR
STRATEGY   153
Phil Stanford

10   THE B-1 BOMBER   166
Robert Berman

11   U.S. TACTICAL NUCLEAR WEAPONS:
A CONTROVERSIAL ARSENAL   176
Barry R. Schneider

12   TACTICAL NUCLEAR WEAPONS:
FOUR PEACETIME SAFETY DILEMMAS   195
Barry R. Schneider

13   THE GLOBAL AUTOMATED BATTLEFIELD   201
Phil Stanford

14   U.S. TACTICAL AIR FORCES: TECHNOLOGY
OUTPACES MANAGEMENT   216
Robert W. Whitaker

15   THE MILITARIZATION OF OUTER SPACE   236
James Willis

INDEX   248

ABOUT THE EDITORS AND CONTRIBUTORS   255

LIST OF TABLES

Table		Page
3.1	Comparative Military Strengths: North and South Korea	49
3.2	U.S. Nuclear Arms in South Korea	52
3.3	U.S. Military Assistance and Sales to South Korea	54
4.1	Japanese Self-Defense Forces	64
4.2	U.S. Military Personnel in Japan	73
4.3	Seventh Fleet Home Port in Japan	73
4.4	Major U.S. Bases in Japan and Okinawa	74
6.1	U.S. Foreign Military Sales and Orders to the Persian Gulf Countries, 1950–75	100
6.2	Conflicts in the Persian Gulf Region	105
6.3	Iranian Military Growth	107
7.1	Acquisition Costs of Major Weapons Systems	117
8.1	U.S. and Soviet Missile Accuracy	132
8.2	U.S. and Soviet Nuclear Weapon Launchers, 1975	133
8.3	U.S. and Soviet Nuclear Destructive Power	136
8.4	U.S. Strategic Megatonnage, 1974	137
8.5	Soviet Strategic Megatonnage, 1974	138
8.6	U.S. and Soviet Strategic Nuclear Weapons, 1970–75	143
10.1	Nuclear Weapons in U.S. Strategic Forces	167
10.2	Performance Characteristics of the B-52 and B-1	170
10.3	B-1 Life-Cycle Costs	173

Table   Page

11.1 U.S. Tactical Nuclear Weapons Widely Dispersed   180

14.1 Four U.S. Air Forces   222

LIST OF FIGURES AND MAPS

Figure

4.1 U.S. Military Forces in the Far East   72

8.1 Soviet Population and Industrial Capacity Destroyed   142

14.1 $42 Billion in New Aircraft Up Over 40 Percent
      from Estimates   218

14.2 15-Year Life-Cycle Costs per Aircraft   219

Map

5.1 Military Facilities in the Indian Ocean Region
     (Western Section)   80

5.2 Military Facilities in the Indian Ocean Region
     (Central Section)   81

5.3 Military Facilities in the Indian Ocean Region
     (Eastern Section)   82

6.1 The Persian Gulf Tinderbox   101

LIST OF ABBREVIATIONS

AABNCP	Advanced Airborne Command Post
AAH	Advanced Attack Helicopter
ABM	Antiballistic Missile System
AEC	Atomic Energy Commission
AFB	Air Force Base
ALCM	Air-launched Cruise Missile
ARPA	Advanced Research Project Agency
ASDF	Air Self-Defense Forces (Japan)
ASROC	Antisubmarine Rocket
ASW	Antisubmarine Warfare
AWACS	Airborne Warning and Control System
BASS	Remotely Monitored Battlefield Sensor System
CEP	Circular Error of Probability
CIA	Central Intelligence Agency
DOD	Department of Defense
DDR & E	Director of Defense Research and Engineering
ECM	Electronic Countermeasures
EMT	Equivalent Megatonnage
FOBS	Fractional Orbital Bombardment System
GSDF	Ground Self-Defense Forces (Japan)
ICBM	Intercontinental Ballistic Missile
JCS	Joint Chiefs of Staff
JDA	Japanese Defense Agency
MARV	Terminally Guided Maneuverable Reentry Vehicles
MBFR	Mutual Balanced Force Reductions (talks between NATO and Warsaw Pact)
MIRV	Multiple Independently Targeted Reentry Vehicles
MIT	Massachusetts Institute of Technology
MSDF	Maritime Self-Defense Forces (Japan)
MST	Treaty of Mutual Cooperation and Security between the United States and Japan
NACF	Naval Air Combat Fighter
NASA	National Aeronautics and Space Administration
NATO	North Atlantic Treaty Organization
NORAD	North American Air-Defense Command
QRA	Quick Reaction Alert (aircraft or missile)
RPV	Remotely Piloted Vehicles
SALT	Strategic Arms Limitation Talks
SAM	Surface-to-Air Missile
SDF	Self-Defense Forces (Japan)
SIAM	Self-Initiating Antiaircraft Munition
SNW	Strategic Nuclear Weapons

SOSUS	Sound Surveillance Under Sea
SUBROC	Antisubmarine Rockets fired by submarine
TACAIR	Tactical Air Forces
TNW	Tactical or Theater Nuclear Weapons
TOW	Antitank missile (Tube-launched, Optically-tracked, Wire-guided)

U.S. FORCES ABROAD

U.S. POLICY
AND THE LESSONS
OF VIETNAM

David T. Johnson

The Vietnam War ended in spring 1975. What is to be learned from this costly experience that stretched over decades at the expense of hundreds of thousands of lives and hundreds of billions of dollars? What are the implications for the United States of the greatest foreign policy disaster in American history? What efforts are American leaders making to learn the lessons of Vietnam and put them into practice? What changes are needed in U.S. defense policy?

A call for "no recriminations" about Vietnam should not be a call for national forgetfulness. It does not preclude reexamination. Some in the Congress have begun an effort to outline foreign policy objectives that incorporate the lessons of the Vietnam experience. Though many feel that the end of the Vietnam War should provide an opportunity for a fundamental reassessment of U.S. policies, the nearness of the tragedy has inhibited discussion. As a result, there has been no extensive national debate on the lessons of Vietnam and the direction of future U.S. foreign policy.

In summer 1975, the Senate initiated an effort to examine the lessons of Vietnam. In the wake of the final collapse of U.S. policy in Indochina, the Senate for the first time in many years made a significant effort to consider the military budget in the context of U.S. foreign policy. The attempt to assure that defense spending serves the aims of U.S. foreign policy and to adjust that policy to new realities sets an important precedent for the future. The Congress adopted a measure requiring the preparation by the executive branch, beginning in 1976, of an annual report explaining the relationship of our military force structure to our foreign policy. This report is to provide a possible focus for future debate. While such a report may help to sharpen the issues and alternatives, additional congressional initiatives may be needed to continue the debate.

Those responsible for recent U.S. foreign policy appear reluctant to support such a national reexamination or to question the assumptions of old policies. For these leaders, the sooner the American people forget Vietnam the better. President Ford says that "the lessons of the past in Vietnam have already been learned, learned by presidents, learned by Congress, learned by the American people."[1] He does not welcome congressional or other inquiry. He suggests that we should put Vietnam behind us, avoid recriminations, and focus on the future. Secretary of State Henry Kissinger agrees that "the Vietnam debate has now run its course."[2]

Have the lessons of Vietnam actually been learned? And what are they? President Ford provides little guidance. No systematic or thoughtful effort has been conducted by the government to examine these issues. President Ford says that we have "learned some lessons concerning how we would conduct a military operation,"[3] but has nothing more profound to suggest beyond such tactical matters. Secretary Kissinger has mentioned several important lessons that he believes have been learned from Vietnam but has not given the public any coherent statement. He is generally complacent and includes "a sound foreign policy design" among the country's "strong assets."[4]

The dominant activity within the executive branch stemming from the Vietnam War is a push to loosen congressional and public opinion restraints on the government's power of intervention and freedom of action abroad. Those who still raise doubts are frequently labeled "isolationists." The American people are to be reawakened to the "realities of power" and their "responsibilities" around the world.

Despite 15 years of U.S. attempts to secure a military solution in Indochina, former Secretary of Defense James Schlesinger stated that for the future our objective, as a great power, is to display a somewhat greater degree of steadfastness and "moral stamina."[5] Secretary Kissinger proclaims the need for "increasing our exertions" and a more "abrasive" policy.[6] In drawing lessons from Vietnam, the dominant thrust of official studies is directed towards increasing military effectiveness, how to "win" future conflicts with new technologies and new techniques, instead of how to avoid them.[7]

The urgency of the task of undertaking a serious, comprehensive, and objective exploration of the lessons of Vietnam is underlined by evidence that lessons have not been learned, despite President Ford's claim. For example, the Mayaguez incident repeated many of the defects in U.S. policy in Vietnam: the inadequate use of political and diplomatic means; a premature resort to force; inadequate consultation with Congress; acting on incomplete and faulty information;

exaggerated justifying rhetoric; and too much concern for "image."
The United States now is moving towards expanding its military
presence in the Indian Ocean, adding to the burden of U.S. military
involvements even though questions have been raised about the wisdom
and ability of the United States to carry out its existing defense commitments. Officials make veiled threats of military intervention to
secure oil supplies in the Middle East when one of the lessons of
Vietnam should be to question military solutions for clearly nonmilitary problems.

No brief discussion of lessons of the Vietnam War can be
adequate or free of defect and exception. The world is too complex,
the choices open for the future are too many, to be comprehended in
short statements or a collection of guidelines. The fact that political
realities around the world do not always correspond to our simplistic
theories and slogans is itself one of the lessons of Vietnam. New
situations need to be perceived in their own time and place—not as
duplicates of earlier ones.

Secretary Kissinger perceives a difference in attitude between
his generation, whose lessons were fundamentally formed in the origins and consequences of World War II and the Cold War, and more
recent generations. He has asserted that "America faces as well the
problem of its new generation. The gulf between their historical
experience and ours is enormous. They have been traumatized by
Vietnam as we were by Munich."[8] But it appears that Secretary
Kissinger continues to give precedence to the traumatic lessons of
Munich and to question the validity of lessons derived from more
recent and more pertinent experience. Is it not possible to learn
from experience without being traumatized by it? One lessons of
Vietnam is that situations need to be seen as they are when they arise.
Viewing the present through the eyes of the past, seeing Munich in
Southeast Asia, can lead to disaster. New challenges must be seen
anew each time they arise.

This analysis identifies major areas where the Vietnam experience indicates that new emphases or directions are needed in U.S.
policy and that they require further debate. This endeavor is a prerequisite for the development of a new foreign policy that seeks to
avoid the mistakes of the past.

LESSON 1: COMMITMENT

In contrast to an earlier period when the United States eagerly
thrust itself militarily into every corner of the world, it is widely
accepted that the United States must now be very careful in the

commitments it makes. Secretary Kissinger has suggested one aspect: "One lesson we must surely learn from Vietnam is that new commitments of our national honor and prestige must be carefully weighed. . . . We must weigh carefully—as we failed to do in the early sixties—the long-term consequences of new engagements. We must not overextend ourselves, promising what is not either in our interest or within our capability."[9]

Although most Americans would agree that the United States needs to define more carefully its role in the world and to be somewhat less ambitious militarily, many American policy makers still have doubts about this lesson and continue to be attracted to the U.S. role as the world's policeman. The overblown conception of the U.S. world role that in great part led to the Vietnam involvement still has strong acceptance within the executive branch. Secretary Schlesinger divined that "historical necessity has thrust upon us" the role of maintaining worldwide military equilibrium. "The burden of responsibility," he stated, "has fallen on the United States, and there is nobody else to pick up the torch if the United States fails to carry it."[10] If the role of the United States is to be somewhat restricted, the difference is that other countries are to be recruited to help be cops on the beat. World police headquarters, however, is still to be in Washington. We have the capacity to exercise a more positive leadership.

U.S. policy of almost unlimited arms sales to the countries on the Persian Gulf, nearly $11 billion since 1972, and the new involvements in the Indian Ocean, also put in doubt whether "the long term consequences of new engagements" are being carefully assessed as Secretary Kissinger asserts. There may be doubts that "we have learned our limits."[11]

If the United States aspires to control rather than influence the flow of international events, the risk of being dragged into new conflicts peripheral to U.S. interests will remain too high. The costs will also be unbearable. Former State Department official Eugene Rostow has said that "American treaties and other commitments are the only cement of the world political system."[12] But most of our alliances were forged in the Cold War confrontations of the 1940s and 1950s. These commitments and involvements must be reexamined to determine if they still serve U.S. and allied interests. We should be careful that our policies dictate our commitments, not the other way around, as has happened too often.

LESSON 2: MILITARY FORCE

One of the most beneficial outcomes of Vietnam has been to raise questions about the limits of military force as an instrument of U.S. foreign policy. The dangers of precipitate use of military force and the inadequacy of military means to solve complex political and economic problems such as were confronted in Indochina are now widely perceived. There are greater inhibitions today on the American propensity toward military intervention and covert operations than there were before the Vietnam War. We recognize that more efforts must be made to resolve problems when they are susceptible to accommodation and compromise instead of waiting until they raise the danger of confrontation and possible use of military force.

The militarization of U.S. foreign policy, however, is still a major concern. Deputy Defense Secretary William Clements has stated a view that, unfortunately, is still widely shared within the executive branch: "In our ever changing world, strength means military strength."[13] The recent report of the Murphy Commission accurately perceived the need to strengthen the State Department and diplomacy in relation to the Defense Department and the military instrument.[14] Policy makers continue to see a very intimate connection between U.S. influence and U.S. military power. It is Secretary Kissinger's belief that "diplomacy which is not related to a plausible employment of force is sterile."[15] In part because of this habitual attachment to armed force as the determinant of national influence, the military budget is increasing substantially, reaching a record $105 billion in fiscal 1976.

A narrow perception of U.S. military power is also strongly held by many U.S. policy makers. Secretary Kissinger said in June 1975 that "America's military strength has always been used to defend, never to oppress."[16] American power has often been employed with good intentions, but its potentially tragic impact on other peoples must not be ignored. One of the lessons of Vietnam is that we should have more care in the righteousness of our purposes and more sensitivity to the human consequences of our military actions.

LESSON 3: ANTICOMMUNISM

Anticommunism has been the dominant theme of U.S. foreign policy for thirty years. The United States became involved in Indochina "to stop the spread of communism." There are real differences in values and practices and the United States must, as it has, maintain sufficient strength to deter the Soviet Union. But too often in the third world we have been indiscriminate and negative in our anticommunism and have seen the competition too much in military terms.

It is a truism that today the communist world is no longer monolithic and that the United States is now following a policy of

detente with both the Soviet Union and China. But it would be difficult
to underestimate the continuing widespread inclination to interpret
world events in terms of the struggle between the "free world" and
the "communists." Secretary Kissinger has asserted "the ability to
prevent major foreign policy successes by countries that profess the
Marxist ideology" as a principle of U.S. foreign policy.[17] Recent
events in Angola, Portugal, Italy, Greece, Turkey, and Korea are
too easily interpreted in terms of the continuing United States-
communist antagonism. For example, a New York Times editorial
in July 1975 held the Soviet Union responsible for internal political
developments in Portugal: "The United States and its NATO allies
need to make it clear to Moscow that the Soviet Union will be held
responsible if Portugal's communists continue on their present
path."[18] The simplification inherent in such a statement is not much
different from the simplification that dominated U.S. policy in Southeast Asia for many years: aggression from the north was the cause
of conflict and Moscow or Peking controlled events.

     The United States encouraged the overthrow of the government
of Chile because, as Secretary Kissinger has been quoted, "I don't
see why we need to stand by and watch a country go communist due
to the irresponsibility of its own people."[19] Uninformed rhetoric
about countries "going communist" is still much too common where
more careful and less ideological analysis is required.

     In the absence of anticommunism as a touchstone, it is difficult
to determine what broad principles motivate U.S. foreign policy.
Secretary Kissinger senses this when he states that "while the cold
war structure of international relations has come apart, a new stable
international order has yet to be formed."[20] The catchword of
"stability" is an inadequate goal, as Secretary Kissinger has occasionally admitted: "our conception of world order must have deeper
purposes than stability."[21]

     Too often the United States continues to align itself instinctively
with the status quo and against social change, siding with the forces
of "stability." Lacking a vision of goals beyond stability, U.S. con-
tainment policies have seldom transcended a reflexive global anticommunism. Vietnam should have taught the lesson that compulsive
resistance to change in the third world can be very damaging to our
interests.

                          LESSON 4: LOCAL ISSUES

     From the beginning of U.S. involvement in Indochina until the
very end, American policy was justified and explained in terms of the

importance of events in Vietnam for other international commitments
and the general strategic position of the United States. Vietnam was
seen as part of a larger struggle, the world-wide strategic conflict
between the United States and other great powers. George Ball noted
in 1966: "We can properly understand the struggle in Vietnam only if
we recognize it for what it is—part of a vast and continuing struggle
in which we have been engaged for more than two decades."[22] Few
Americans understood the local issues and conflicts that were the
determining factors in Indochina. We never understood the people of
Indochina and their perceptions of their own problems. We ignored
the Asian realities underlying the war.

A lesson of Vietnam in this regard is that we must make a
greater effort to understand other peoples' perceptions and also to
try to see ourselves as others see us. It is a most difficult task. Our
ability to dictate outcomes is limited by our inadequate political understanding. A reassertion of the principle of nonintervention in other
peoples' affairs would be most healthy.

Theodore White has asserted the importance of improving our
political understanding:

> The episode in Vietnam can be allowed to become unmiti-
> gated disaster or it can be reduced to a tragedy that we
> must mourn but can live with, depending on what we have
> learned. What we should have learned is clear: the reach
> of American power is not the reach of our bombers, our
> helicopters, our fleet, our logistics. The reach of Amer-
> ican power extends only as far as the reach of American
> political understanding. [23]

LESSON 5: DISENGAGING FROM MISTAKES

The lesson here is easy to state, but very hard to follow in
practice: Our national welfare and honor can be better served by
early disengagement from a mistaken policy than by compounding the
mistake by continuing it. First, it is very hard to recognize a mistake and to admit that one has been wrong. Second, the inclination
on the part of policy makers to continue policies once they have become committed to them is extraordinarily powerful. The United
States stayed in Vietnam long after most Americans had come to see
that it served a doubtful purpose. Internal Pentagon analyses indicate
that the "avoidance of humiliation" was a dominant factor in why the
United States stuck it out so long after reason dictated the need to
disengage. [24] Vice Admiral William Mack, recently retired as

superintendent of the U.S. Naval Academy, has pointed out that dissenters within government were dealt with severely. [25]

One positive consequence of the war has been the decline of executive branch domination of foreign policy and a shaking of the former belief that foreign affairs is a matter only for insiders and "experts." The Congress has asserted a more active role to share responsibility and provide corrective, critical perspectives. Although there is no guarantee that mistakes will not continue to be made, a more democratic foreign policy with shared responsibility, more varied inputs, and greater attention to critics may make it easier to correct future mistakes.

Part of the difficulty of American disengagement from Vietnam was due to distorted views by U.S. policy makers that other countries somehow wanted the United States to persevere, to "maintain its commitment." In fact, most U.S. allies, including European countries and Japan, came to support U.S. withdrawal sooner and more strongly than did Americans. They recognized that U.S. obsession with Vietnam damaged U.S. ability to meet responsibilities in other parts of the world.

LESSON 6: SECRECY

The Vietnam War divided the American people more than any event since the Civil War. Disillusionment stemming from official deception was one of the major causes of popular disenchantment. We have become suspicious of attempts to cloak official activities and purposes with the cover of "national security." We now recognize that executive secrecy and secret commitments can deny the public and its representatives their necessary voice in foreign policy and can lead to mistaken and unpopular involvements. Excessive secrecy and policy elitism can cause great damage to democratic processes. The continuing distrust between Congress and the executive branch is a legacy of past and present abuses.

Secretary Kissinger sensibly states that the only viable U.S. foreign policy is one that has the support of the people: "No foreign policy has any chance of success if it is born in the minds of a few and carried in the hearts of none."[26] Unfortunately, policy makers see their job more as trying to regain public approval for old policies than in revising these policies.

Full sharing of information and the opportunity for adequate debate and examination of alternatives are essential prerequisites for good policy and public support. The Congress in 1973 passed the War Powers Act to reassert the Congress' constitutional role. The first significant opportunity to apply this act, in the Mayaguez incident, indicated that in a climate of crisis the country can again be plunged into military action without full debate and in ignorance of the facts.

Covert actions by U.S. military and intelligence agencies played a major role in involving the United States in Southeast Asia. Recent revelations stemming from Watergate have begun to raise the curtain on the extensive secret world of the Central Intelligence Agency and other overseas covert operations. We are beginning to see that covert operations often can lead to overt involvement and that secret commitments can take place without members of Congress having any control or even knowledge of what is going on.

LESSON 7: MILITARY AID

Some believe that one of the lessons of Vietnam is that where U.S. troops should not be involved in fighting, U.S. military assistance and military training programs can help accomplish the same purposes. This was the message of the Nixon Doctrine. In fact, however, this conception of the role of military aid as a substitute for direct U.S. military involvement dates back to the 1950s and was the major rationale for early U.S. involvement in Indochina. As late as July 1975, after the biggest U.S. aid program in history, President Ford still believed that military aid could have saved the day: "I felt that in the case of Vietnam and Cambodia if we had had the opportunity to make military assistance available there might have been another solution in Vietnam."[27]

If the goals that one is pursuing are wrong or not achievable, military aid is not a panacea. Too often U.S. aid programs have served to support corrupt and repressive regimes that are incapable of solving the political and economic problems confronting them. U.S. arms and U.S. advisors become identified with such regimes and great damage is done to the reputation and prestige of the United States.

The executive branch and the Congress are headed in different directions on the question of U.S. arms transfers. The State Department and the Defense Department, as they did in Indochina, view military aid activities as one of the major instruments of U.S. foreign policy and adopt a permissive attitude towards satisfying foreign demands for U.S. arms and training. Congress, however, is increasingly critical of extensive U.S. arms deals with Persian Gulf and Middle Eastern countries and wants to have greater control.

The real lesson of the experience in South Vietnam is that military aid, the Nixon Doctrine, Vietnamization, whatever it may

be called, failed. There may be other situations in which military aid
is desirable, but Americans are now more skeptical about bestowing
such aid. We have also learned that military assistance is a critical
step towards national involvement. It can lead to military intervention.

LESSON 8: SELF-RELIANCE

A truism that has been reinforced by the Vietnam experience
is that we can only help those who are willing and able to help themselves. U.S. efforts in Western Europe and in Japan after World
War II are examples of mutually successful programs. But in much
of the rest of the world the conditions for the United States to play a
useful role, particularly militarily, have been absent. We have en-
deavored mightily, as in Vietnam, with little accomplishment.

Secretary Kissinger has some wise words in this connection:
"We have learned important lessons from the tragedy of Indochina—
most importantly that outside effort can only supplement, but not create, local efforts and local will to resist. . . . There is no question
that popular will and social justice are, in the last analysis, the
essential underpinning of resistance to subversion and external
challenge. "[28]

We have too often tried to equate military power with effective
government. We have been intimately involved with governments that
cannot obtain the support of their own people and have little legitimacy,
regimes that do not deal with the causes of discontent and violence.

The humility that we should have learned from our costly failures
in Indochina should encourage us really to put into practice our statements about supporting those who are successfully dealing with social
justice and obtaining genuine popular support. We should not let
blustering about "national security" or "anticommunism" distract us
from this fundamental lesson of Vietnam or make us deaf to the voices
of those who may be telling us unpleasant truths that we do not wish
to hear.

John Stuart Mill warned us more than a century ago:

> A government which needs foreign support to enforce
> obedience from its own citizens is one which ought not
> to exist; and the assistance given to it by foreigners is
> hardly ever anything but the sympathy of one despotism
> with another. [29]

MILITARY LEGACY

There will certainly be continuing disagreement about the foreign policy lessons of Vietnam but the hardware and tactics generated by that conflict will be with us for many years. The weapons and technologies developed for Vietnam are proliferating around the world, increasing the potential for destructive conflict. The basic components of the electronic battlefield of the future were first used in Vietnam, and many urgently generated weapons from the Vietnam War are now part of our conventional military arsenal.

U.S. military forces fought a long, frustrating war against a persistent and elusive opponent in Vietnam. Weapons and equipment were developed in the drive to locate and destroy enemy forces and their supplies. It was hoped that mobility, massive firepower and technological gadgetry would save American lives and win the war. The war was not won. There were no panaceas for an American-South Vietnamese victory. At best, there were some tactical successes.

Yet the Vietnam War was and is today viewed by many military officials as a successful laboratory for the development of tactics and technology suitable for future conflicts. General George Brown, chairman of the Joint Chiefs of Staff, recently said: "Because of our long involvement in Southeast Asia, we have today the most combat-experienced and battle-tested forces in the world. And I know of no other profession in which experience better prepares a man for the tasks which lie ahead. Notwithstanding the recent tragic consequences, the Vietnam experience had better prepared our military forces for the task ahead."[30] General Brown may be correct, but the country has paid dearly for this on-the-job training.

When President Ford states that he has "learned some lessons concerning how we would conduct a military operation"[31] he is probably thinking about bombing. Secretary Schlesinger elaborated on the new importance that the United States attaches to strategic bombing when he warned North Korea in these words: "One of the lessons of the Vietnamese conflict is that rather than simply counter your opponent's thrusts, it is necessary to go for the heart of the opponent's power: destroy his military forces rather than simply being involved endlessly in ancillary military operations."[32] General Brown stresses that "airpower is now, more than ever, the decisive factor in warfare."[33]

Between 1966 and 1973, 7.5 million tons of high explosives were dropped over Indochina by U.S. planes.[34] This was the most intensive bombing campaign ever conducted by the United States. More tonnage

was dropped over Indochina than in both theaters of World War II and
the Korean War combined.

As American troops were withdrawn, the bombing became the
centerpiece of U.S. strategy in Indochina. But how successful was
the bombing? Its purpose was to destroy Hanoi's capability and, even
more, its willingness to support the war in the south. With few industrial targets, North Vietnam's capabilities could not easily be destroyed. According to one RAND study,[35] as early as 1965 Hanoi
anticipated a virtually unlimited American bombing campaign and
began to adjust its industrial and transportation systems. North Vietnam also effectively used the bombing to extract larger amounts of
aid from the Soviet Union and China. The bombing increased the
number of people available for military service, and boosted popular
support for the war. The infiltration rates into the south actually
increased after we started bombing.[36] Throughout the war the U.S.
military underestimated the opponent's strength and perseverance.
Our technological power could make them change tactics, but it could
never make them abandon the war.

General Brown has recently criticized American tactics and
"restraint" in Indochina: "It violated the basic military principles of
surprise and mass as the way to achieve prompt success with minimum loss."[37] While these may be good principles of war, they
require certainty of purpose and there is a potential danger that in
future crises the United States will be prone to premature escalation
or overreaction.

The option of using tactical nuclear weapons is also being
pushed. If it appears to the rest of the world and ourselves that we
cannot credibly threaten intervention with American troops in the
wake of Vietnam, then perhaps we can threaten "limited nuclear
responses." Secretary Schlesinger's 1975 report on tactical nuclear
weapons in Europe discussed the first use of such weapons in language
that military officials have also applied to other parts of the world:
"The attack should be delivered with sufficient shock and decisiveness
to forcibly change the perceptions of the Warsaw Pact leaders and
create a situation conducive to negotiations."[38]

The attempt to wring political leverage from nuclear weapons
is a most dangerous development that has been accentuated by U.S.
foreign policy failures in Southeast Asia. The root of the problem is
the persistence of the unfortunate belief that the United States must
aspire to a messianic global mission. Secretary Schlesinger has
proclaimed the U.S. world role by saying that "without the constable
there can only be anarchy."[39] Unfortunately, that notion of America's
indispensability as the world's policeman persists among U.S. policy
makers, despite Vietnam.

NOTES

1. President Gerald Ford, taken from a May 6, 1975 press conference in Washington, D. C.

2. Secretary of State Henry Kissinger, taken from an April 17, 1975 speech in Washington, D. C. before the American Society of Newspaper Editors.

3. President Ford, taken from a June 9, 1975 press conference.

4. Secretary Kissinger, taken from an April 17, 1975 speech in Washington, D. C. , op. cit.

5. "Now—A Tougher U. S. ," U.S. News and World Report, May 26, 1975, p. 20.

6. Secretary Kissinger, taken from an April 17, 1975 speech in Washington, D. C. , op. cit. See also interview, Thomas Ross, Chicago Sun-Times, May 12, 1975.

7. See, for example, Colonel Richard W. Smith, Military Intervention In A Changing World (Washington: The National War College Strategic Research Group, October 14, 1974).

8. Secretary Kissinger, taken from an April 17, 1975 speech in Washington, D. C. , op. cit.

9. Secretary Kissinger, taken from a May 12, 1975 speech in St. Louis, Missouri, before the St. Louis World Affairs Council.

10. U. S. Department of Defense, Annual Defense Department Report FY1975, March 4, 1974, p. 1.

11. Secretary Kissinger, taken from a June 23, 1975 speech in Atlanta, Georgia, before the Southern Council on International and Public Affairs, and the Atlanta Chamber of Commerce.

12. Eugene Rostow, Commentary, July 1975, p. 77. Contribution to symposium on "America Now: A Failure of Nerve?"

13. Deputy Defense Secretary William Clements, taken from an April 10, 1975 speech in Dallas, Texas.

14. Report of the Commission on the Organization of the Government for the Conduct of Foreign Policy (Washington, D. C. : Government Printing Office, June 1975).

15. Henry A. Kissinger, Nuclear Weapons and Foreign Policy (New York: Harper and Row, 1957), p. 201.

16. Secretary Kissinger, taken from a June 23, 1975 speech in Atlanta, Georgia, op. cit.

17. Secretary Kissinger, in an interview with William F. Buckley, Jr. , "Firing Line," WETA-TV, September 13, 1975.

18. The New York Times, July 17, 1975.

19. Quoted in Seymour Hersh, "Censored Matter in Book on CIA," the New York Times, September 11, 1974.

20. Secretary Kissinger, taken from a May 12, 1975 speech in St. Louis, Missouri.

21. Henry A. Kissinger, American Foreign Policy: Three Essays (New York: W. W. Norton and Co. , 1969), p. 94.

22. George Ball, taken from a January 30, 1966 speech.

23. Theodore White, "Putting Down the Whiteman's Burden," New York, May 12, 1975.

24. See memorandum from John T. McNaughton, assistant secretary of defense for international security affairs, for Secretary of Defense Robert S. McNamara, March 24, 1965. See also the New York Times edition of The Pentagon Papers (New York: Bantam Books, 1971), p. 432.

25. Vice Admiral William Mack, taken from his retirement speech, August 1, 1975 in Annapolis, Maryland.

26. Secretary Kissinger, taken from an August 2, 1973 speech before the International Platform Association.

27. President Ford, "Excerpts from President Ford's Interview Assessing First Year in Office," the New York Times, July 25, 1975.

28. Secretary Kissinger, taken from June 18, 1975 speech before the Japan Society in New York.

29. John Stuart Mill, quoted in Skeptic, Special Issue Number 8, 1975, p. 64.

30. General George Brown, taken from a May 17, 1975 speech in San Antonio, Texas.

31. President Ford, from a June 9, 1975 press conference.

32. James R. Schlesinger, in an interview in U.S. News and World Report, May 26, 1975.

33. General Brown, op. cit.

34. Data obtained from the Defense Department Public Affairs Office, June 1975. See also Raphael Littauer and Norman Uphoff, eds. , The Air War in Indochina (Boston: Beacon Press, 1972).

35. Oleg Hoeffding, Bombing North Vietnam: An Appraisal of Economic and Political Effects (Santa Monica: RAND Corporation, December 1966).

36. See staff study prepared for the use of the Senate Foreign Relations Committee, Bombing as a Policy Tool in Vietnam (Washington, D. C.: Government Printing Office, October 12, 1972).

37. General Brown, op. cit.

38. James R. Schlesinger, The Theater Nuclear Force Posture in Europe: A Report to the United States Congress, April 1975, p. 15. See also Jack Anderson and Les Whitten, "Tactical A-Weapons Called 'Option,'" the Washington Post, July 8, 1975.

39. James R. Schlesinger, taken from an April 15, 1975 speech before the Overseas Press Club in New York.

2

U.S. FORCES
FOR EUROPE AND
THE MBFR TALKS
David T. Johnson

The annual cost to the United States of peacetime preparations for conflict in Europe is higher than the cost of the Vietnam War at its peak. The yearly price tag on U.S. armed forces for defense in Europe is about $35 billion. The annual cost of the war in Southeast Asia at its high point, when 600,000 U.S. servicemen were serving in Southeast Asia, was $21.5 billion in fiscal year 1969.[1]

Providing forces for the defense of Western Europe against possible invasion by the Soviet Union is the most expensive item in the Defense Department budget, exceeding outlays on strategic forces. The total defense budget can be roughly divided between 75 percent for conventional forces and 25 percent for strategic forces.[2] Public attention is usually directed to controversial strategic missiles, submarines, and aircraft, but it is the $75 billion spent each year on maintaining the capability to fight conventional wars overseas that uses the bulk of the military budget.

The size of U.S. general purpose forces is largely determined by the North Atlantic Treaty Organization commitment. As former Secretary of Defense James Schlesinger has said, "most of our forces already are or soon will be oriented toward a war in Europe."[3] This is in line with the declaration of President Ford that "NATO is the cornerstone of United States foreign policy."[4] The Defense Department has acknowledged that the level and composition of U.S. conventional forces are not driven by the need to directly defend the territory of the United States. Because of its advantageous geographic position and powerful strategic forces, the United States requires only small conventional forces to defend itself against foreign threats. Assistant Secretary of Defense Leonard Sullivan confirmed this conclusion when he stated that "practically no U.S. forces are planned to fight on or over the soil of our own continent."[5]

Most U.S. conventional forces are purchased for forward defense of our allies. The size, composition, and cost of U.S. conventional forces are established primarily to support plans for war in Europe. U.S. forces in Europe, in Secretary Schlesinger's view, are "the political and military backbone of NATO."[6] Army Chief of Staff General Fred C. Weyand has said that "we are structured in the U.S. Army pretty much keyed to NATO."[7] For the U.S. Air Force, "the NATO scenario is the dominant factor in determining the level and capabilities of our tactical forces."[8] U.S. Navy ships and aircraft are also being developed principally for a lengthy conventional war in Europe. In recent years, this stress on Europe has become even more pronounced. Secretary Schlesinger stated that "with the end of our involvement in Vietnam, we now emphasize Europe in our general purpose force planning."[9]

COMPOSITION OF CONVENTIONAL FORCES

U.S. conventional forces consist of land, sea, and air components. The U.S. Army is being increased from 13 to 16 active combat divisions by 1977. There are also three active Marine Corps divisions, 13 aircraft carriers around which the Navy is structured, and 68 Air Force fighter and attack squadrons and other tactical air units. To augment this active force, there are 1 million Ready Reserve and National Guard troops immediately available to be called.

The United States formally commits a specific number of units in support of the NATO alliance each year, although there is no formal treaty requirement to do so. The official numbers are classified, but a reasonably complete listing can be derived from congressional hearings and other open sources. In fiscal year 1976 there are about 300,000 U.S. military personnel in Europe including 198,000 Army and 73,000 Air Force, organized primarily in five Army divisions, two armored cavalry regiments, and 22 tactical fighter squadrons.[10] There is also in Europe prepositioned equipment for an additional 2.6 divisions located in the United States but designated for rapid airlift to Europe in case of conflict. The troops in Europe are accompanied by about 250,000 dependents,[11] 18,000 U.S. civilian employees, and 70,000 foreign national civilian employees. There are 139 principal U.S. military bases in Europe.[12]

The United States has more than 7,000 tactical nuclear weapons in Europe[13] and some 2,000 associated delivery systems, like missiles

and aircraft. The United States maintains 780 combat aircraft, including carrier aircraft, in the European theater. The Sixth Fleet,
permanently stationed in the Mediterranean, normally has 40 ships
and submarines, structured around two aircraft carriers. Conventional forces in the continental United States, primarily for conflict
in Europe, include almost the entire Atlantic Fleet, with five carriers,
one Marine division, and seven Army divisions. Of the 22 Air Force
wings, seven are permanently based in Europe and 12 wings are based
in the United States, oriented toward Europe. [14] Most Reserve and
Guard units with modern combat equipment are also oriented toward
Europe.

CALCULATING THE FULL COSTS OF
U.S. NATO FORCES

The Defense Department produces a complicated array of
figures for the cost of U.S. NATO forces. It has never, however,
revealed publicly the extent of NATO-designated forces. The
financial figures must, of necessity, be inexact because of the complexities involved in detailing the direct and indirect costs in department accounting. For fiscal year 1975, the Defense Department
calculated that the cost of forces based in Europe was $8.8 billion. [15]
Forces based in the United States and committed for quick deployment to Europe cost an additional $10.6 billion in fiscal 1975. These
U.S. rapid-reinforcement forces are only part of the total U.S. forces
that would be used for European defense. The Defense Department
calculated that it spent an additional $10.7 billion in fiscal 1975 on
conventional forces that could be used in a NATO conflict, if necessary, but that are also available for fighting in Third World countries.
As Secretary Schlesinger has stated, "NATO itself, in an emergency,
could well draw in something on the order of 12 or 13 U.S. divisions
not currently deployed in Europe." [16] This leaves three or four
divisions for a "secondary contingency."
    The Pentagon's calculations of the financial cost to the United
States of defense of Europe do not include a number of items that
bring the total annual cost to $35 billion or more. As Senator John
McClellan, chairman of the Senate Appropriations Committee, has
observed of portions of strategic forces, research and development,
and Defense Department administration, "obviously a good deal of
these costs are NATO-related." [17] The Europeans enjoy whatever
benefits there are under the nuclear umbrella provided by the United
States without contributing to the costs of U.S. strategic forces. The
United States would probably retain most of its strategic forces in

the absence of a commitment to the defense of Europe. However,
much of the impetus toward the development of new strategic weaponry
that could be used in counterforce or "flexible response" nuclear
warfare stems from the demanding requirements of the U.S. commitment to European defense. The effort to give "extended deterrence"
to Europe sets a requirement for U.S. strategic forces that is, in
Secretary Schlesinger's words, "much more demanding than the kind
of deterrent that merely protects the homeland."[18] Some perhaps
unquantifiable amount of U.S. spending on strategic forces can be
attributed to the costs of the U.S. defense of Europe and the need to
continually reassure the Europeans that we would actually use nuclear
weapons against the Soviet Union in the case of invasion of Western
Europe.

Additionally, a major portion of the $10 billion spent each year
on research and development by the Defense Department must be
added to the costs of defending Europe. New and expensive conventional weapons systems are being developed primarily for war in
Europe.[19] Our NATO allies contribute little toward paying for new
U.S. weapons that will be used primarily for their defense. Recently,
under pressure from Congress, the executive branch has been trying
to stimulate increased cooperation on weapons development between
the United States and other NATO countries, but little progress has
yet been achieved. Examples of major weapons that are primarily
for use in a European war include the F-15 and F-14 fighters, the
SAM-D missile system, the XM-1 tank, and the AWACS warning and
control aircraft. The $10.8 billion F-15 aircraft program is being
produced to defend NATO ground forces against Soviet air attack in
Europe. The proposed $5.6 billion SAM-D surface-to-air missile
system is intended principally for deployment in Europe for similar
purposes. Additionally, small tactical nuclear weapons ("mininukes")
are being considered for use in Europe.

The Defense Department includes a share of the cost of newly
procured weapons and equipment in its calculations of the cost of
U.S. NATO forces. It is doubtful, however, that DOD takes fully
into account the degree to which weapons are procured for NATO
purposes. The Senate Armed Services Committee studied this matter
several years ago and concluded:

> That defense of NATO is uppermost in defense planning
> is clearly illustrated by review of justifications pre-
> sented to support procurement of weapons systems. A
> review of selected general purpose weapons systems
> estimated to cost $30 billion shows that $21-$25 billion
> of that cost can be identified with the requirement to
> support NATO defense.[20]

Finally, Defense Department figures do not include the retirement pay for U.S. NATO forces, nor the overhead administrative costs of these forces. In addition, although recent efforts have been made to increase the payments of European allies to help offset the cost of U.S. forces stationed in Europe, in compliance with the Jackson-Nunn amendment, there are indications that the executive branch has tended to exaggerate the European contribution in order to allay congressional pressures.[21]

FOR THE FUTURE—MORE EMPHASIS ON ARMS FOR EUROPE

For more than 20 years, the United States has borne the major burden for organizing and supporting the defense of Western Europe against possible attack by the Soviet Union. Even so, Pentagon planners foresee even greater emphasis and spending on conventional arms and European defense in the future. In 1973 Lieutenant General George Seignious, then Director of the Joint Staff of the Joint Chiefs of Staff, said that "the evolution in the U.S. forces you will see in the coming years will be more and more identifiable with our mission in NATO."[22] In addition to the shift of attention after the Vietnam War from Asia to Europe, it is argued that the development of approximate parity between the United States and the Soviet Union in strategic weapons has increased the need for NATO to have stronger conventional forces. From the Pentagon point of view, paradoxically, the requirement for conventional forces, and presumably the danger of conventional war, is greater than 15 years ago when relations with the Soviet Union were far more strained.

This is not the place to address in detail the argument that nuclear deterrence somehow makes conventional war more likely, but the view of Bernard Brodie casts doubt on generally accepted assumptions: "If fear of what major war brings is greatly augmented by nuclear weapons, which it unquestionably is, any conflict that appears to increase the risk of such a war is bound to become less likely, not more so."[23] Nuclear weapons diminish the likelihood of war with the Soviet Union, including a conventional war in Europe.

The United States and some of its NATO allies are engaged in a major effort to increase the capability of their military forces. The expansion of the U.S. Army from 13 to 16 divisions is justified to Congress primarily on the basis of the NATO commitment. Though reducing excessive support forces in Europe, the United States is adding two new brigades in Europe and other ground combat forces. The air force is being expanded from 22 to 26 wings primarily to support European defense. New airlift programs have been proposed that will approximately double the forces that the United States will be able to lift to Europe. [24] Refinements in tactical nuclear weapons and tactics are being contemplated. The focus of U.S. efforts is on increasing this nation's and allied combat ability in the early phases of a possible conflict and on achieving increased capability for rapid deployment of reinforcements. One indicator of what has been achieved in recent years is that during and immediately following the Vietnam War, the United States had no combat-ready divisions in Europe, while today all the divisions there are combat ready. [25]

The other major area for improving NATO forces concerns improvement of military cooperation between the United States and its allies. According to Assistant Secretary of Defense William Brehm, "what NATO needs to improve most is the ability of its forces to fight together."[26] Air Force Chief of Staff General David C. Jones agrees that "NATO capabilities, which are already substantial, can be markedly improved, without dramatically increased budgets, through restructuring, standardization, specialization, and improved interoperability."[27] The need for increased standardization of weapons in NATO is indicated by DOD studies that show that currently in Central Europe NATO forces have 23 different families of combat aircraft, seven different families of main battle tanks, 22 different families of antitank weapons, and more than 100 different separate tactical missile systems. [28] A recent report of the Senate Armed Services Committee states that "it has been estimated that such duplication totals $10-15 billion each year, and the lack of standardization leads to a 30-40 percent loss in combat effectiveness."[29]

While Secretary Schlesinger periodically journeyed around Western Europe pressing for standardization of weapons and logistics and criticizing European nationalism and parochialism, from the European point of view the U.S. position often is one of U.S. demands to buy more American weapons. The decision of the Netherlands, Norway, Denmark, and Belgium to purchase the American F-16 aircraft is a recent example. The political and economic divisiveness of the new U.S. push to sell the United States as "the arsenal of democracy" has not yet fully emerged, but Senator John Culver has sounded a warning: "We talk to our NATO partners about the need for standardization, but will our powerful obsession with selling our own products permit us to make the compromises necessary to lead the way?"[30]

BACKGROUND TO MBFR

In the period from 1966 to 1973 the issue of reducing the U.S. military involvement in Europe was frequently raised in the Congress, with Senator Mike Mansfield as the chief proponent of U.S. reductions. The beginning of the MBFR (mutual and balanced force reductions) talks between NATO and the Warsaw Pact nations in October 1973 and uncertainties raised by the collapse of the U.S. position in Southeast Asia have somewhat lessened public discussion of U.S. military policy toward Europe. But the factors that have led some to question a relationship between the United States and Western Europe involving such a heavy U.S. military responsibility for the region's defense are likely to stimulate continued debate. The economic growth of Western Europe and the improvement in Europe's military and political position in relation to the Soviet Union are powerful arguments for the European NATO partners taking over a greater share of their own defense.

Western Europe has regained its wealth since World War II. In 1951, the combined gross national product of all the European members of NATO was $47 billion. By 1974, it jumped to $1,242 billion, nearly twice that of the Soviet Union. The European Economic Community has replaced the United States as the world's largest trading unit. [31] By almost any measure, the combined industrial might of NATO Europe surpasses that of the Soviet Union. The greater economic and manpower resources of NATO Europe provide a basis for a strong military potential as well. As Secretary Schlesinger stated, "a comparison of NATO's and the Warsaw Pact's Gross National Products, defense expenditures, populations, and numbers of men under arms reveals no inherent reason for NATO to be inferior."[32]

The vastly improved political situation in Europe is an important reason to question U.S. policies. Judging by their level of defense expenditures and contacts with the Soviet Union and Eastern Europe, our European allies, although closer at hand, seem to take a less worried view of the Soviet threat than the United States. Although aware of Soviet military capabilities, they discount the Soviets' aggressive intent and rightly consider the chances of war in Europe to be vastly less today than in the past. A Soviet conventional attack on Western Europe is increasingly implausible. It has become more difficult to see what Soviet interests would be served by an attack on Western Europe. Economic threats to stability are widely viewed in Europe as far more immediate than the threat from Soviet military power. Chancellor Helmut Schmidt of West Germany seemed to be expressing these sentiments when he told a NATO meeting in June

1975 that the Atlantic alliance was threatened "more by the world economic situation than in any particular geographic area."[33]

The political situation in Europe has changed dramatically from
when the North Atlantic Treaty was signed in 1949. General Andrew
Goodpaster, former Supreme Allied Commander in Europe, has
graphically described the prevailing perception of the Soviet threat
at the time that NATO was founded:

> In those days the question was not, "Will there be war?"
> but rather, "In what month will war start?" An exhausted
> Western Europe, weakened and weary of war, faced a
> new threat—and it seemed only a matter of time until the
> threat would be carried out. That was the climate—the
> harsh, numbing, almost paralyzing climate—into which
> NATO was born.[34]

The division of the world between a bloc led by the United States
and a Soviet-led bloc has been eroded. The emergence of China as
the Soviet Union's most hostile opponent has fundamentally altered
old conceptions of the balance of power. Increasingly, the conflict
between the Soviet Union and the West has been channeled into nonmilitary spheres, on which basis a wealthy and confident Western
Europe already competes as an equal. Many of the European Cold
War tensions of the 1950s and 1960s can be traced to dilemmas
arising from the Berlin situation and the German problem. Today,
the Berlin accords and the normalization of relations between West
Germany and Eastern Europe have resolved most of the old disputes.
The conclusion of the Conference on Security and Cooperation in
Europe on August 1, 1975 was intended to signal a further step away
from the old hostilities and military confrontations.

With the growth of European economic strength and the waning
of the Cold War, many Americans have expressed doubts about the
United States devoting so much of its military efforts to the possibility
of a major war in Europe. Recent polls indicate that although Americans support a general commitment to NATO, only a minority would
favor U.S. military involvement if Western Europe were invaded.[35]
Public opinion is changeable, but the reluctance of the public to
continue America's post-World War II role in maintaining military
security abroad seems clear.

NEGOTIATIONS ON MUTUAL REDUCTIONS OF FORCES (MBFR) AND ARMAMENTS

In response to the domestic pressures for change in U.S. policy,
the U.S. government since 1966 has been promoting the concept of

mutual and balanced force reductions in Central Europe as a substitute
for independent U.S. reductions. The Nixon administration tied any
cut in U.S. forces in Western Europe to corresponding and larger
reductions in Soviet forces in Eastern Europe. Former President
Nixon stated the policy that has been continued by President Ford:

> Given the existing strategic balance and similar efforts
> by our allies, it is the policy of this government to main-
> tain and improve our forces in Europe and not reduce
> them except through reciprocal reductions negotiated
> with the Warsaw Pact. [36]

The United States has approached the MBFR talks preoccupied with
NATO problems and the presumed need to stimulate Western Europeans to step up their military activities.

The long-awaited "Negotiations on Mutual Reductions of Forces
and Armaments and Associated Measures in Central Europe" began
in Vienna on October 30, 1973. These talks between the members of
NATO and the Warsaw Pact are among the most complicated international negotiations in history. Certainly they are much more complex than the Strategic Arms Limitation Talks, if only because 19
instead of two countries are participating. Eleven states are full
participants and eight are observers.

Little progress was made in the first two years of negotiation.
Each side presented proposals for reduction that were emphatically
rejected by the other. Each perceives the military balance differently and emphasizes differing aspects of it. As Secretary Schlesinger
has said, "the conceptual bases of the Eastern and Western proposals
are fundamentally different. "[37] NATO's plan seeks to reduce ground
combat manpower levels, primarily Soviet, to a common ceiling of
about 700,000 soldiers each for NATO and the Warsaw Pact in the
central European region—the territories of West Germany, Belgium,
Netherlands, Luxembourg, East Germany, Czechoslovakia, and
Poland. [38] In the first phase of NATO's proposal, the United States
would withdraw 29,000 soldiers and the Soviets would withdraw
68,000. In the second phase, NATO would reduce by 48,000 more
and the Warsaw Pact by an additional 157,000. In 1975, according to
Western figures, the Warsaw Pact had 925,000 ground soldiers,
including 460,000 Soviet troops, in the central region and NATO had
777,000, including 193,000 U.S. Army personnel.

The Soviet MBFR proposal seeks to preserve what the Warsaw
Pact considers to be the existing stable correlation of military
forces. [39] Its force reduction scheme envisages equal percentage
reductions of NATO and Pact forces and would include air forces
and tactical nuclear weapons in addition to ground combat forces.

The NATO position has been to concentrate on cutting Soviet ground forces. However, in 1975 the United States considered a new proposal[40] that would exchange a cut of 1,000 of the 7,000 tactical nuclear weapons that the United States has in Europe for a 1,700 cut in Soviet tank forces. Such a reduction of the extremely large number of tactical nuclear weapons in Western Europe would probably have no impact on NATO's military capability for, as Assistant Secretary of Defense Leonard Sullivan has remarked, "there is probably more, quasi-obsolete nuclear capability in Europe than we absolutely need to have today."[41]

The head of the U.S. delegation in Vienna has been Stanley Resor, a former secretary of the army. In describing the Soviet threat to NATO and the need for Soviet forces to be reduced by much larger amounts than those of the NATO allies, Ambassador Resor has stressed the Soviet superiority in numbers of ground forces, numbers of tanks, and disparities in geography that could affect U.S. and Soviet reinforcement capabilities. Resor has outlined the NATO assessment:

> There are three major disparities: the Warsaw Pact has more active duty ground force personnel in the agreed area of reductions, it has more tanks, and the Soviet Union is much closer to Central Europe than the United States. We regard these disparities in numbers of men, numbers of tanks, and distance of the United States and the Soviet Union from the areas as basic to the present situation. They all work to the advantage of the Warsaw Pact.[42]

Louis Michael, director of the Defense Department's MBFR Task Force, adds that "our MBFR position is structured especially to attack those disparities."[43] Michael has also indicated that the U.S. approach to MBFR is very much concerned with keeping up incentives for Western European military efforts: "Essentially, we are . . . applying MBFR, or participation in MBFR, in support of the basic objectives . . . namely, strengthening of our conventional defenses, and getting our Allies to do more in terms of supporting their share of the burden."[44]

DIFFERING ASSESSMENTS OF THE
MILITARY BALANCE

The Soviet Union, while providing very little data on its own and apparently not disputing that it has numerical advantages in tanks

and ground forces in the area, emphasizes that NATO forces are
superior to Warsaw Pact forces in other respects that may be as
important as or more important than the particular disparities upon
which NATO has focused. Soviet Ambassador to the MBFR talks,
O. Khlestov, has indicated the difficulty of singling out a few measures of military power:

> Modern armed forces, ground forces, air forces and
> the appropriate weapons, including contingents armed
> with nuclear weapons, are integrated. They form a
> single military complex. . . . The exclusive reduction
> of ground forces could lead to an endeavor to strengthen
> other services—air forces and nuclear contingents—
> which might lead to a race in these types of armaments. [45]

New technologies and new tactics can indeed have a decisive
impact on the effectiveness of military forces. U.S. Army Chief of
Staff General Fred Weyand summarizes some of the new weapons
developments that are revolutionizing warfare:

> Advances in conventional weaponry have been rapid and
> far reaching in recent years. The battlefield is a far
> more lethal place than it used to be. . . . Missiles,
> "smart" bombs, and other weapons only recently con-
> sidered as technologically advanced, are now common-
> place. The electronics technological explosion has
> substantially altered the conduct of battlefield command,
> while everything from satellites to sensors has changed
> our approach to reconnaissance. Battlefield mobility
> and firepower have increased markedly in less than
> a decade. [46]

General George Brown, chairman of the Joint Chiefs of Staff, states
that "air-to-ground munitions for close air support, particularly in
the antiarmor role, are being modernized and stockpiled in Europe.
These munitions offer the fastest way by which the ground battle can
be influenced with reinforcements."[47] He also projects the increasing
importance of air power: "Both the U.S. and the USSR ground forces
face an air threat in the 1980s consisting of large quantities of versatile, well-equipped aircraft, which will be fast, maneuverable,
possess electronic devices to neutralize defense systems, and deliver
ordnance with extreme accuracy."[48]
    The American and NATO advantage in new munitions and air
power is substantial. As General David Jones, air force chief of
staff, has stated, "in one area, we, in the United States, have

tremendous superiority and that is in designing and building airplanes
and equipping these aircraft with the proper avionics and weapons."[49]
The in-place tactical air forces in Europe are approximately 3,000
on each side.[50] But NATO aircraft are superior to their Warsaw
Pact counterparts in range and staying power and NATO pilots are
better trained and far more experienced than Pact pilots. Most Pact
aircraft are intended for air defense rather than offensive roles.[51]
Warsaw Pact air forces are markedly inferior to NATO in the kinds
of ordnance available to them. NATO forces have a greater variety
of more effective air-to-ground missiles, "smart" bombs, and air-
to-air missiles. Optically and electronically guided "smart" bombs—
because of their great accuracy—could potentially enable one plane to
do what had required many planes in the past. This gives a substantial advantage to NATO air forces that is not likely to be eroded in
the foreseeable future because, apparently, the Soviet Union lags
considerably in the development of comparable weapons.

It is not surprising that the Soviets have opposed NATO proposals
in the MBFR talks that focus exclusively on reducing alleged Soviet
advantages and that leave untouched important areas where the Warsaw Pact lags significantly. Nor is it surprising that NATO has
rejected Pact suggestions that preserve the disparities that most
concern NATO.

U.S. officials are ambivalent in characterizing the existing
military balance in Europe. In the MBFR negotiations, the emphasis
is on rectifying imbalances, but in other contexts, U.S. military
leaders have frequently expressed satisfaction with NATO's military
strength. Secretary Schlesinger has made a number of such statements. For example:

- With regard to the numerical elements, we have in the central
  region something approaching a numerical balance.[52]
- We have the numerical ingredients in balance.[53]
- There is an approximate balance between the immediately
  available forces of NATO and the Pact in the Center Region.[54]
- There is no vast or overwhelming numerical difference between
  the forces put together by NATO and the Warsaw Pact. . . .
  The Soviets continue to have very substantial respect for the
  conventional capabilities of NATO.[55]
- The force balance with regard to conventional forces is one that
  gives us a high degree of confidence in deterrence.[56]
- The conventional deterrent provided there [Central Europe] by
  American-German forces is sufficient to deal with any Soviet
  attack.[57]

In part, these optimistic assessments are based on recent
studies within the Defense Department that have revised old con-

ceptions of Soviet strength and NATO weakness. [58] As Deputy Assistant Secretary of Defense Robert Murray has said, "we are now able
to see things more clearly than we were a few years ago. "[59] The new
studies differ from old ones in the following respects:

Previous studies had only considered forces that are formally
committed to NATO. The new analyses include all forces of NATO
countries that could reasonably be expected to fight in Central Europe.
The new assumptions have raised the number of forces available to
NATO.

Old studies assumed that all Warsaw Pact divisions are as well
equipped and manned as the best Soviet divisions. NATO forces were
excessively downgraded by comparison. More realistic assessments
on both sides are now incorporated, lessening the estimated numbers
and quality of opposing Pact forces.

Previous studies had assumed very short Soviet reinforcement
times "because they ignored the Pact's need to make logistical preparations. "[60] More realistic assumptions about lengthier Soviet reinforcement and logistical problems are now used.

Old methods of comparing opposing weapons systems had been
quite crude and mechanistic. "The new system places less value on
tanks and artillery, which the Pact holds in large numbers, and more
value on the lighter weapons systems, where NATO has some advantages in numbers. "[61]

William Brehm, assistant secretary of defense for manpower
and reserve affairs, has summarized some of the newly acknowledged
Warsaw Pact weaknesses that have led to more accurate, and more
optimistic, assessments of NATO's defensive capability:

> The Soviets rely to a great extent on mobilization, many
> divisions are supplied with older equipment, their ability
> to move large numbers of men and equipment quickly
> seems to have been exaggerated, most of their aircraft
> are intended for defensive roles and many are obsolete
> and of quite limited capability, and the reliability of some
> Pact members in war would be uncertain. [62]

Secretary Schlesinger has agreed that "NATO possesses important
quantitative or qualitative advantages in tank destroyers, antitank
weapons, trucks, logistic support and modern fighter aircraft. "[63]
He believes that "it is clear that NATO is in better shape conven-
tionally than had been anticipated. "[64]

It seems evident, however, that the old tendency to understate
NATO capabilities and overstate Warsaw Pact capabilities underlies
the position of NATO in the MBFR negotiations. Stress is placed on
a handful of indicators of Pact strength. NATO spokesmen exaggerate
the importance of those areas in which the Pact has some numerical

advantage. The Pact manpower advantage, the Soviet tank threat, and the presumed vastly superior Soviet reinforcement capability are the constant themes of NATO discussions of the MBFR talks, as well as being prominent in arguments against any reduction of U.S. forces stationed in Europe. The actual situation, however, is not as starkly black and white as is often alleged. NATO has strengths that may more than compensate for any areas of supposed Soviet advantage.

MANPOWER COMPARISONS

The Warsaw Pact outnumbers NATO in ground troops in Central Europe, but as Secretary Schlesinger has noted, "with the inclusion of forces from the United Kingdom, France, and Denmark, the NATO allies have greater forces available than those available to the Warsaw Pact in the NATO guidelines area."[65] General Brown has observed that "in all three NATO regions, national ground forces amount to 1.78 million [for NATO], while Warsaw Pact forces amount to 1.62 million in the Eastern European countries and the three western [Soviet] military districts abutting NATO territory."[66] Interestingly, in contrast to trends in NATO toward reducing support forces and increasing combat forces, the Defense Department reports that during the past few years there has been a trend toward increasing the proportion of support troops within Warsaw Pact forces.[67]

There are some advantages that accrue to NATO, a presumably defensive alliance, in fighting a defensive battle. They mitigate Warsaw Pact manpower advantages. General Michael S. Davison, former commander of the U.S. Army in Europe, states that "military history is replete with examples of smaller forces destroying superior forces through a superior defense."[68] He adds that "an often-used military axiom is that an attacking force should have a numerical force superiority of about three to one."[69] New technological developments and the experience of the 1973 Mideast war also indicate that the defense has regained the advantage in conventional warfare.[70]

A relatively new factor that has substantially changed the balance of forces confronting the Soviet Union has been the emergence of China as a second major potential military threat. In the east, the Soviet Union faces the Chinese, who are armed with nuclear weapons and have a regular armed force of about 3.5 million.[71] According to the Defense Department, the Soviets have 43 divisions with 562,000 men[72] in far eastern regions facing China. Secretary Schlesinger has said that "Soviet ground forces are divided almost evenly east and west of the Urals."[73] Schlesinger also comments wryly that China is now the world's foremost supporter of NATO.[74]

The recent massive military build-up of Iran also cannot be anything but disquieting for the Soviet Union. It raises the prospect of a third important military front that the Soviets must take into account in their defense planning.

The substantial growth of West German military power is another important factor. From 1956 to 1975, West German active armed forces have increased from 66,000 to 495,000. [75] Secretary Schlesinger has observed that "even in the mid-1960s, German forces possessed limited capabilities. In recent years, the German forces have grown to be a very formidable deterrent, indeed, as reflected, I think, in the Soviet attitudes toward the Bundeswehr."[76] He stated that the Germans are capable of putting 1.2 million men in the field on short notice.[77] Presently, West Germany has responsi- bility for defending about 50 percent of the Central Region front, the U.S. Army about 30 percent, and the remaining 20 percent is assigned to the Belgian, British, and Dutch forces.[78] A very impor- tant, perhaps dominating, Soviet concern in the MBFR talks has been to bring about some control or reduction of the German forces con- fronting them.[79] The United States has opposed such efforts and sought to focus MBFR on Soviet and U.S. forces.

An additional consideration that must be taken into account in analyzing the Soviet manpower threat to NATO is that Soviet troops in Eastern Europe are there in some measure as occupation forces to preserve political stability and Soviet hegemony. Former Secre- tary of Defense Elliot Richardson commented in 1973 that since 1955, when the Warsaw Pact was established, Soviet troops in Eastern Europe had been used in a military sense "not against NATO, but against two of the Pact member states—Hungary in 1956 and Czecho- slovakia in 1968."[80]

Compared to NATO, the Warsaw Pact is politically a much more dubious and potentially flawed alliance. Despite the presumed advantages of greater standardization of equipment within the Pact, their military exercises have been found to be less than memorable. Secretary Schlesinger, speaking of a recent Warsaw Pact exercise, called it "an unimpressive affair."[81] General David Jones, former commander of U.S. Air Forces in Europe, states that there is great inflexibility and lack of local initiative in the Soviet military: "Having spent most of the last 10 years in Europe . . . I would say they are very inflexible in the way they do things."[82]

TANK COMPARISONS

NATO has approximately 6,000 tanks in the Central European region compared with about 15,500 for the Warsaw Pact.[83] The quality of NATO tanks, however, as measured by long-range firepower, armor protection, cruising range, human engineering, safety, ammunition load, and overall maintainability and reliability, is superior to that of Soviet tanks. [84] General Fred Weyand, army chief of staff, states that "the U.S. force in Europe is a tank heavy, mobile force trained and equipped to meet this [Soviet tank] thrust."[85]

More important, over the past decade the tank has become increasingly vulnerable because of the development and proliferation of comparatively inexpensive but effective antitank weapons, delivered both from the ground and from the air. NATO has an advantage of over 23,000 antitank weapons[86] and, in such weapons, outnumbers the Warsaw Pact in Central Europe by a ratio of 2.2 to 1. [87] NATO antitank weapons are more advanced technologically than those of the Pact. New TOW and Dragon antitank missiles are now being deployed throughout NATO forces in Europe.

The Middle East war in October 1973 demonstrated the continued vulnerability of the tank. The Arabs and the Israelis suffered substantial losses of tanks, totaling about 2,000. Evidently, antitank missile technology had overcome protective countermeasures currently available to tanks. The cost-effective comparison also puts the tank in a questionable position. A $500,000 tank can be destroyed by a very inexpensive man-carried antitank weapon like the $4,000 TOW missile. A tank is not required to counter another tank. These developments prompted Colonel Edward B. Atkinson to write an article in Army magazine entitled "Is the Soviet Army Obsolete?"[88]— so titled because of the great reliance that the Soviets put on tanks and tank-dependent tactics that stem from World War II experiences. Major General Howard H. Cooksey, army acting deputy chief of staff for research and development, observes that "certainly in the Mideast war, the Israelis found out, the hard way, that blitzkrieg tactics will not work."[89]

The geography of Central Europe is less suitable for tank warfare than is the Sinai in the Middle East, and could present grave difficulties for any rapid Soviet armored advance. NATO has a marked advantage in modern offensive aircraft and in helicopters carrying antitank weapons. As General Jones has said, "the NATO air forces are a far more potent combat force than their Warsaw Pact counterparts."[90] Helicopters, able to hug the nap of the earth and take advantage of natural obstacles, might be effective in taking a toll of tanks in Central Europe. [91] As a factor in measuring the military balance in Europe, comparisons of numbers of tanks can be a misleading indicator of real military capability.

GEOGRAPHY AND REINFORCEMENT

The United States has built a large airlift capability for rapidly moving troops and equipment between the United States and Europe. This airlift capacity is largely provided by the 77 C-5 and 276 C-141[92] aircraft of the Military Airlift Command and the approximately 345[93] commercial aircraft made available in case of emergency through the Civil Reserve Air Fleet. The Soviet Union, by comparison, has only 40 heavy military transport aircraft. [94]

Secretary Schlesinger has suggested that the United States may not be at a severe disadvantage in reinforcement capability when compared with the Soviet Union: "With our airlift capabilities, we are able to redeploy combat troops very quickly, in fact more quickly in a number of respects than the Soviets can in a location closer at hand. . . . The difficulties of redeployment may be less for us than they are for our possible opponents."[95] The Defense Department requested $1.6 billion in the fiscal 1976 budget,[96] not approved by Congress, for expanded airlift programs that would, if implemented, double the force that the United States could airlift to Europe in the same time span. [97]

The Soviets' reinforcement distance is about 1,500 miles compared with 3,500 miles for the United States,[98] but the supply of Soviet troops in Central Europe, and the advance of reinforcements, present difficulties not often realized. Land, unlike open ocean or air, can be cut in many places by air strike, partisan actions, and conventional mining. Geographic obstacles can be exploited to make overland travel difficult. The Soviet Army relies heavily on railroads for transportation and is deficient in road-based transport. [99] The Pact rail system is very vulnerable to crippling interdiction. NATO's tactical air forces are structured for quick destruction and disruption of Warsaw Pact supply and reinforcement routes. There are also the transportation difficulties resulting from the Soviet possession of a five-foot gauge rail, while the other Pact nations have a smaller track size. [100] In general, considering the volume of traffic involved, NATO capability for land-interdiction, and the vulnerability of rail lines, Soviet reinforcement would have serious problems. The railway net that connects the Soviet industrial centers and supply routes across the territory of unreliable allies could be as vulnerable to disruption, if not more so, as the lengthier reinforcement routes between the United States and Europe. NATO has its own reinforcement problems, but the logistical constraints on the Soviets' ability to support large-scale, sustained offensive warfare are considerable.

Pentagon planners have essentially ruled out the possibility that the Soviet Union could launch a massive surprise attack on Western Europe. Soviet forces cannot be moved westward in substantial numbers without lengthy and visible mobilization. U.S. intelligence resources, most importantly satellite reconnaissance, would provide advance warning. NATO devotes considerable resources to strategic warning. Secretary Schlesinger has criticized a "Pearl Harbor complex"[101] in the United States and reported that "the total list of potential indicators of a Soviet attack in Europe is long, several hundred items. "[102]

The Defense Department summarizes the situation this way:

It is also our belief that the nature and magnitude of Pact repositioning and reinforcement activities which would be required to reach even a minimally adequate attack posture against NATO could not remain unobserved by NATO intelligence sources. Hence, we have concluded that the Warsaw Pact cannot build up and redeploy in such a way as to enable a complete surprise attack to occur. [103]

The existence of such warning times permits a substantial increase in the number of both U.S. and NATO Europe forces available to oppose Soviet attack. In Secretary Schlesinger's words, "our ability to deploy forces rapidly could do much to offset the Soviet Union's geographic advantage, particularly in the early weeks of a confrontation in Europe. "[104]

FUTURE OF MBFR

The complexities that are behind NATO's concentration on the "three disparities" of manpower, tanks, and geography in the MBFR talks help to explain why these negotiations have stalled during the first two years. It will be extremely difficult to achieve "balanced" reductions of forces, because so many different kinds of units and complex weapons are involved. The differing force postures, mobilization procedures, and geographic situations of NATO and the Warsaw Pact make the technical difficulties of negotiating agreed reductions almost insurmountable. Numbers of troops and amounts of weapons cannot be translated with precision into levels of security. Differing national perspectives also produce conflicting conceptions of what constitutes a fair balance. These talks are likely to drag on for years.

A basic problem is that for supporters of the continuation of the present level of U.S. forces in Europe, there is no right time to cut. There is little or no interest in reducing troops except in return for Soviet cuts that would be so large that the Soviet Union would have a very difficult time accepting them. There appears to be minimal interest in seeking and defining workable compromises and adjustments.

The role of the MBFR talks for the United States has, in large part, been to forestall pressures in the Congress to reduce U.S. troops. The first chairman of the NATO Working Group on MBFR, General T. R. Milton, states that "the work was begun in NATO in 1970 with one principal objective: the pacification of Senator [Mike] Mansfield, who seemed determined to cut U.S. forces in Europe."[105] The talks have also been used to keep the pressure on West European governments to increase their military expenditures to enhance NATO's "bargaining position."

Former Secretary Schlesinger has said that "there is a tangled web of motivations with regard to MBFR."[106] The probable outcome would be a small, symbolic reduction to prevent larger reductions enforced by Congress or carried out independently by European governments. A danger is that the levels frozen by an MBFR treaty will then be immune to further reexamination and very large military establishments in Europe will be legitimized for decades more.

One positive feature of the MBFR dialogue is that hopefully representatives of NATO and the Warsaw Pact will, in the process of exchanging views, learn more about each other and develop greater sensitivity to how the other perceives the military situation. Such a learning experience is reported to have occurred in the SALT talks and there are indications that MBFR is also helping to dissolve stereotypes.[107] A possible ironic conclusion to MBFR could be a further easing of tensions between East and West, but no accompanying significant reductions of military forces.

Secretary Schlesinger has said that the United States does not see MBFR as "a force reduction exercise" or "a budget reduction exercise."[108] He does not say so, but in many respects the United States uses MBFR as a force expansion exercise. Schlesinger has also stated that even if MBFR leads to some reduction of U.S. troops stationed in Europe, the United States has no plan to cut them out of the military.[109] Forces withdrawn from Europe would presumably be reassigned in the United States and provided with added equipment and expensive airlift capability to make possible a quick return to Europe. As General Andrew Goodpaster, former NATO military chief, has stated, "the net of it could well be an increase in the funds that would be required"[110] for defense.

In order to make the MBFR talks really work, a new approach
may be needed that is not dominated by excessive attachment to the
decades-old military confrontation in Europe. The tendency on the
part of American officials to attribute problems in Europe to military
factors also makes progress in MBFR difficult. New proposals are
needed that recognize that there is more than one valid perception of
the military balance. On the surface, the MBFR negotiations are
about hardware and troop strengths, but their real importance is
political. They should not become stalled by emphasis on one-sided,
technical details. Unfortunately, both sides in the talks seem to lack
a full commitment to making them work.

NOTES

1. U.S. Department of Defense, The Economics of Defense
Spending: A Look At the Realities (Washington, D.C.: Government
Printing Office, July 1972), p. 149.

2. For example, former Defense Secretary James R. Schles-
inger has stated that "we estimate that more than 70 percent of our
Defense expenditures [are] attributable to the general purpose forces
and activities related to them." See Annual Defense Department
Report FY 1975 (Washington, D.C.: Government Printing Office,
March 4, 1974), p. 81.

3. U.S. Department of Defense, Annual Defense Department
Report FY 1976 and FY 197T (Washington, D.C.: Government Printing
Office, February 5, 1975), p. III-10.

4. President Ford, quoted in the New York Times, May 29,
1975.

5. U.S. Congress, 93rd Congress, Senate Armed Services
Committee, Fiscal Year 1976 and July-September 1976 Transition
Period Authorization for Military Procurement, Research and Devel-
opment, and Active Duty, Selected Reserve, and Civilian Personnel
Strengths (Washington, D.C.: Government Printing Office, April 7,
1975), Part 5, p. 2513.

6. U.S. Department of Defense, Annual Defense Department
Report FY 1976 and FY 197T, op. cit., p. III-28.

7. U.S. Congress, House, Armed Services Committee, Military
Posture Department of Defense Authorization for Appropriations for
Fiscal Year 1976 (Washington, D.C.: Government Printing Office,
1975), February 26, 1975, Part 1, p. 592.

8. Senate, Armed Services Committee, op. cit., Part 5,
p. 2560.

9. House, Armed Services Committee, op. cit., Part 1,
p. 219.

10. Senate, Armed Services Committee, op. cit., Part 5, p. 2251.

11. Senator Sam Nunn, ibid., p. 2169.

12. As of the end of fiscal 1974. Senate Armed Services Committee, Fiscal Year 1974 Authorization for Military Procurement, Research and Development, and Active Duty, Selected Reserve, and Civilian Personnel Strengths (Washington, D.C.: Government Printing Office, 1973), Part 8, p. 5343.

13. See James R. Schlesinger, The Theater Nuclear Force Posture in Europe: A Report to the United States Congress (Washington, D.C.: Government Printing Office, April 1975) and Jeffrey Record, U.S. Nuclear Weapons in Europe: Issues and Alternatives (Washington, D.C.: Brookings Institution, 1974).

14. Senate, Armed Services Committee, Fiscal Year 1976, op. cit., Part 2, p. 556.

15. Ibid., Part 1, p. 324.

16. House, Appropriations Committee, Department of Defense Appropriations for 1976 (Washington, D.C.: GPO, 1975), Part 1, p. 105.

17. Senate, Appropriations Committee, Department of Defense Appropriations Fiscal Year 1975 (Washington, D.C.: GPO, 1974), Part 5, p. 111.

18. House, Appropriations Committee, op. cit., p. 270.

19. Dr. Malcolm R. Currie, director of defense research and engineering, has said that "the environment for which we design our systems is Central Europe." Program of Research, Development, Test and Evaluation FY 1976 (Washington, D.C.: Government Printing Office, 1975), p. VI-4.

20. Senate, Armed Services Committee, Report on Military Procurement Authorization, Fiscal Year 1972 (Washington, D.C.: Government Printing Office, September 7, 1971), p. 16.

21. See General Accounting Office, Some of the Issues Involved in Maintaining U.S. Forces in Europe (Washington, D.C.: Government Printing Office, September 12, 1975), pp. 6-10.

22. Senate, Foreign Relations Committee, U.S. Forces in Europe (Washington, D.C.: GPO, July 27, 1973), p. 84.

23. Bernard Brodie, War and Politics (New York: Macmillan Co., 1973), p. 404.

24. Robert Murray, deputy assistant secretary of defense (manpower and reserve affairs), Senate, Armed Services Committee, op. cit., Part 5, p. 2246.

25. Ibid., p. 2246.

26. Ibid., p. 2174.

27. General David C. Jones, Senate, Armed Services Committee, op. cit., Part 2, p. 488.

28. Senate, Armed Services Committee, op. cit., Part 5, p. 2200.

29. Senate, Armed Services Committee, Report on Military Procurement Authorization, Fiscal Year 1976 (Washington, D.C.: Government Printing Office, May 19, 1975), p. 119.

30. Senator John Culver, Congressional Record, September 30, 1975, p. S17081.

31. Senate, Armed Services Committee, op. cit., Part 5, p. 2203.

32. Senate, Appropriations Committee, op. cit., Part 1, p. 67.

33. Helmut Schmidt, quoted in Craig R. Whitney's, "Schmidt Says Economic Crisis is Threat to NATO," New York Times, June 2, 1975, p. 10.

34. SHAPE and Allied Command Europe: Twenty Years in the Service of Peace (Belgium: NATO, 1971), p. 9.

35. See Charles R. Foster, "American Elite and Mass Attitudes Towards Europe," NATO Review, June 1975, pp. 13-15. A Gallup Poll in 1973 indicated that a majority of the public who had an opinion on the issue of withdrawal of troops from Europe favored it; Washington Post, October 8, 1973; and New York Times, October 9, 1973.

36. President Richard Nixon, report to the Congress, United States Foreign Policy for the 1970s, February 9, 1972, p. 44. At a NATO meeting on May 29, 1975, President Ford reaffirmed this position: "Our commitment not to engage in any unilateral reduction of U.S. forces committed to NATO remains valid." Quoted in NATO Review, June 1975, p. 3.

37. Senate, Armed Services Committee, Fiscal Year 1976, op. cit., Part 1, p. 321.

38. For details of NATO and Warsaw Pact proposals see: House, Armed Services Committee, Review of Arms Control and Disarmament Activities (Washington, D.C.: Government Printing Office, December 10, 1974), pp. 3-4; David Binder, "NATO Hesitance Reduces U.S. Ability to Deal on Cuts in European Forces," New York Times, September 10, 1975; Richard J. Levine, "Europe as an Armed Camp," Wall Street Journal, September 22, 1975.

39. V. Biktorov, "The Vienna Talks," International Affairs (Moscow), August 1974, pp. 22-30; O. Khlestov, "Mutual Force Reductions in Europe," Survival, November-December 1974, pp. 203-98 (reprinted from World Economics and International Relations, No. 6, 1974).

40. Kingsbury Smith, "European Forces Linked to N-Arms," Boston Herald-American, September 12, 1975; Craig R. Whitney, "Talks Open on Troops in Europe but Cuts Seen Far Off," the New York Times, September 27, 1975.

41. House, Armed Services Committee, Military Posture and H.R. 3689 Department of Defense Authorization for Appropriations for Fiscal Year 1976 and 197T (Washington, D.C.: Government Printing Office, 1975), Part 2, p. 2961.

42. United States Arms Control and Disarmament Agency (ACDA), mimeographed, Selected Background Documents Relating to Mutual and Balanced Force Reductions, Part III, May 5, 1975, p. 49.

43. Senate, Armed Services Committee, Fiscal Year 1976, op. cit., Part 5, p. 2227.

44. Ibid., p. 2226.

45. ACDA, op. cit., p. 29.

46. Senate, Armed Services Committee, Fiscal Year 1976, op. cit., Part 2, p. 387.

47. Ibid., Part 1, p. 323.

48. Ibid., pp. 233–34.

49. House, Armed Services Committee, Military Posture 1976, op. cit., p. 460.

50. Assistant Secretary of Defense Leonard Sullivan, Senate, Armed Services Committee, Fiscal Year 1976, op. cit., p. 2512.

51. General George Brown, Senate, Armed Services Committee, Fiscal Year 1976, op. cit., Part 1, p. 244.

52. House, Appropriations Committee, Appropriations for 1976, op. cit., p. 251.

53. Ibid., p. 253.

54. Senate, Appropriations Committee, Department of Defense Appropriations Fiscal Year 1975, op. cit., p. 106.

55. House, Armed Services Committee, Military Posture 1976, op. cit., p. 178.

56. Ibid., p. 179.

57. House, Appropriations Committee, Appropriations for 1976, op. cit., p. 27.

58. For discussions of the new studies, see: Michael Getler, "Study Insists NATO Can Defend Itself," the Washington Post, June 7, 1973; Senate, Armed Services Committee, Military Procurement Authorization, Fiscal Year 1974, op. cit., Part 8, pp. 5249, 5279, 5304; Part 1, p. 310; Senate, Armed Services Committee, Fiscal Year 1976, op. cit., Part 1, pp. 321–22.

59. Senate, Armed Services Committee, Fiscal Year 1976, op. cit., Part 5, p. 2235.

60. Ibid., Part 1, p. 322.

61. Ibid.

62. Ibid., Part 5, p. 2171.

63. Senate, Appropriations Committee, Department of Defense Appropriations, Fiscal Year 1975, op. cit., Part 5, p. 106.

64. James R. Schlesinger, taken from a June 8, 1973 press conference.

65. House, Appropriations Committee, Appropriations, Fiscal Year 1976, op. cit., p. 251.

66. Senate, Armed Services Committee, Fiscal Year 1976, op. cit., Part 1, p. 250.

67. Ibid., Part 5, p. 2279.

68. General Michael S. Davison, "The Military Balance in Central Army Group," Strategic Review, Fall 1974, p. 15.

69. Ibid., p. 16.

70. Gwynne Dyer, "Why Outmanned NATO Can Hold," the Washington Star, October 5, 1975.

71. Senate, Armed Services Committee, Fiscal Year 1976, op. cit., Part 1, p. 78.

72. Senate, Armed Services Committee, Military Manpower Issues of the Past and Future (Washington, D.C.: Government Printing Office, 1974), p. 18.

73. Senate, Armed Services Committee, Fiscal Year 1976, op. cit., Part 1, p. 80.

74. House, Armed Services Committee, Military Posture 1976, op. cit., p. 102.

75. International Institute for Strategic Studies, The Military Balance 1975-1976 (London: IISS, 1975), p. 22.

76. House, Armed Services Committee, Military Posture 1976, op. cit., p. 179.

77. House, Appropriations Committee, Appropriations for 1976, op. cit., p. 27.

78. Senate, Armed Services Committee, Fiscal Year 1976, op. cit., Part 5, p. 2279.

79. Ibid., p. 2229.

80. Elliot Richardson, Senate, Armed Services Committee, Fiscal Year 1974, op. cit., Part 1, pp. 175-76.

81. House, Appropriations Committee, Appropriations for 1976, op. cit., p. 248.

82. General David Jones, ibid., Part 2, p. 71.

83. Craig R. Whitney, "Rise in East-Bloc Troops Noted," New York Times, September 29, 1975, p. 3.

84. House, Appropriations Committee, Department of Defense Appropriations for 1973 (Washington, D.C.: GPO, 1972), Part 1, p. 447; Jeffrey Record, Sizing Up the Soviet Army (Washington, D.C.: Brookings Institution, 1975), p. 25.

85. General Fred Weyand, Senate, Armed Services Committee, Nomination of Tankersley, Brownman, Marcy, Penisten, and Weyand (Washington, D.C.: GPO, October 3, 1974), p. 41.

86. House, Armed Services Committee, Military Posture 1976, op. cit., Part 1, p. 210.

87. Ibid.

88. Colonel Edward B. Atkinson, "Is the Soviet Army Obsolete?" Army, May 1974, pp. 10-16.

89. Senate, Armed Services Committee, Fiscal Year 1976, op. cit., Part 4, p. 1811. On Soviet tank tactics, see also Jeffrey

Record, "Armored Advance Rates: A Historical Inquiry," Military
Review, September 1973, pp. 63-72.

90. Senate, Armed Services Committee, Fiscal Year 1976,
op. cit., Part 2, p. 489.

91. Brooke Nihart, "Score: TOW/Cobra 20, Armor 1,"
Armed Forces Journal, September 1972, p. 20.

92. General Accounting Office, Airlift Operations of the
Military Airlift Command During the 1973 Middle East War, April 16,
1975, p. 1.

93. Ibid., p. 3.

94. Senate, Armed Services Committee, Fiscal Year 1976,
op. cit., Part 5, p. 2508.

95. Senate, Armed Services Committee, Nomination of
James R. Schlesinger to Be Secretary of Defense (Washington, D.C.:
Government Printing Office, 1973), p. 96.

96. Senate, Armed Services Committee, Fiscal Year 1976,
op. cit., Part 1, pp. 143-47.

97. Ibid., Part 5, p. 2246.

98. General George Brown, ibid., Part 1, p. 265.

99. Jeffrey Record, Sizing Up the Soviet Army, op. cit., p. 45;
General Michael S. Davison, op. cit., p. 16.

100. House, Appropriations Committee, Military Construction
Appropriations for 1976, Part 3, p. 205; Record, Sizing Up the Soviet
Army, op. cit., pp. 45-46.

101. Senate, Foreign Relations Committee, U.S. Forces In
Europe, op. cit., p. 86.

102. House, Appropriations Committee, Appropriations for
1976, op. cit., p. 262.

103. Ibid., p. 255.

104. James R. Schlesinger, Senate, Armed Services Committee, Fiscal Year 1976, op. cit., Part 1, p. 143.

105. General T. R. Milton, "On Used Cars and MBFR," Air
Force, October 1975, p. 34.

106. House, Armed Services Committee, Military Posture
1976, op. cit., Part 1, p. 136.

107. Craig R. Whitney, "Rise in East-Bloc Troops Noted,"
New York Times, September 29, 1975, p. 3.

108. James R. Schlesinger, taken from a December 11, 1974
press conference in Brussels.

109. General Accounting Office, Some of the Issues Involved
in Maintaining U.S. Forces in Europe, September 12, 1975, p. 13.

110. House, Foreign Affairs Committee, Fiscal Year 1975
Foreign Assistance Request (Washington, D.C.: Government
Printing Office, 1974), p. 414.

3

KOREA AND U.S.
STRATEGY FOR
NORTHEAST ASIA
Stefan H. Leader

The end of more than 30 years of war in Southeast Asia and the American withdrawal from the region have set in motion political and military changes throughout Asia. Many Asian countries have reassessed their relations with the United States as well as with other important countries in the region, including the Soviet Union, the People's Republic of China, Japan, and North Vietnam. A new multipolar pattern of relations has emerged in which no one country can be said to dominate the Asian region and many countries are competing for influence. All the countries in the region, but especially the Soviet Union, China, and Japan, are adjusting in various ways to a changed international environment, the outlines of which are only beginning to emerge.

The United States has also had to adjust to the new realities of Asian international relations. This has taken the form of a shift in attention away from Southeast Asia as an area of high priority to a renewed emphasis on Korea and Japan. The process of adjustment has produced neither a long-range conception of American policy for Asia, nor a new policy, but rather a stopgap strategy based on reaffirmation of old military commitments. The most salient American objective in Northeast Asia has become the preservation of the existing state of affairs—both in terms of existing political arrangements and existing American military forces in the region. Instead of new imaginative departures, we find renewed emphasis on old commitments, old balance of power theories, and an absence of policy instruments beyond reliance on American military forces.

This chapter is an attempt to survey the current state of U.S. policy toward Korea and its broader Northeast Asian context. Because U.S. military forces continue to be an important—indeed a dominant instrument of American policy—we will give special attention to these forces and the political issues raised by them.

U.S. MILITARY FORCES IN KOREA

More than 20 years after the end of the Korean War, the center-piece of American policy in Northeast Asia continues to be the large American military presence on the peninsula and the commitment to defend South Korea—The Republic of Korea—represented by this force. This commitment is the focus of much criticism and debate. As of June 30, 1976 the United States will have nearly 40,000 military personnel stationed in South Korea. This includes 31,700 soldiers, 8,014 airmen, 216 sailors, and 32 marines. The total has been slowly rising from 37,663 as of June 1974 and moving closer to the Defense Department's ceiling of 42,100.[1]

The largest component of the American military force in Korea consists of 14,600 troops of the Second Infantry Division and the 11,000 men of the 19th Support Group who back them up. Air force combat units consist of two squadrons of supersonic F-4 fighter bombers. There are a total of approximately 50 U.S. F-4 fighter bombers currently based in South Korea.

The most politically sensitive component of the American military force in South Korea is, of course, the large number of nuclear weapons based there. Former Secretary of Defense James Schlesinger recently acknowledged what has been well known for some time—that the United States has nuclear weapons based in South Korea.[2] It is estimated that there are several hundred—perhaps as many as 686—nuclear weapons of various types, including artillery shells, missile warheads, bombs, and land mines, in South Korea. (See Table 3.2, below.)

POLITICAL ISSUES

Numerous questions have been raised regarding the commitment to defend South Korea and our military presence there. The most important questions are whether the defense of South Korea is vital for American defense and whether American troops need to remain in South Korea, for how long, and under what circumstances they might be withdrawn. In addition, public discussion has focused on a number of other related issues: What is the existing military balance on the Korean peninsula and what is the likelihood of a renewal of hostilities there? What is the proper role of U.S. forces while they remain in South Korea and how should they be deployed? Are the nuclear weapons based in South Korea necessary and under what circumstances might they be used? How much military and economic aid should be provided to the Republic of Korea government and for how long? What impact will the domestic policies of the Park government have on the stability of the peninsula and the willingness of the United States to continue to support the Republic of Korea?

The most basic issues are whether the U.S. commitment to the defense of South Korea is necessary and is consistent with U.S. national interests, and whether U.S. troops need to remain in South Korea.

Few analysts—even those who support the continuation of the U.S. defense commitment to South Korea—insist that the defense of South Korea in itself is essential to the defense of the United States. Instead, they argue that the American commitment to defend South Korea is of some political importance for protecting our global position and our interests in Northeast Asia. Thus, to understand our commitment to South Korea, it is essential to examine it in its broader Northeast Asian and global context.

U.S. STRATEGY FOR ASIA

A basic theme of U.S. defense and foreign policy worldwide, especially under former Secretary of Defense Schlesinger and Secretary of State Henry Kissinger, has been the importance of maintaining "worldwide military equilibrium." While in office Secretary Schlesinger was particularly forceful in stating this theme. In his FY 1975 annual report he asserted, "The United States today . . . bears the principal burden of maintaining the worldwide military equilibrium which is the foundation for the security and survival of the free world."[3] In applying this strategy special emphasis has been placed on Northeast Asia and particularly South Korea and Japan.

The major justification given for the continued maintenance of U.S. troops in South Korea is consistent with this broad conception of the U.S. role in the world and, as Secretary Schlesinger argued, is fundamentally political, not military.[4] This was given further emphasis by Leonard Sullivan, assistant secretary of defense for program analysis and evaluation, when he told the Senate Armed Services Committee that U.S. troops in South Korea "maintain a perception of balance in that corner of the world where the interests of the Chinese, the Soviets, the Japanese and the United States come together."[5]

In a more fundamental sense American purposes continue to be
what they have been since the early 1950s, to support U.S. client
states by preventing what some have seen as the expansion of Soviet
power in Asia. Assistant Defense Secretary Sullivan has pointed out
that American force levels are "dictated primarily by the Soviet
threat, which is gradually becoming a worldwide threat at sea and on
all portions of the Eurasian continent."[6] To a lesser degree there is
still concern about the possibility of Chinese intervention in a renewed
war in Korea.[7]

The commitment to this strategy combined with the fall of South
Vietnam and the continuing American withdrawal from Southeast Asia
has led American policy makers to emphasize a single short-run
goal. As of October 1, 1975, 17,000 U.S. military personnel remained
in Thailand, though this total continued to decline consistent with the
wishes of the Thai government. All American troops are scheduled
to leave Thailand by July 1976.

The short-run goal is to maintain the present U.S. troop level
in Asia so as to demonstrate continued American interest in the area.
American policy makers also do not want to create the impression
that the United States is withdrawing from Asia.[8]

In fact, the United States is not withdrawing from Asia and the
possibility of war in Northeast Asia continues to be one of two major
events used to justify the size of U.S. military forces. The other is
a war in Europe.

Forces earmarked specifically for Asian contingencies include
two Army divisions (one in Korea and one in Hawaii) and one Marine
division (on Okinawa), the Third and Seventh Fleets, and 29 tactical
air squadrons.[9] In addition, four divisions and an infantry brigade
based in the United States are earmarked as strategic reserves for
worldwide deployment and could also be used in Asia. The total cost
of these forces has been estimated by Barry Blechman of the Brookings Institution at $23 billion per year.[10]

The need to protect the security and independence of Japan is
also used to justify the presence of U.S. troops in South Korea.
While the security and independence of Japan are certainly in the
U.S. national interest, the presence of U.S. troops in Japan is not
essential for the defense of Japan. Far more important is the ability
of both Japan and South Korea to defend themselves.

There is no doubt that U.S. withdrawal from Korea would make
many Japanese uneasy and could confront Japan with a serious decision
about the adequacy of its own defenses and the reliability of the defense
commitment by the United States. Nevertheless, it should be clear
that the commitment to Japan has far stronger support in the United
States than the commitment to South Korea. Furthermore, as former
Ambassador to Japan Edwin Reischauer has indicated, it is more

sensible to rely for the defense of Japan on naval forces in the straits
between Japan and Korea than on ground forces on the Korean peninsula. [11] Such a posture would pose a far easier task for the United
States since it would be politically more acceptable to most Americans than the present arrangement. A U.S. naval presence would
also allay Japanese fears about U.S. abandonment and would be
consistent with the U.S. role as a Pacific, not an Asian, power.

The advantages of air and naval forces over ground forces were
pointed out by Army Colonel Zeb Bradford. Writing in Military Review,
Bradford pointed out that as a result of Vietnam:

> we have learned that, in strategic terms, ground power
> can be quite inflexible once committed however much
> flexibility it may provide on a tactical level . . . While
> aircraft and ships can often reverse course and make a
> clean break, ground forces rarely can do so once engaged.

He went on to point out that the use of ground forces "burns bridges
of easy political or logistical withdrawal."[12]

The question of how long American troops will remain on the
peninsula, as well as when and under what circumstances they might
leave, continues to be an important issue. For several reasons it is
clear that U.S. military forces will be withdrawn at some time in the
future. There continues to be widespread concern among the general
public and on the part of some government officials that war might
break out and the United States might be drawn into another land war
in Asia. The House Defense Appropriations Subcommittee has recommended that U.S. forces be reduced to 20,000 by 1978. Public opinion
continues to be sharply divided on the question of whether U.S. forces
should be used to help defend South Korea in the event of renewed
war. A Harris poll released in June 1975 indicated that although 43
percent would favor using American land, air, and naval forces in
the event of a North Korean attack, 37 percent opposed such action.
When the question was worded slightly differently, the same poll found
only 28 percent in favor of U.S. military involvement and 52 percent
opposed. Even if we accept the higher figure in support of intervention,
the results are not encouraging.[13] In May 1975, the following question
was asked: "If North Korea invaded South Korea we have a firm commitment to defend South Korea with our own military forces. If South
Korea were invaded would you favor or oppose the United States using
troops, airpower and naval power to defend South Korea?" The results
were 43 percent in favor, 37 percent opposed, and 20 percent not sure.
Also in May 1975 the following question was asked: "There has been a lot
of discussion about what circumstances might justify U.S. military involvement, including the use of U.S. nuclear weapons. Do you feel if

North Korea attacked South Korea you would favor or oppose U.S.
military involvement?" Without the leading opening statement about
"a firm commitment" only 28 percent favored military involvement,
52 percent were opposed, and 20 percent were not sure.

As was demonstrated so clearly by Vietnam, the issue is not
whether a majority favors intervention but whether there is a sizable
minority that strongly opposes it. During much of the Vietnam War,
opposition was restricted to a minority of the American public, though
opposition expanded to a majority near the end of the war. Our experience in Vietnam demonstrated that the domestic costs of intervention
in the face of strong minority opposition can make such a policy unten-
able, tear the country apart, and in the long run weaken the United
States. Finally, the South Korean government has said that in five
years—assuming continued American aid to modernize their armed
forces—it will no longer need American ground troops. [14]

So long as American troops remain in Korea there will continue
to be concern over how and where they are deployed. One battalion
of the Second Division is based north of the Imjin river on the southern
edge of the demilitarized zone. The remainder of the division is
located about 20 miles to the rear of the South Korean army's defensive
positions at Camp Casey.

In the event of an attack, U.S. forces would have no choice but
to become quickly involved in the fighting. While this might be desirable from the perspective of some theories of deterrence, nevertheless it leaves American policy makers with few choices and may not
be desirable in light of sharp public division on whether to fight in
Korea again. [15] This would be particularly troublesome in the event
of a renewed Korean war of purely Korean origins. Because of the
danger of a renewed Korean war leading to a U.S.-Soviet confrontation, it would be in the U.S. interest not to become a belligerent if
the origins of the war were purely Korean.

On April 7, 1975 Assistant Defense Secretary Sullivan told a
subcommittee of the House Armed Services Committee that he had
doubts about the positioning of the American division in Korea. He
pointed out that it is squarely in the middle of the most likely North
Korean invasion route. [16] Secretary Schlesinger has said, "We would
prefer that those forces be deployed further back but that would
require very large expenditures for military construction."[17] While
executive branch spokesmen have cited the problem of cost as the
major impediment to basing the Second Division further south, the
Army plans to spend about $30 million between 1976 and 1980 on new
barracks and other facilities including almost $5 million on the existing
base at Camp Casey. This suggests that in spite of their avowed concern with positioning U.S. troops, the Pentagon does not plan to move

the Second Division farther south.[18] It also suggests that the Pentagon plans to keep American forces in South Korea beyond 1980.

MILITARY BALANCE

The military capability of South Korea is at least equal to and in some respects greater than that of North Korea. South Korean ground forces outnumber those of North Korea by 580,000[*] to 410,000 and are more experienced than the North Koreans. Three hundred thousand South Koreans are tough combat veterans of the Vietnam War. In contrast, the North Korean army has not had any combat experience since the Korean War. In addition, South Korea has reserves, the Homeland Defense Reserve Force, of about 2.7 million men, compared to militia of approximately 1.5 million for North Korea. While North Korea may have an advantage in number of tanks[19] (approximately 1,300 to 1,000 for South Korea), the South Korean army has already been equipped with approximately 700 TOW antitank missiles, and will have more than 1000 by the end of 1976.[20]

The TOW is a highly effective weapon that makes it possible for two soldiers to destroy one tank at ranges of more than a mile. The effectiveness of such weapons against tanks, especially when fired from prepared defensive positions, was graphically demonstrated by the Egyptians in the October 1973 Yom Kippur War.[21]

Secretary Schlesinger said in Congressional testimony in 1974 that South Korea is capable of repulsing a North Korean attack without American ground support. The Pentagon has said, "With our assistance the South Koreans have developed a significant military capability, especially in ground forces, which we believe are adequate for defense against North Korea."[22]

There are some areas in which the South Koreans do not have as much equipment as they would like. An example is combat aircraft. The Center for Defense Information estimates that the North Koreans have about 573 combat aircraft, compared to 330 for South Korea.[23] These aggregate statistics, however, do not tell the whole story. If one compares the two air forces in terms of modern, high performance aircraft, one finds that the South Koreans have an advantage of 203[†] to 153.[‡] This is because a larger part of the North

---

[*] Total includes 20,000 Marines.

[†] Thirty-six F-4C/D, 154 F-5A/E/F and 10 RF-5A. In addition, 18 F-4E's and 87 F-5Es are on order.

[‡] One hundred twenty-five MIG-21, 28 SU-7.

TABLE 3.1

Comparative Military Strengths: North and South Korea

	South Korea	North Korea
Military Forces		
Army	560,000	410,000
Air Force	25,000	40,000
Navy	20,000	17,000
Marines	20,000	—
Total	625,000	467,000
Reserve Forces and		
Civilian Militia	2,700,000	1,600,000
Combat Planes	330	573
Tanks	1,000	1,300
Combat Ships	143	177
Population	35,000,000	15,400,000
Military Expenditure as		
a Percentage of GNP	5.2	9.4
Number of Soldiers		
per 100 people	2.0	2.5

Sources: International Institute for Strategic Studies, "The Military Balance," 1975-76, p. 56. Also, Time, June 30, 1975; Republic of Korea Military Attache, Washington, D.C.; The Department of Defense; World Military Expenditures and Arms Trade (Washington, D.C.: Arms Control and Disarmament Agency, 1974); and Ruth Sivard, World Military and Social Expenditures (New York: Institute for World Order, 1974).

Korean air force consists of obsolete aircraft (MIG 15/17/19). The South Koreans also have a substantial advantage in the ability to conduct both long-range offensive attacks deep inside North Korea—deep interdiction—and to provide close support to their troops. South Korean F-4 Phantoms have three times the range and three times the payload of the fighter-bombers (MIG-19s and SU-7s) in the North Korean air force, and South Korean F-5Es have approximately 50 percent more range and payload than North Korean aircraft. South Korean Sparrow and Sidewinder air-to-air missiles would likely give them a significant advantage in air combat. Finally, most of the North Korean air force consists of defensive interceptor aircraft.

Because of the nominal North Korean advantage in numbers of fighter aircraft, and their fear of a North Korean surprise attack, the South Koreans have built many aircraft shelters. This has largely neutralized the possibility that the South Korean air force could be destroyed on the ground by a North Korean surprise attack. As was pointed out in a 1973 Senate report, "U.S. Air Force officers in Korea argue that the disparity in fighters and bombers (between North and South Korea) is more than compensated for by the shelter program since shelters and not planes then become targets in case of a surprise attack."[24] In short, what is militarily significant is not the total number of aircraft on each side, but their relative capabilities. From this perspective it is clear that the larger number of fighter aircraft in the North Korean inventory is simply not militarily significant.

The Republic of Korea is also making a substantial effort to improve its ability to defend itself. The South Korean government will double its military spending in fiscal 1976 to nearly $1.5 billion. This will comprise more than 30 percent of its total budget. In contrast, North Korea is reported to have spent approximately $880 million last year on its military forces.

Table 3.1 concisely summarizes the comparative military capabilities of North and South Korea. These data, as well as the Pentagon's assessments, make it quite clear that the South Koreans do have the capacity to defend themselves without U.S. ground support and are rapidly acquiring the capacity to defend themselves without U.S. air and naval support.

NORTH KOREAN AGGRESSION?

Estimates of the likelihood of a North Korean attack have fluctuated somewhat in recent years. After the fall of South Vietnam, many American officials expressed concern that this defeat might encourage Kim Il Sung of North Korea to launch an attack against the South.[25] This war talk was encouraged somewhat by both the bellicose statements of Kim Il Sung and by the Park government, which was anxious to secure reaffirmation of the American commitment to defend Korea. The Park government, moreover, has effectively used the threat of war to suppress internal opposition.

However, Secretary Schlesinger subsequently played down his concern over a possible North Korean attack. Upon his return from Japan and South Korea in early August 1975, he made it clear that he did not consider a war in Korea to be likely. "Deterrence is working," he said.[26] In the same news conference, he said the conventional "force balance in the Korean peninsula is not unsatisfactory . . . "

and, further, that he regarded the possibility of using nuclear weapons as unlikely. [27]

It has been clear for some time that, for their own reasons, neither the Soviet Union nor China is prepared to support a North Korean attack on South Korea. [28] It is apparent that renewed war in Korea would severely damage Soviet-American and Chinese-American relations. Further, it is doubtful that North Korea could support such a war by itself for very long without substantial aid from China, the Soviet Union, or both. [29] There is sufficient evidence to suggest that this is precisely the message conveyed to Kim by the Chinese when he visited Peking in April 1975. Chinese statements at the time referred very pointedly to Chinese support for the peaceful unification of Korea. [30] Kim received an even colder response from the Soviets, who discouraged Kim's visit to Moscow.[31]

U.S. NUCLEAR WEAPONS: HELPFUL OR HARMFUL?

The presence of American nuclear weapons in Korea poses serious problems because there is serious doubt about their military utility. There is considerable difference between U.S. tactical nuclear weapons in Korea and those in Europe. In the case of nuclear weapons in Europe there are comparable weapons—though not as many—on the other side, and consequently U.S. nuclear weapons serve an important deterrent function. [32] In contrast, there are no nuclear weapons in North Korea. Thus, there is no need for them as nuclear deterrents in the South. The Pentagon's intention is obviously to create fear in the minds of the North Koreans that the United States might resort to nuclear weapons if they were to attack the South. However, the likelihood that the United States would use nuclear weapons against a nonnuclear country is very low. The political costs would be great. Also, there is no need for nuclear weapons if the South Koreans can defend themselves, as the Department of Defense believes. Shortly before his departure from the Defense Department, Secretary Schlesinger backed away from his original threat to use nuclear weapons in Korea. Instead, he has acknowledged that because of the conventional force balance, their use would not be necessary. [33] Under the circumstances, withdrawal of U.S. nuclear weapons from Korea appears to be the most appropriate policy.

TABLE 3.2

U.S. Nuclear Arms in South Korea

Service	System	Number of Nuclear-Capable Systems	Load and Reload (number per system) (estimates)	Total (estimated)	Explosive Power per Warhead (maximum kilotonnage)
USAF	(Fighter-Bomber)				
	F-4	48	4	192	10kt
U.S. Army	(Artillery)				
	M-110 (203 mm)	28	2	56	1kt
	M-109 (155 mm)	76	2	152	1kt
	(SAM)				
	Nike-Hercules	144	1	144	5kt
	(SSM)				
	Honest John	4	20	80	100kt
	Sergeant	2	6	12	100kt
	Atomic Mine	25–50	1	25–50	5kt
Total				661–686	

Methodology used: Nuclear capable systems in Korea were identified and then, using estimates based on European load and reload experience, a total for each system was computed. The maximum total kilotonnage available might be understood in terms of the bomb dropped on Hiroshima: 14 kilotons. The total kilotonnage is, therefore, between 816 and 944 Hiroshima equivalents.

Source: Center for Defense Information.

U.S. MILITARY AID TO KOREA

U.S. military efforts in Korea have been extensive and costly.
The cost to the United States since 1950, including the cost of the
Korean War, all economic and military aid, and the cost of U.S.
troops in Korea, has been about $38 billion. Since the end of the
Korean War the United States has spent about $11 billion to maintain
its military forces in Korea. Military grants to the Korean government since 1950 have cost the United States about $4 billion. Military
sales on favorable credit terms have amounted to about $300 million,
all since 1971. [34]

In recent years, the issue of U.S. military aid to Korea, and
indeed all forms of aid, has been closely tied to the level of American
troops, to judgments of the military balance on the peninsula, and to
the human rights question. In 1971, the withdrawal of 20,000 U.S.
troops was accompanied by a commitment by the United States of
$1.5 billion, over five years, to modernize the South Korean armed
forces. The modernization plan called for grants under the Military
Assistance Program of $1.25 billion, including $350 million to support
operations and maintenance costs of Korean armed forces, and additional grants of $250 million in Excess Defense Articles. Equipment
given under this program is valued at a third of acquisition cost. The
bulk of this $1.5 billion was to be in new hardware and equipment like
aircraft, tanks, and missiles. The total value of all U.S. military
aid to South Korea during the period 1971 to 1975 has actually reached
almost $1.8 billion, though not all of this total went for new equipment.
If the FY 1976 request of $210.8 million is fully funded, it will bring the
total of American military aid to the ROK to nearly $2 billion for the
1971-76 period.

While the South Koreans have legitimate military needs that
should be treated sympathetically, future requests for military aid
need to be examined carefully. The South Koreans have become adept
at concealing or understating their own strength to justify more
assistance. Furthermore, attention to the equipment that the South
Koreans receive is essential. Our objective should be to improve
their defensive, not offensive, capabilities. Aircraft like the F-4—
of which South Korea has 36—that have range and sufficient payload
to make possible attacks deep into North Korea can destabilize the
military balance and raise the specter of attack on the North from the
South. The United States should not provide this kind of offensive
capability. Also, we should not complicate the Koreans' operations
and maintenance problems by providing them with a large variety of
sophisticated aircraft or weapons.

TABLE 3.3

U.S. Military Assistance and Sales to Korea
(millions of dollars)

Programs	1971	1972	1973	1974	1975	1976	Total
Military Assistance Program (Grants including the Foreign Military Training Program)	291.2	155.5	149.6	94.1	82.6	76.5[a]	849.5
Credit Sales (FMS Credit Sales)	15.0	15.0	25.0	56.6	59.0	126.0[a]	296.6
Excess Defense Articles (Grants) (1/3 of acquisition value)	17.1	14.3	9.1	5.9	1.0	8.3[a]	55.7
Other Grants (including PL 91-652, PL 480, sec. 104)	106.2	184.7	0.2	0	0	0	291.1
Ship Loans	0	3.2	5.7	0	0	0	8.9
Administrative Costs of U.S. Advisers (JUSMAG)	15.0	14.6	14.9	10.8	7.0	7.3	69.6
Subtotals	444.5	387.3	204.5	167.4	149.6	218.1	1,571.4
Military Assistance included in Defense Department Budget (MASF)[b]	208.2	188.9	133.5	0	0	0	530.6
Grand total	652.7	576.2	338.0	167.4	149.6	218.1	2,102.0

[a]Proposed.

[b]These funds were for the support of South Korean forces that fought in South Vietnam. The money went for the operation and maintenance of South Korean forces as well as new equipment and supplies, some of which were returned to South Korea.

Sources: Department of Defense, Defense Security Assistance Agency, Agency for International Development, U.S. Overseas Loans and Grants, July 1, 1945–June 30, 1974, Department of Defense, "Report on Transfer of U.S. Resources to Foreign Nations for Security Assistance," in U.S. Senate, Committee on Foreign Relations, Hearings, Foreign Assistance and Related Programs, Appropriations, FY 1973, Appendix II.

The United States should be moving towards an agreement to reestablish the armistice provision restricting introduction of weapons into the Korean peninsula. Obviously, this cannot be done unilaterally. It must be undertaken with the full agreement of North Korea and its suppliers. This is crucial to the future stability of the peninsula.

Finally, military aid to both sides has helped to make the Korean peninsula one of the world's most heavily militarized regions. South Korean society is heavily dominated by the military. It is clear that the military, North and South, has a vested interest in continuing the high level of tension that has existed in recent years. If we are to succeed in reducing tension in Korea and encouraging democratic reforms in South Korea, greater efforts need to be made to strengthen the nonmilitary institutions of Korean society. In practical terms, this means larger amounts of economic aid aimed at strengthening universities, political parties, and voluntary associations as counter-weights to the military.

HUMAN RIGHTS AND MILITARY AID

South Korean violations of human rights are a continuing issue and could have a bearing on future military and economic aid to South Korea because of a provision in the Foreign Assistance Act of 1974 and new amendments to the 1975 Military Assistance Authorization Bill passed by House and Senate committees. The 1974 law directs the president to "reduce or terminate military or economic assistance to any government which engages in a consistent pattern of gross violations of internationally recognized human rights, including torture, or cruel, inhuman or degrading treatment or punishment: prolonged detention without charges or other flagrant denials of the right to life, liberty, and the security of the person." Under another provision of the law, the president may furnish security assistance in spite of human rights violations by advising the Congress that extraordinary circumstances require it. In more recent actions, House and Senate committees have gone beyond these provisions and approved amend-ments to the 1975 military assistance bill which would in some instances place the final decision in the Congress. The amendments require the State Department to prepare reports on the status of human rights in various countries and permit the Congress to termi-nate assistance by concurrent resolution upon finding violations of human rights.

These legislative provisions demonstrate the seriousness with which many members of Congress view human rights violations. A number of supporters of these provisions in Congress fear that

oppressive policies of the government of the Republic of Korea will in
the end undermine the support of its own people and damage its ability
to defend itself. Representative Donald Fraser said in April 1975,
"A continuation of such policies can lead to dangerous instability
within South Korea . . . "

Former Ambassador Edwin Reischauer recently wrote, "Park
is embarked on a policy that seems almost designed to destroy popular
support for his regime and make the distinction between the North
and the South seem no longer very important."[35] There may not be
sufficient evidence to support a firm conclusion that violations of
human rights will erode the support of the Korean people, though the
possibility cannot be dismissed. It is clear that South Korean government actions are eroding the support of the American people. In a
Harris poll conducted in June and July of 1975, 42 percent of those
questioned agreed with the statement "South Korea is a dictatorship
and takes away the rights of political opposition and it is wrong for
us to support such a government." Only 32 percent disagreed with
the statement. [36]

The Republic of Korea government has promulgated a series
of "emergency decrees" prohibiting criticism or action aimed at
revision of the existing constitution and providing for severe punishment for those who oppose the decrees. Several reports on the subject
of human rights in Korea have impressed members of Congress.
Amnesty International's mission to Korea in 1975 reported violations
of due process of law, violations of academic freedom, and violations
of other internationally recognized standards of human rights.

There is at least one rather troubling similarity between Korea
and Vietnam. During the entire course of the Vietnam War much was
made of the great importance of Vietnam for the American political
and military position throughout the world. Vietnam was almost always
discussed in terms of its worldwide strategic significance and not in
terms of its own unique history and problems. Since the fall of South
Vietnam we have discovered that the worldwide significance of South
Vietnam was far less than we had supposed. The same tendency is
apparent in Korea. Again, former Secretary of Defense Schlesinger
and President Ford have made much of the global geopolitical significance of Korea and our commitment to its defense, but have paid
little attention to the domestic situation within Korea, which has the
potential to destabilize the peninsula. The apparent conflict between
the demands of deterrence and internal democracy in South Korea
disappears if it is understood that deterrence of a North Korean
attack and defense of South Korea may depend on South Korean public
support for their government. The issue becomes even more important in light of the concern expressed by the South Korean government
that the North Koreans are intent on fomenting an insurgency in South

Korea that they could then exploit politically and militarily. Nothing is likely to produce support for such efforts in South Korea as quickly as the continued, brutal repression of legitimate criticism of the Park regime.

The substantial South Korean ground capability makes it clear that U.S. ground forces can be gradually withdrawn from South Korea over the next few years without any significant destabilizing impact on the peninsula. This would eliminate the danger that U.S. troops might quickly become involved in a war, and would restore some of the flexibility that their presence so near the demilitarized zone sacrifices. U.S. air forces could remain in the area, preferably in Japan and on carriers in the waters near Korea. The presence of these forces would be sufficient to perform the political functions—maintenance of a regional balance, deterrence of North Korea, symbol of U.S. interest in the region—that American strategy in the region necessitates. Finally, U.S. military assistance should be so structured that it increases the military self-sufficiency of the South Koreans to make possible a gradual reduction of South Korean dependence on the United States and a discontinuance of U.S. assistance.

One of the fundamental lessons of the last 25 years of U.S. defense and foreign policy in Asia is that the United States is essentially a Pacific power, not an Asian power. American interests in the Far East, which are largely economic, reside not on the Asian mainland, but rather in Japan and the Pacific Ocean basin. The United States does not have vital security interests on the Asian mainland and certainly none that justify becoming involved in another land war there. It is essential that American policy makers recognize this and adjust the American military presence in the region to reflect properly this fact.

It is also essential that American policy makers recognize that nationalism—the most potent political force in this century—is also the most potent political force in Asia today. U.S. setbacks in Asia—our trauma and national hysteria over the so-called "loss of China," and more than 20 years of lost opportunities for American diplomacy that resulted, as well as our defeat in Vietnam—have been the result of our insufficient understanding of the force of nationalism. At the same time, we insisted on treating the Chinese civil war and the war in Vietnam as skirmishes in our worldwide struggle to resist first Soviet, and then Chinese, communist hegemony.

A more realistic American policy in Asia would recognize the vitality and power of nationalism and our limited ability to influence it. Chinese concern for growing Soviet interest and involvement in Asia should be viewed in this light. The Soviets have no magic formula for political success in Asia. On the contrary, they are likely to encounter the same nationalist resistance that the United States has encountered, and they give no indication of having any better understanding of it than the United States has had. A lower military profile in Asia and greater reliance on diplomacy are likely to be the most productive American policies over the next ten years.

NOTES

1. See Korea Week, vol. 8, no. 15 (August 15, 1975), p. 1. A substantial part of this increase is caused by the replacement of Korean soldiers assigned to the Second Division (KATUSA's) by Americans. This was undertaken at the urging of Congress, which directed that the Second Division's mission be broadened beyond simply defense of South Korea. Congress directed that the Second Division be converted into a Pacific-area reserve force capable of deployment throughout the entire Pacific area. See also Army Times, March 12, 1975.

2. James R. Schlesinger, taken from a June 20, 1975 news conference at the Defense Department.

3. James R. Schlesinger, Annual Defense Department Report, FY 1975 (Washington, D.C.: Department of Defense, 1975), p. 1.

4. U.S. Congress, House, Appropriations Committee, Department of Defense Appropriations, FY 1976 (Washington, D.C.: GPO, February 26, 1975), Part I, p. 355.

5. U.S. Congress, Senate, Armed Services Committee, Fiscal Year 1976 and July-September 1976 Transition Period Authorization for Military Procurement, Research and Development and Active Duty Selected Reserve and Civilian Personnel Strengths (Washington, D.C.: GPO, April 7, 1975), Part 5, p. 2517.

6. Ibid., Part 5, p. 2513.

7. Ibid.

8. Ibid.

9. U.S. Department of Defense, Manpower Requirements Report for FY 1975 (Washington, D.C., February 1974), pp. XVI-8-XVI-11. Eleven squadrons are specifically designated by the Department of Defense as necessary for Asian contingencies. In addition, 37 squadrons in the United States and Iceland are designated as reinforcements for Europe and Asia. We have counted half of these, 18 squadrons, in arriving at the total of 29 squadrons for Asia.

10. Senate, Armed Services Committee, op. cit., Part 5, p. 2620.

11. Edwin Reischauer, "Back to Normalcy," Foreign Policy, no. 20 (Fall 1975): 207.

12. Colonel Zeb Bradford, "American Ground Power After Vietnam," Military Review, April 1972, p. 4.

13. Jae Un Lee, "South-North Dialogue: A North Korean Peace Offensive?" Journal of Korean Affairs 5, no. 2 (July 1975): 34; Louis Harris Associates, New York, 1975.

14. The New York Times, August 21, 1975.

15. See, for example, Thomas Schelling, Arms and Influence (New Haven, Conn.: Yale University Press, 1966), pp. 35-91.

16. Korea Week, op. cit.

17. Senate, Budget Committee, 1976 First Concurrent Resolution on the Budget (Washington, D.C.: Government Printing Office, March 21, 1975), vol. 2, p. 1110.

18. Korea Week, September 30, 1975, p. 3.

19. International Institute for Strategic Studies, The Military Balance: 1975-1976 (London: 1975), p. 56; Republic of Korea Military Attache, Washington, D. C. The estimate of 1300 North Korean tanks is an average of the figures provided by these two sources.

20. U.S. Department of Defense, Defense Security Assistance Agency, Foreign Military Sales and Military Assistance Program, FY 1976-197T, Congressional Presentation Document (Washington, D.C.: Government Printing Office, 1975), p. 21.

21. Elizabeth Monroe and A. H. Farrar-Hockley, "The Arab-Israeli War, October 1973, Background and Events," Adelphi Paper no. 111 (London: IISS, 1975), pp. 33-34.

22. Department of Defense, Manpower Requirements Report for FY 1976 (Washington, D. C., February 1975), p. V-6.

23. These estimates are based on several sources, including: Norman Polmar, personal communication; The Military Balance, op. cit.; and Defense Security Assistance Agency, Security Assistance Program, FY 1976 and 197T, Congressional Presentation Document (Washington, D.C.: Government Printing Office, 1975).

24. Senate, Foreign Relations Committee, Staff report, Korea and the Philippines, November 1972 (Washington, D.C.: GPO, 1973), p. 23.

25. The Christian Science Monitor, May 27, 1975.

26. James R. Schlesinger, taken from a September 1, 1975 news conference at the Department of Defense, Washington, D. C.

27. Ibid.

28. William Spahr, "The Military Security Aspects of Soviet Relations with North Korea," Journal of Korean Affairs, vol. 4, no. 1 (April 1974): 7; and Jae Un Lee, op. cit., p. 33.

29. Department of Defense, Manpower Requirements Report for FY 1975 (Washington, D. C., 1974), p. V-7.

30. Peking Review, May 2, 1975, p. 11.

31. U.S. News and World Report, June 15, 1975, p. 11.

32. It is estimated that there are approximately 2,250 Soviet tactical nuclear weapons in Europe compared to approximately 7,000

for the United States. See Jeffrey Record, Sizing Up the Soviet Army (Washington, D. C.: Brookings Institution, 1975), p. 40.

33. James R. Schlesinger, taken from a September 1, 1975 news conference at Andrews Air Force Base, Maryland.

34. House, Appropriations Committee, Foreign Assistance and Related Agencies, Appropriations for 1975 (Washington, D.C.: GPO, 1974), p. 1181; Department of Defense, Defense Security Assistance Agency, Foreign Military Sales and Military Assistance Facts (Washington, D.C.: GPO, November 1975), p. 19.

35. Edwin Reischauer, "The Korean Connection," The New York Times Magazine, September 22, 1974, p. 99; Congressional Record, U.S. House of Representatives, April 8, 1975, p. 1570.

36. Poll conducted in June and July, 1975, by Louis Harris Associates, New York. Results provided by Louis Harris Associates in telephone conversation.

4

**JAPAN UNDER
U.S. PRESSURE**
Dennis F. Verhoff

During his August 1975 visit to Japan, former Secretary of Defense James R. Schlesinger urged Japan to increase its military forces. He alleged that Japan's military capability is inadequate to defend Japan: "At the present time . . . it is not sufficiently ample to fulfill the mission."[1] It is not at all clear that the Japanese government or the Japanese people see the situation the same way. Other U.S. military officials have also differed with Secretary Schlesinger. Assistant Secretary of Defense Leonard Sullivan has stated that the Japanese "do have adequate defenses for the islands."[2]

The reason for Schlesinger's urging Japan to expand its military forces may be more related to U.S. military plans for the defense of South Korea than to the defense of Japan itself. If the Korean factor is dominant, we may be pressuring the Japanese government into a course of action that could have dangerous consequences for its relationship with the Japanese people and the rest of Asia. Japanese rearmament, for whatever purpose, is the most explosive domestic issue in Japan and of tremendous concern to the rest of Asia.

AN ANOMALY IN A MILITARY WORLD

The Japanese constitution stipulates, and the great majority of Japanese agree, that Japan should maintain military forces that are purely defensive in nature. Japan has no military forces capable of waging an offensive war against any nation. This has made it possible for Japan to spend less of its gross national product for military force than any major nation in the world. Without raw materials and without

61

offensive military forces, Japan has become a world power with peace
and prosperity at home—an anomaly in today's world of growing reliance on weaponry.

In 1974, Japan spent $4.3 billion on self-defense. This figure
is equivalent to 0.9 percent of Japan's GNP, 6.4 percent of its national
budget, and $39 per capita. [3]

By contrast, the United States spent $85 billion on military
forces in 1974. This was 6.0 percent of our GNP, 26.9 percent of
our national budget, and $395 per capita. [4] In the wake of the debacle
in Southeast Asia, the United States is making a fundamental reassessment of the need to maintain military forces around the world and particularly in Asia and the western Pacific. In the name of partnership
we are urging allies to assume more of the burden of their own defense
to cut U.S. costs and permit removal of U.S. military forces from
foreign countries. Serious problems can arise if American military
policies and overseas military deployments are not consonant with the
defense needs of our allies.

U.S.-JAPANESE RELATIONS: HEIGHTENED CONCERN

The nature of Japan's future military role has emerged as a
major issue of U.S. post-Vietnam policy in Asia. The level and pace
of American-Japanese diplomatic exchanges have increased sharply
since the U.S. exodus from Southeast Asia. President Ford's visit to
Japan in November 1974, Japanese Prime Minister Miki's visit to
the United States in August 1975, Secretary of Defense James Schlesinger's visit to Japan in that same month, and Emperor Hirohito's
visit to the United States in October 1975 reflect the increased attention given to Japanese-American military relations.

The key military issues are: 1) the size and purpose of the
Japanese Self-Defense Forces (SDF) and American pressures to
increase them; 2) the future of the Treaty of Mutual Cooperation and
Security (MST); and 3) American bases and their uses in Japan. Lurk-
ing behind all three issues is the question of a nuclear-armed Japan.

While the American-Japanese relationship has undergone
numerous adjustments, American initiatives have dominated bilateral
relations throughout the postoccupation period. Remnants of an occupation mentality still prevail on both sides. When problems and crises
have occurred, they have occurred largely as a result of inadequate
communication of intentions and goals and American insensitivity to
Japanese needs. The most blatant example of this lack of communication was former President Nixon's failure to inform the Japanese
of his intention to visit the People's Republic of China in July 1971.

This announcement came as a severe shock to the Japanese government because American officials had failed to consult or even inform the Japanese of this American initiative. The Japanese government, however, can also be faulted for its complacency and lack of initiative on foreign policy issues over the years. [5] Japan has placed almost total reliance on the spirit and intent of the Treaty of Mutual Cooperation and Security of 1960 with the United States that calls for consultation concerning any changes in the Asian region.

The American diplomatic opening to Peking is symptomatic of past Japanese-American relations in that it dramatically demonstrated the subordination of Japan to American interests in Asia and the Pacific. American officials have frequently circumvented Japanese policy makers because it was felt that they lacked an appreciation of realpolitik. These diplomatic failures are certain to produce fundamental changes in Japanese attitudes.

MILITARY RELATIONS

Detente and the American diplomatic opening to Peking in 1971 have created new incentives and opportunities for Japan to pursue a foreign policy that is more independent of the United States and that takes into account the uniquely Japanese political, cultural, social and historical experience. Despite the room for political maneuver that detente has created, however, military issues threaten to continue to be the primary focus of Japanese-American relations.

American government officials, particularly Secretary Schlesinger, have recently advocated an expanded Japanese defense effort. [6] This theme originated during the Korean War, when American occupation forces were quickly shifted from Japan to the Korean peninsula. It is also argued that Japan has basically had a "free ride" on the American commitment to the conventional and nuclear defense of Japan. In the absence of a credible military threat to Japan, the free ride argument is questionable. In strict cost-accounting terms, Japan has contributed valuable real estate and subsidized the maintenance of American bases in Japan. [7] The U.S.-Japanese military relationship has benefited the United States more than it has benefited Japan. The United States has utilized American bases in Japan and Okinawa during our involvements in the Korean and Vietnam Wars. American military officials continue to see these bases as convenient for U.S. military operations in East Asia.

JAPAN'S SELF-DEFENSE FORCES

Since the creation of the Self-Defense Forces in the early 1950s, Japan has moved slowly but steadily to develop a strong, modern, well-equipped military force capable of defending Japan against attack. Today, Japan's Self-Defense Forces, of 236,000 officers and men, [8]

TABLE 4.1

Japanese Self-Defense Forces

Self-Defense Forces	Number
Air	
Actual Manpower	42,000
Fighter Aircraft	595
Other Aircraft	454
Air Defense Missiles (NIKE)	180
Ground	
Actual Manpower	155,000
Reserves	39,000
Tanks	690
Artillery	4,190
Artillery Rockets	50
Air Defense Missiles (HAWK)	170
Aircraft	449
Maritime	
Actual Manpower	39,000
Reserves	600
Destroyers-Frigates	49
Submarines	16
Other Ships	150
Aircraft	230
Totals	
Manpower	236,000
Tanks	690
Aircraft	1,720
Ships	215
Air Defense Missiles	350

although characterized by some weaknesses, have significant defensive
capabilities. Japan's Air Self-Defense Force with 42,000 men and an
inventory of almost 600 combat aircraft is comparable in size to
North Korea's.[9] Approximately 270 of those aircraft are modern
Japanese-built F-4 Phantoms and F-104 Starfighters with specifically
designed defensive configurations.[10] In addition, the Japanese are
 adding the Japanese-designed-and-built FS-T2 supersonic trainer-
attack planes. Moreover, a Japanese delegation toured the United
States in June 1975 and looked at the whole range of new U.S. fighters
with a view toward buying between 100 and 125. The estimated value
of this purchase is over $1 billion.[11]

Japan's Maritime Self-Defense Force (MSDF) with 215 ships
and 39,000 men has been gradually increasing in size with the addition
of modern Japanese-designed-and-built ships, including destroyers
and submarines.[12] The MSDF is planning to improve its antisubmarine warfare capability by acquiring as many as 50 U.S. P-3C
patrol aircraft at a cost of at least $1 billion.[13] The MSDF has, by
conscious design, virtually no capability to support its ships beyond
Japanese coastal waters. The MSDF is essentially a defensive coast
guard, which is consistent with Japan's constitutional proscription on
deploying military forces abroad.[14]

IMPEDIMENTS TO EXPANSION

The Japanese are modernizing their Self-Defense Forces (SDF),
but progress has been restrained for a number of reasons. The major
impediment to any significant expansion of Japan's Self-Defense
Forces is the constitutional ambiguity surrounding the military in
Japan. Article 9 of the American-drafted Japanese constitution states
that "the Japanese people forever renounce war as a sovereign right
of the nation and the threat or use of force as means of settling international disputes."[15] Although the Japanese Diet (Parliament)—the
highest organ of state power—has interpreted this article to mean that
military forces for defensive purposes are not prohibited, the consti-
tutionality of this interpretation is still being challenged before
Japan's Supreme Court, and, more importantly, in the hearts and
minds of the Japanese people. Only 58 percent of the Japanese people
in a recent poll supported the SDF.[16] In a country with a political
tradition that places a high value on consensus, this is not overwhelm-
ingly supportive. This less than enthusiastic support for the SDF, in
large measure, explains the low status of the military in Japan and
the shortfalls in authorized strength—29,000 for all three branches of
the Self-Defense Force in 1975. An indicator of the low status of the

military in Japanese society is that the military rarely wear their
uniforms in public, even commuting to and from duty stations in
civilian clothes.

Japan perceives no immediate, direct threat to the integrity and
security of the Japanese islands. Foreign Minister Mayazawa recently
termed this "the relatively favorable international environment surrounding Japan."[17] Japanese judgments on this matter are realistic.
The only adversary capable of attacking Japan is the Soviet Union.
However, the probability of such an attack is low for several reasons.
An attack on Japan would severely tax the minimal Soviet logistical
and amphibious capabilities in the Far East. The Sino-Soviet dispute
requires the Soviets to maintain large military forces on the Chinese
border, and the Soviet Warsaw Pact commitments keep substantial
military forces tied down in Europe.

Japan's view of today's world is that large scale wars involving
the major powers or wars involving nuclear weapons are highly
unlikely. On the other hand, the Japanese note that limited wars and
guerrilla wars caused by ideological confrontation, nationalism, anti-
colonialism, territorial disputes, and racial disputes have occurred
frequently in recent years and can be expected in the future.[18] Specifically, Japan regards military conflict on the Korean peninsula as
an indirect threat to Japanese interests. The Miki-Ford Joint Announcement issued at the end of the Japanese prime minister's visit
to the United States in August 1975 stated: ". . . the security of the
Republic of Korea is essential to the maintenance of peace on the
Korean peninsula, which in turn is necessary for the peace and
security in East Asia, including Japan."[19] The United States has
been pressuring Japanese leaders to cooperate more closely with the
United States in military preparations related to Korea.

JAPAN AND KOREA

The United States, the Soviet Union, and the People's Republic
of China seem to want to avoid conflict on the Korean peninsula. Conflict leading to unification of the two Koreas, whether initiated by
North or South Korea, would threaten the interests of all three powers.
Japan, as the fourth Asian power, would then be placed in a very difficult position. Any role beyond Japan's agreed-to provision of minimal logistical support for the American defense of South Korea would
adversely affect Japan's relations with the Soviet Union and the People's
Republic of China. This would also undermine ongoing Japanese efforts
to mediate the conflict between North and South Korea.

Instability on the Korean peninsula would also threaten Japanese economic interests and trade with both Koreas. More importantly, it could cause domestic problems because of the 600,000 or more Korean residents in Japan, at least two-thirds of whom are estimated to be sympathetic to the Kim Il Sung regime in North Korea.[20] Conflict on the Korean peninsula could be the spark that inflames the present animosity between Japanese and Korean residents in Japan. Domestic political issues, such as the generally low socioeconomic status of Koreans living in Japan and Japanese perceptions of these people as economic parasites, could easily be thrown into stark relief by conflict on the Korean peninsula.[21]

Although the stability of Korea is important to Japan, Prime Minister Miki has stated that Japan would not become militarily involved in a war in Korea and in any case, thinks such a war highly unlikely.[22] Former Secretary Schlesinger reiterated this same point on his visit to Tokyo in August 1975. The absence of any perceived immediate, direct military threat to Japan is one reason Japanese policy makers have found it difficult to respond to American pressure to significantly expand their Self-Defense Forces.

SELF-DEFENSE?

Although the Japanese see their SDF as a strictly defensive force that would form the nucleus of Japan's limited response to any overt or covert aggression, it is not at all clear that American officials share this perception. For instance, in his posture statement for fiscal 1976, the Chairman of the Joint Chiefs of Staff, General George Brown, stated that: "It is in our interest to encourage Japan to build on our common interest for peace and stability by maintaining forces adequate for the defense of the Japanese homeland and contiguous areas."[23] What General Brown meant by "contiguous areas" is not clear, but if he is encouraging deployment of Japanese Self-Defense Forces outside Japan, he is suggesting that Japan violate its constitution. Any hint of Japanese military reinvolvement on the Korean peninsula would resurrect Korean and other Asian fears of a rebirth of the Japanese militarism of the 1930s and 1940s. Although American military leaders pay lip service to the constitutional restraints on Japanese Self-Defense Forces, they would undoubtedly consider Japanese acceptance of a wider role in American East Asian military matters in a very favorable light.

FISCAL RESTRAINTS

In addition to the constitutional restraint and the absence of an immediate, direct threat to Japan, another restraint on any Japanese effort to increase further the SDF is the current economic situation. Japan's Finance Ministry sets an overall spending limit to which Japanese Defense Agency (JDA) planners must adhere. An inflation rate of 24 percent in 1974 and increases in personnel costs have largely consumed the 12.4 percent increase in the defense budget from FY 1973 to FY 1974.[24] Shortfalls in acquisition of some equipment also reflect this realistic Japanese thinking that defense spending must mirror the general health of the economy. For example, JDA's Fourth Five-Year Defense Plan (1972-76) calls for acquisition of 68 Japanese-built FS-T2 attack aircraft, but the number actually in the Air Self-Defense Force's (ASDF) inventory at the end of the plan (March 31, 1976) will only be 18.[25] This is also typical of the slow rate of equipment acquisition in the Ground Self-Defense Forces (GSDF) and the Maritime Self-Defense Forces (MSDF).

Another economic restraint on defense spending is Japan's need to remedy social and economic inadequacies much neglected during the phenomenal growth years of the 1960s and early 1970s. As Japan's expenditures for education, social security, medical care, and pollution control increase, military spending will necessarily be restrained.[26]

REVIVAL OF JAPANESE MILITARISM?

An additional impediment is the historical impact of Japanese militarism on the rest of Asia and on the Japanese people themselves. For the Japanese, the militarism of the 1930s and 1940s produced the ignominy of defeat in August 1945. The reaction of the Japanese public to anything that smacks of militarism is indicative of Japanese policy makers' problems in dealing with defense issues. In 1970, the ritual suicide of Yukio Mishima, an advocate of traditional martial arts and patriotic values, met with derision. The return in 1974 of an Imperial Army holdout from the jungles of the Philippines first produced a wave of romantic admiration that later turned into contempt for someone who would waste his life so foolishly. These reactions make clear how far Japan has come from the Bushido spirit of the 1930s and 1940s.

Any proposed expansion of the defense budget or of Japan's military role generates charges of a "revival of Japanese militarism" from other Asian countries. Japanese government officials are keenly aware of this problem and work to avoid the charge even to the extent that they worry about the amount of capital investment and level of trade with Asian countries once occupied by the Japanese Imperial Army.

NUCLEAR WEAPONS

Some military analysts in this country regard a nuclear-armed Japan as inevitable.[27] They reason that without nuclear weapons, Japan will be unable to play the game of great-power politics commensurate with its economic status. The American government is concerned over the failure of the last Diet session to ratify the Nonproliferation Treaty and is currently making efforts, such as offering international inspection of American nuclear reactors, to persuade Japan to do so. The Miki government has gone on record in favor of ratification and the next Diet session may ratify it.[28]

A number of factors, often overlooked by American analysts and policy makers, loom large in Japanese thinking on the nuclear issue. First of all, 1975 marked the 30th anniversary of the American opening of the nuclear age with the bombing of Hiroshima and Nagasaki. Japan is the only country to have experienced the horror and destruction of atomic weapons. The resultant Japanese "nuclear allergy" and the maintenance of the three nonnuclear principles—no manufacture, no introduction, and no possession of nuclear weapons— are deeply ingrained in the Japanese conscience. These events have produced a militant reaction to all things nuclear. One example of this attitude is the five-week blockade of Japan's first nuclear-powered cargo ship, the Mutsu, by Japanese fishermen in 1974.[29]

Another indication of the general state of Japanese attitudes toward nuclear weapons was the furor provoked in late 1974 by the testimony of retired Rear Admiral Gene La Rocque that U.S. Navy ships do not generally offload their nuclear weapons before entering any foreign ports.

JAPANESE VULNERABILITY

Possession of nuclear weapons by Japan would be tremendously destabilizing throughout Asia. In testimony before Congress last year, Deputy Secretary of State Robert S. Ingersoll, a former U.S. Ambassador to Japan, summed up the situation quite well:

If ever Japan were judged to be returning to an earlier
militarism, tensions would rise throughout Asia, countries would arm and China in particular would react
strongly. The situation would be thrown into even more
serious relief were Japan to acquire a nuclear capability. [30]

In order to possess a credible nuclear deterrent, Japan would
have to spend billions of dollars with very uncertain results, given
the fact that there is essentially no defense against nuclear attack
except the threat of counterattack.

The geographical and demographic composition of the Japanese
islands makes Japan peculiarly vulnerable to nuclear attack. Japan
is a chain of narrow islands—no more than 250 miles across at the
widest point—with most of the population concentrated in a very small
area. Ninety percent of the people, farms, and factories of Japan are
located within 50 miles of a line drawn from Tokyo through the main
cities of the Pacific seaboard to Fukuoka on the island of Kyushu. To
destroy Japan through a nuclear attack would be an easy task. This
extreme vulnerability may be uniquely Japanese, but nuclear vulnerability is a fact of life common to all countries, nuclear and nonnuclear.

It should be noted that Japan does have the capability to produce
nuclear weapons. In addition to the necessary fissionable material,
Japan clearly possesses the technology to produce nuclear weapons
within a matter of months. However, even though Japan has not yet
ratified the Nonproliferation Treaty, it is highly unlikely that Japan
will decide to acquire nuclear weapons. [31]

THE U.S. NUCLEAR UMBRELLA?

In the eyes of many Japanese and Americans the U.S. nuclear
umbrella has played an important role in the defense of Japan for
many years. The concept of "nuclear umbrella" is vague and impre-
cise, and the recent Miki-Ford Joint Announcement did little to clarify
it. In that announcement it was stated that Japan and the United States
recognize that "the U.S. nuclear deterrent is an important contributor
to the security of Japan."[32] It further stated that "the U.S. would
continue to abide by its defense commitment to Japan . . . in the event
of an armed attack against Japan, whether by nuclear or conventional
forces."[33] Thus, according to these statements, the nuclear umbrella
implies a U.S. commitment to defend Japan with nuclear weapons
against nuclear and conventional attack. However, the United States
and the Soviet Union can clearly destroy each other with nuclear

weapons regardless of who strikes first. Therefore, it is unlikely
that the United States will accept the destruction of the United States
in order to save Japan.

In short, there is reason to doubt the existence of such an
umbrella, despite President Ford's recent assurances. This should
be of small concern, however, since the incentives for any country
to threaten or attack Japan with either nuclear or conventional weapons
are small and the disincentives very great. There are many less dangerous ways to influence Japan. Furthermore, each of Japan's nuclear
armed neighbors has a strong interest in seeing that Japan is not
dominated by, nor too friendly with, the other. This fact, more than
the security link with the United States, protects Japan and provides
considerable opportunities for Japanese diplomacy.

SOURCES OF TENSION

While the United States-Japan Treaty of Mutual Cooperation and
Security (MST) remains the cornerstone of our relations with Japan,
U.S.-Japanese relations often suffer from differences in interpretation
of the treaty. Total coincidence of perceptions between any two countries, allies or adversaries, is rare, but the striving for such agreement is perhaps the most important function of diplomacy. From the
American perspective, emphasis has largely centered on the military
aspects of the treaty. For the Japanese, emphasis is placed on all
aspects of U.S.-Japanese relations, military, economic, political,
and cultural.

Three specific clauses of the Mutual Security Treaty represent
sources of tension in American-Japanese relations. One is Article VI,
or the so-called "Far East clause," which grants the United States
use of areas in Japan for its land, air, and naval forces to insure the
security of Japan and "the maintenance of international peace and
security in the Far East."[34] The maintenance of peace in the Far
East, especially on the Korean peninsula, is obviously of great concern to Japan. However, the Japanese are fearful of being dragged
into a conflict against their better judgment or that the United States
may insist on using military force as a solution where other solutions
are possible and involve the Japanese in the ensuing conflict.

A sore point for the United States is the "prior consultation"
arrangement under which U.S. troop movements and use of equipment
are subject to prior approval by Tokyo.[35] Our Department of Defense
thinks this may delay prompt action in an emergency. This is again
indicative of the differences in perception each party has of the MST.

FIGURE 4.1

U.S. Military Forces in the Far East

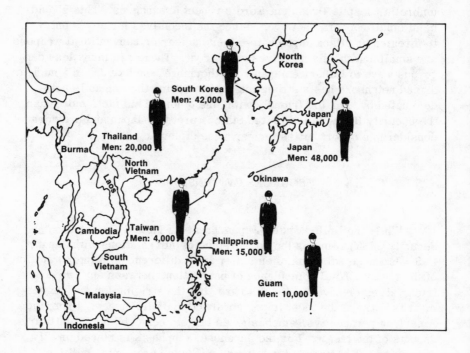

Source: Department of Defense.

The third source of tension is the presence of American bases
in Japan. For many Japanese, these bases represent a continuation
of the occupation and an unnecessary guarantee of the questionable
American nuclear umbrella. Furthermore, they occupy valuable real
estate in densely populated areas. As of 1972, 70 percent of U.S.
base area and 77 percent of American military personnel in the home
islands were located within 60 miles of Tokyo.

While U.S. bases in Japan have more political than military
importance, the Pentagon continues to see them as staging areas and
jump-off points for a land war in Asia. This was pointed out by
General Brown in his FY76 posture statement. He said that these
bases represent American military power "in plain sight, close at
hand and ready to fight."[36] As such, he said, they reassure our allies
that we intend to live up to our treaty commitments. Nevertheless, it
is a foregone conclusion that in time they will be removed. The South

TABLE 4.2

U.S. Military Personnel in Japan

Region	Number
Home Islands	16,000
Okinawa	32,000
Total	48,000

TABLE 4.3

Seventh Fleet Home Port in Japan

Type of Ship	Number	Total Number of Crew Members
Combat store ship (AFS)	2	790
Guided missile light cruiser (CLG)	1	867
Attack aircraft carrier (CVA)	1	2,328
Destroyer (DD)	4	1,103
Guided missile destroyer (DDG)	1	316
Escort ship (DE)	1	338
Guided missile frigate (DLG)	1	344
Total	11	6,086

Koreans, for example, have said that in five years they will not longer need American ground forces. It is possible that Secretary Schlesinger's recent statements urging an expanded Japanese Self-Defense Force could be seen by Japan as a hint that we will withdraw from Japan in time and that the Japanese will be on their own.

During the height of the Korean War, the United States had as many as 4,000 military facilities and more than 250,000 military personnel in Japan.[37] Since then, the American presence has slowly been reduced to 143 military installations[38] and 48,000 military personnel[39]--most of the reductions having occurred in the last few

TABLE 4.4

Major U.S. Bases in Japan and Okinawa

Base	Facility
Home Islands	
Yokota	Headquarters, U.S. Forces Japan, and of the 5th Air Force
Camp Zama	Headquarters of the U.S. Army in Japan (25 miles southwest of Tokyo)
Yokosuka	Headquarters, U.S. Naval Forces in Japan and Homeport for nine ships of the Seventh Fleet
Sasebo	Naval base and homeport for two ships of the Seventh Fleet
Atsugi	Seventh Fleet naval air facility
Iwakuni	Air base for First Marine Air Wing (part of Seventh Fleet)
Sagami	Repair depot for the Army
Misawa	Air Force base
Okinawa*	
White Beach	U.S. Naval facilities
Kadena Air Base	Fleet flying activities
Camp Courtney	Headquarters for Third Marine Division and Third Marine Amphibious Force

*
U.S. bases on Okinawa occupy 20 percent of the island.

years. Of the 48,000 military personnel in Japan, approximately two-thirds are based on Okinawa where American bases occupy 20 percent of the island. Today, the military justification for U.S. forces stationed in Japan, as in Korea, has diminished. They could gradually be further reduced over the next five years in close consultation with Japan.

JAPAN'S FUTURE COURSE

Since the opening of Japan in the middle of the last century, Japan has run a frenetic race to catch up with the West. The catching-up process has led to various extremes—the militarism of the 1930s and 1940s and the pollution and congestion of today's urban, industrial society. Today, Japan has no model to emulate. It faces the same indeterminate future all nations face. (Problem issues such as global economic interdependence, the role of force in international relations, and the quality of life are not amenable to easy solution. No nation, however, has yet provided an example for other nations to follow in attempting solutions.) If Japan, in clinging to the status quo, maintains its past complacency and acquiescence to American initiatives, it will miss a golden opportunity to chart a course of action unemcumbered by heavy military expenditures and nuclear fears.

If Japan succumbs to the current American pressure to expand its defense efforts for whatever reasons—maintenance of the American nuclear umbrella, hoped-for concessions in other areas of American-Japanese relations, or sheer inertia of the existing state of affairs—it may be setting out on a course of ever-increasing military expenditures that will feed on its own reasoning and be difficult to reverse. There would be no advantage for Japan to trade its nuclear allergy for the tremendous risks and uncertainties of a nuclear arms race. If the world has learned anything in recent years, it is that possession of nuclear weapons creates more uncertainties than it removes.

Japan has a unique opportunity to become a leader of the post-industrial world—a world that has yet to tackle seriously the problems which industrialization, interdependence, and nuclear proliferation have created. A significantly expanded Japanese military effort or a nuclear-armed Japan would only add to the problems.

CONCLUSIONS

1) The level of Japan's military expenditures reflects an accurate judgment about threats to its security and the usefulness of military force in its international relations. Japan does not need to increase its own military forces.

2) The "rush to growth" of the Japanese economy has created inadequacies in Japan's social infrastructure—for example, education, health care, pollution, welfare—that will encourage the Japanese to continue their stringent controls on military spending.

3) The Japanese "nuclear allergy" and three "nonnuclear principles"—no possession, no manufacture, no introduction of nuclear weapons—are still very significant impediments to Japan's acquisition of nuclear weapons.

4) Japan's military establishment is adequate to defend the Japanese islands. U.S. military forces stationed in the area,

ostensibly to protect Japan, serve more political than military functions and could gradually be reduced over a five-year period.

5) The U.S. government is pushing Japan down the path of
rearmament. It is, however, in America's interests to encourage
the possibility of a nonmilitarized Japan. Admission of Japan to
permanent membership on the United Nations Security Council would
serve to recognize Japan as a nonnuclear great power.

NOTES

1. The Washington Post, August 30, 1975.

2. U.S. Congress, Senate, Armed Services Committee,
Hearings on S. 920, 94th Cong., 1st sess. (Washington, D.C.: Government Printing Office, 1975), Part 5, p. 2517.

3. These figures are extracted from Military Balance 1975-76
(London: International Institute for Strategic Studies, 1975), pp. 76-77.

4. Ibid.

5. See Donald Hellmann, Japan and East Asia (New York:
Praeger Publishers, 1972), pp. 140-67, for an analysis of the
domestic factors involved in Japanese foreign policy making. Hellmann characterizes the defense decision-making process as one of
"fundamental immobilism."

6. Christian Science Monitor, August 29, 1975.

7. Japan provided $255 million for U.S. base maintenance in
FY 1974. Japan is preparing to spend $600-700 million over the next
couple of years for U.S. base relocation and consolidation within
Japan. Report of Senator Strom Thurmond and Senator William Scott
to Senate, Armed Services Committee (Washington, D.C.: Government
Printing Office, 1975), p. 7.

8. Military Balance, op. cit., p. 55.

9. Ibid.

10. These figures are compiled from Military Balance, op. cit.,
p. 55; Hisao Iwashima, "Japan's Defense Policy," Strategic Review,
Spring 1975, p. 20; and information obtained from the Embassy of
Japan, Office of Military Attache, Washington, D.C.

11. "Defense Industry Notes," International Defense Review
vol. 8, no. 3, June 1975, p. 445; and Aerospace Daily, September 10,
1975, p. 49.

12. Military Balance, op. cit.

13. International Defense Review, op. cit.

14. See Theodore McNelly, Politics and Government in Japan
(Boston: Houghton Mifflin Co., 1972), pp. 261-70, for the full text
of the Japanese constitution.

15. Ibid.

16. Sanki Jiji, September 15, 1973, cited in J. Rey Maeno, "Japan 1973: The End of an Era," Japan Survey, January 1974, p. 57.

17. Foreign Minister Kiichi Miyazawa, "Japan's Diplomacy in Today's World," speech at the Foreign Correspondents Club, Tokyo, Japan, July 10, 1975.

18. Japan Defense Agency, Japan's Fourth Five-Year Defense Plan, Tokyo, Japan, 1972, p. 6.

19. Japan Times, August 8, 1975.

20. Nathan White, "Japan's Interests in Korea," paper prepared for delivery at the American Political Science Association convention, September 1975, p. 17.

21. McNelly, op. cit., p. 234.

22. Christian Science Monitor, August 7, 1975.

23. General George Brown, Senate, Armed Services Committee, op. cit., Part 1, p. 258.

24. Robert Bowie, "Japan's Sun Still Rising," Christian Science Monitor, June 11, 1975.

25. Iwashima, op. cit., p. 20; and information obtained from the Embassy of Japan, Office of Military Attache, Washington, D.C.

26. See Henry Rosovsky, "Japan and the United States: Notes from the Devil's Advocate," in Priscilla Clapp and Morton H. Halperin, eds., United States Japanese Relations (Cambridge, Mass.: Harvard University Press, 1974), pp. 79-93, for a discussion of the growth-at-any-cost philosophy of Japan's recent past and the implications of this for the future.

27. See Fred Greene, Stresses in U.S.-Japanese Relations (Washington, D.C.: Brookings Institution, 1975), pp. 92-104, for a discussion of American and Japanese views on Japan's nuclear option.

28. Miki's commitment to ratification was contained in the Miki-Ford Joint Announcement, Japan Times, August 8, 1975.

29. See Shunji Taoka, Japan's Defense and the American Presence (Washington, D.C.: Georgetown Center for Strategic and International Studies, 1975), p. 30, for a more lengthy discussion of the Mutsu incident.

30. Deputy Secretary Robert S. Ingersoll's testimony is cited in Keyes Beech, "Japan—the Ultimate Domino?" Saturday Review, August 23, 1975, p. 17.

31. See "Japan's Nuclear Option," Strategic Survey 1972 (London: International Institute for Strategic Studies, 1973), pp. 40-44, for a succinct discussion of the issue.

32. Joint Announcement, op. cit.

33. Ibid.

34. See Senate, Foreign Relations Committee, United States Security Commitments Abroad, vol. 2, Parts 5-11 (Washington, D.C.: GPO, 1970), pp. 1433-38, for the entire text of the treaty.

35. Ibid., p. 1436.

36. Senate, Armed Services Committee, op. cit., p. 259.

37. The Baltimore Sun, July 13, 1975.

38. Far Eastern Economic Review, May 2, 1975, p. 33.

39. U.S. Department of Defense, news release, "U.S. Military Personnel Outside the United States," September 12, 1975.

5

THE INDIAN OCEAN: A
NEW NAVAL ARMS RACE
David T. Johnson

In November 1974, an eight-ship U.S. Navy task force, together with ships from Britain, Iran, Pakistan, and Turkey, took part in the largest naval exercises ever held in the Indian Ocean.[1] The 80,000-ton aircraft carrier Constellation toured the Persian Gulf, the first time a U.S. carrier had been there since 1948. The primary purpose of this operation was to demonstrate U.S. naval strength in the approaches to the Persian Gulf and to the world's largest oil reserves.

Since the October 1973 war in the Middle East, the United States has increasingly been displaying its military power in the Indian Ocean. For approximately one-third of the time since then, the U.S. Navy has kept either a cruiser or a carrier task force in the region, in addition to the three ships of the Mideast force that has been based at Bahrain in the Persian Gulf since 1949. As the Defense Department has stated, "We do foresee a requirement by our national command authorities to maintain militarily significant forces in the Indian Ocean, for periods of time amounting to 30 to 60 days each quarter. Since October 1973 that is what has been done."[2]

Much of the debate over the increasing U.S. military presence in the Indian Ocean has focused on the Defense Department's efforts to build a naval and air base on the island of Diego Garcia in the middle of the Indian Ocean. The proposed base expansion has assumed a symbolic importance beyond its strictly military significance. For some, Diego Garcia represents the continuation of the same impulses to be the world's policeman that led to the Vietnam involvement. For others, Diego Garcia is a necessary step to counter the Soviet Union in a region of the world that has become increasingly important to the United States. Although the expansion of facilities on Diego Garcia has gone forward, after lengthy congressional debate, the long-term

MAP 5.1

Military Facilities in the Indian Ocean Region
(Western Section)

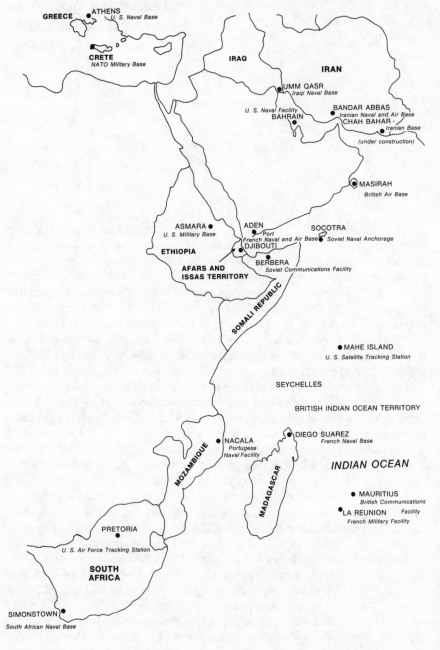

Source: Center for Defense Information.

MAP 5.2

Military Facilities in the Indian Ocean Region
(Central Region)

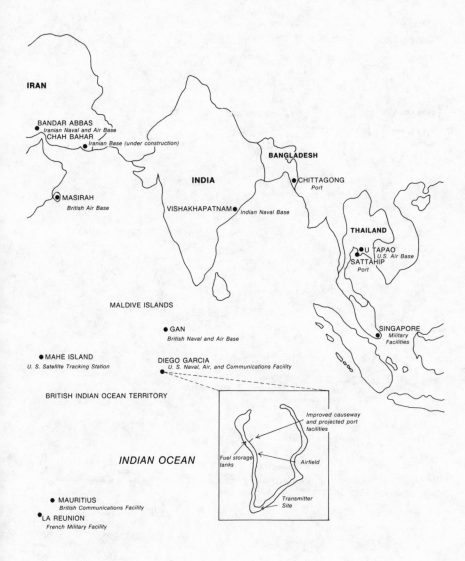

IRAN

BANDAR ABBAS
Iranian Naval and Air Base
CHAH BAHAR
●*Iranian Base (under construction)*

BANGLADESH

INDIA

●CHITTAGONG
Port

●MASIRAH
British Air Base

VISHAKHAPATNAM●
Indian Naval Base

THAILAND

●U TAPAO
U.S. Air Base
SATTAHIP
Port

MALDIVE ISLANDS

●GAN
British Naval and Air Base

SINGAPORE
*Military
Facilities*

●MAHE ISLAND
U. S. Satellite Tracking Station

DIEGO GARCIA
U. S. Naval, Air, and Communications Facility

BRITISH INDIAN OCEAN TERRITORY

Improved causeway
and projected port
facilities

INDIAN OCEAN

Fuel storage
tanks

Airfield

●MAURITIUS
British Communications Facility
●LA REUNION
French Military Facility

Transmitter
Site

Source: Center for Defense Information.

81

MAP 5.3

Military Facilities in the Indian Ocean Region
(Eastern Section)

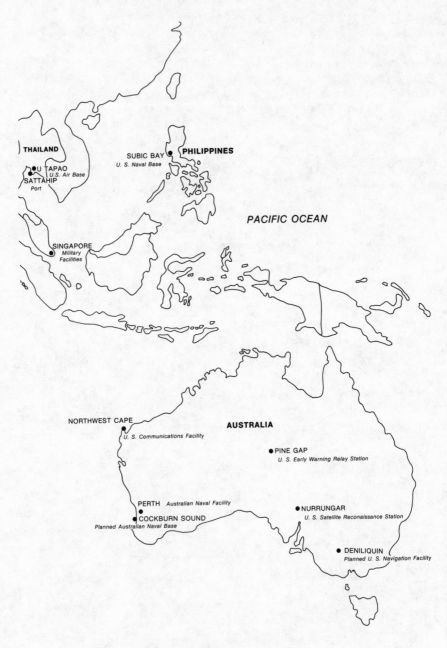

Source: Center for Defense Information.

direction of U.S. policy in the Indian Ocean remains uncertain, bound
as it is with such complex and potentially explosive matters as the
conflict over oil, conditions in the Middle East and Persian Gulf, the
great power rivalry between the United States and the Soviet Union,
and the possibility of violent change in southern Africa.

Before the 1973 Mideast war, U.S. policy toward the Indian
Ocean generally followed a pattern of low-profile and minimal military
involvement. There were, of course, important exceptions like the
"tilting" exercise in gunboat diplomacy during the India-Pakistan war
in 1971, when the United States sent a carrier task force into the
Indian Ocean. It is also true that U.S. Navy planning for increased
U.S. military presence in the Indian Ocean, including the base at
Diego Garcia, dates to the early 1960s, if not before. Before 1973,
however, most U.S. policy makers seemed to agree that the United
States had no vital interests at stake in the region and that U.S.
security interests there were comparatively limited and best served
through nonmilitary means.

The position of the State Department was concisely stated in
1971 by Ronald Spiers, then director of the Bureau of Politico-Military
Affairs:

> There appears to be no requirement at this time for us
> to feel impelled to control, or even decisively influence,
> any part of the Indian Ocean or its littoral given the
> nature of our interests there and the current level of
> Soviet and Chinese involvement. We consider, on balance,
> that our present interests are served by normal com-
> mercial, political, and military access.[3]

Assistant Secretary of State David Abshire added that "U.S. security
interests in the Indian Ocean are quite limited."[4] The Pacific, Atlantic, and Mediterranean were perceived as areas of much higher priority. U.S. policy makers acknowledged that in the highly improbable
event of a conventional conflict between the United States and the
Soviet Union, the Indian Ocean was a most unlikely area for confrontation. Congressman Don Fraser capsulized the case for restraint
when he observed that "an approach that defines the Indian Ocean as
vital to the security of the United States leaves little room for reasonable dialog."[5]

Prevailing Defense Department policy seemed to support the
low-profile policy consensus. Former Navy Secretary John Chafee
said in 1972 that "We ought to go slowly here and not escalate the
thing and see what happens."[6] Former Defense Secretary Melvin Laird
downplayed the need for a permanent military presence in the Indian
Ocean.[7]

The U.S. Navy, however, has long had ambitious plans for the Indian Ocean and has been pushing for a base there since the early 1960s. Negotiations between the United States and Great Britain led to the creation of the British Indian Ocean Territory (BIOT) and the December 1966 agreement to make the islands comprising the BIOT, including Diego Garcia, available to both countries for military purposes for a period of 50 years. U.S. initiative in the creation of the BIOT and the acquisition of Diego Garcia were directly related to a belief that the United States had to move into the region to fill the alleged vacuum that was being created by the reduction of British military activity "east of Suez." Diego Garcia was selected because of its central location, the minimal political problems that it seemed to raise, and because it had ideal qualities for a naval facility. Admiral John McCain, former commander-in-chief of the U.S. Pacific Fleet, said that "as Malta is to the Mediterranean, Diego Garcia is to the Indian Ocean."[8]

In the late 1960s, before the substantial expansion of Soviet naval presence in the Indian Ocean and before public attention had become focused on the Persian Gulf as a source of oil, the Navy proposed the establishment of a communications facility and a support base on Diego Garcia. In 1969 and 1970, Congress rejected naval proposals for a support base, but agreed to the establishment of a limited communications facility. Opposition to new commitments in the Indian Ocean on the part of a number of powerful senators stopped the navy for the time being. Senator Mike Mansfield, chairman of the Senate Appropriations Subcommittee on Military Construction, has quoted a comment of the late chairman of the Senate Appropriations Committee, Senator Richard Russell, who expressed the view of many: "If we make it easy for the Navy to go places and to do things, we will find ourselves always going places and doing things."[9]

The turning point in the abandonment of a U.S. policy of restrained military presence in the Indian Ocean was the October 1973 Mideast war and the associated oil embargo. On November 30, 1973, former Secretary of Defense James Schlesinger announced that a decision had been made "to reestablish the pattern of regular visits into the Indian Ocean and we expect that our presence there will be more regular than in the past."[10] The carrier Hancock was sent into the Ocean in November 1973 and was soon followed by the carrier Oriskany. When the new military budget was sent to Congress in early 1974, it contained a request for $32 million to expand the facility at Diego Garcia to support increased naval deployments and to build a larger airfield. Congressional opposition delayed appropriations until 1975, but in the end the Defense Department got what it had sought.

FUNCTIONS OF THE DIEGO GARCIA BASE

The original U.S. Navy impetus for obtaining base rights on the island of Diego Garcia was to fill the presumed vacuum left by the reduction of British military power in the region and to be able eventually to have a permanent naval and air base from which to support operations in the Indian Ocean as the navy carrier fleet was reduced and other overseas bases became less reliable.

The first prerequisite for the development of an expanded U.S. naval presence in the Indian Ocean was the existence of a series of radio, navigation, and communications facilities to handle the anticipated increase in naval traffic. Diego Garcia was added to the network extending from Asmara, Ethiopia, to the North West Cape in Australia.

These communications facilities have also fulfilled the function of making possible periodic patrols of Polaris and Poseidon submarines into the Indian Ocean. There has been some controversy about whether the United States stations ballistic missile submarines in the Indian Ocean; but although the United States may not as yet permanently station missile submarines in the Indian Ocean, it is probable that parts of that ocean have at least occasionally been used as patrol areas. No one disputes that excellent coverage of Soviet and Chinese targets can be achieved from the area. For example, the February 1974 issue of Seapower, the magazine of the Navy League, in discussing the U.S. communications facility in Australia at North West Cape, stated that "classified messages to Polaris/Poseidon submarines deployed in the Indian Ocean are sent from this station."[11] It is likely that the U.S. Navy intends to deploy strategic submarines in the Indian Ocean more frequently in the future as additional Poseidon submarines carrying longer-range missiles enter the inventory and as the Trident submarine is acquired.

After the existence of a communication and surveillance network, the next step in the creation of the necessary infrastructure for increased naval deployments was the development of a supply and reapir base in the Indian Ocean to make possible more efficient and expanded naval patrols. The first increment of funding for the construction of such a substantial support base, initially rejected by Congress in 1969, was resubmitted by the Defense Department for congressional approval in early 1974, in the time of renewed interest in the Indian Ocean-Persian Gulf region following the oil embargo.

The naval communications station on Diego Garcia and the related airfield on which work began in March 1971 are manned by about 430 military personnel. There is an 8,000-foot runway that is used by cargo aircraft and long-range P-3 naval patrol planes. By mid-1975 $70 million had been spent on the construction of facilities on Diego Garcia, including some dredging of the harbor. Additional projects to expand facilities on Diego Garcia consist of the following:[12]

1. Increasing the fuel storage capacity from the present 60,000 barrels of aviation fuel to a total of 380,000 barrels of aviation fuel and 320,000 barrels of fuel oil for ships;

2. Deepening and widening the harbor to provide anchorage for a carrier task force, normally one carrier and four destroyers, and the construction of a pier to provide about 550 feet of berthing, primarily for the loading or unloading of fuel;

3. Lengthening the runway to 12,000 feet to permit large cargo aircraft (C-5s), tankers (KC-135s), and strategic reconnaissance aircraft (EC-135s and SR-71s) to operate efficiently and safely. B-52s could use the airfield on an occasional basis.

4. Expansion of airfield facilities—hangar and parking areas— to permit expanded aircraft staging and maintenance and other construction to provide storage of ammunition and other supplies.

5. Construction of additional personnel quarters to accommodate the approximately 600 military personnel whom the Defense Department plans to station permanently on Diego Garcia.

The total cost of the construction of the base on Diego Garcia is approximately $200 million. However, the cost of new commitments in the Indian Ocean could be substantially more. The navy may request new ship construction because of its added responsibilities in the Indian Ocean. One new aircraft carrier with associated ships and aircraft costs about $3 billion. To keep one carrier on station requires two to back it up. Thus, a new commitment to keep one carrier in the Indian Ocean could cost as much as $9 billion. The need for more ships has not yet been made explicit by the navy but the logic of the situation seems inescapable in view of navy complaints about the difficulty of meeting commitments in other oceans even before the increase in naval patrols in the Indian Ocean.

Improvements to the harbor, runway, and refueling and support facilities on Diego Garcia will substantially increase the capability of the United States to sustain military activity in the Indian Ocean. Its utilization will be constrained, however, by the fact that everything on the island, including all the fuel to be stored there, has to be shipped from thousands of miles away. Diego Garcia also lies at some distance from the regional areas of primary U.S. concern, the approaches to the Persian Gulf and the Red Sea.

Secretary Schlesinger stated in 1974 that "there is no intention at the present to maintain a specific Indian Ocean fleet"[13] and President Ford has assured Congress that "there is no intent to permanently station operational units there [Diego Garcia], and the installation would not imply an increase in the level of U.S. forces deployed to that region."[14] The attempt to separate the issue of the base at Diego Garcia from the issue of increased military activity in the region is, however, strained. It seems clear that the existence of Diego Garcia will encourage further military buildup. Admiral Elmo Zumwalt, then Chief of Naval Operations, said in 1974 that "the greatest virtue of having the support base, on an austere basis, at Diego Garcia, is that . . . it will be possible to maintain a larger number [of ships] in the Indian Ocean."[15]

Although sometimes concealed from public view, the navy's intention to create a substantial military presence in the Indian Ocean is evident. The impetus accelerated with the winding down of the Vietnam War, as the navy began looking for post-Vietnam missions with which to occupy itself, and subsequently as the navy began to push an expanded role for itself as the keeper of "the oil lifelines." The "austere" communications station on Diego Garcia was a way station on the road to something bigger and better. As Admiral Zumwalt said in 1972, "in order for the United States to maintain a superior position in the Indian Ocean, it needs to have facilities."[16] At the same time that Secretary Laird was still downplaying the need for a permanent presence, Admiral Zumwalt was saying that "I think a permanent presence is mandatory."[17]

THE SOVIET NAVY AND THE INDIAN OCEAN

Admiral Zumwalt and other supporters of a U.S. military expansion in the Indian Ocean have stressed the Soviet naval threat in the region. Admiral Zumwalt said "their tentacles are going out like an octopus into the Indian Ocean."[18] Unfortunately, the tendency has been to exaggerate Soviet naval strengths and understate U.S. naval strengths in the effort to justify the need for the Diego Garcia base.

One frequently used measure of Soviet and U.S. naval presence in the Indian Ocean is the number of "ship-days" spent by naval vessels of the two countries in the Indian Ocean. Ship-days are produced by multiplying the number of ships in the ocean by the number of days they spend there. In 1971, for example, the Soviet Union is said to have accumulated 3,970 ship-days versus 1,337 for the United States.[19] Less prominently displayed, however, because they tell a different story, are the data on comparative port calls. Port calls are perhaps a more accurate indication of impact and influence in the region. In 1971 Soviet naval units, one to three ships per visit, made 18 port calls to countries in the Indian Ocean region. The U.S.

Navy made 177 port calls.[20] The Soviet advantage in ship-days and
the U.S. advantage in port calls has continued. Part of the explanation
for the discrepancy is that the Soviet naval units tend to spend much of
their time at open sea anchorages, out of sight and perhaps out of
mind of the people of the region.

The U.S. Navy helps to make up for this lack of publicity by
providing the Soviet Navy a lot of free advertising. Secretary Schlesinger has said in his defense posture statements that perceptions of
military capabilities by third parties are as important as actual capabilities. If this is so, the U.S. Navy may be harming its own interests
by emphasizing the Soviet naval threat and degrading U.S. capabilities.
Overrating of the Soviet Union's naval strength in the Indian Ocean,
or elsewhere, yields the Soviets unnecessary and undeserved political
gains, particularly in third world countries.

Ship-day comparisons also ignore the actual nature of the kinds
of ships in the Indian Ocean and their combat capabilities. Minesweepers are equated with aircraft carriers. Any time that the
United States chooses to put a carrier task force into the Indian Ocean,
it has unquestioned military superiority over Soviet naval forces in
the region. Most of the Soviet ships in the Indian Ocean are noncom-
batants, support ships and auxiliaries: for example, oilers, repair
ships, distiller ships, space support ships, minesweepers, oceanographic ships, tenders. In general, the most common Soviet combat
presence in the Indian Ocean since 1968 has been in the range of
three or four surface combatants.

The Soviet Union has important nonmilitary maritime interests
in the Indian Ocean. George Vest, director of the State Department's
Bureau of Politico-Military Affairs, observes that "it is the natural
trade route for them, being largely land-locked, this is their natural
transit point."[21] Several years ago some 12 percent of the merchant
ships transiting the Indian Ocean were Soviet.[22] With the continued
expansion of its merchant fleet, it is likely that the level of Soviet
merchant activity in the Indian Ocean has increased. The Soviet Union
also has a growing Indian Ocean fishing fleet, which several years ago
accounted for almost one-third of the Soviet total annual catch.[23] The
Soviets have numerous civilian oceanographic, hydrographic, and
space and missile test support ships in the Indian Ocean. In addition
to trade with and aid to many of the countries along the Indian Ocean,
Soviet merchant ships passing between the eastern and western parts
of the Soviet Union frequently transit through the Indian Ocean. The
Indian Ocean is a sea lane connecting the vast expanses of the eastern
and western regions of the Soviet Union. Admiral James Holloway,
chief of naval operations, states that "the Indian Ocean is an all
weather transit route for the Soviet Navy between European and Asiatic
Fleets."[24] From the Soviet point of view the presence of Soviet naval

ships in the Indian Ocean also probably has some relationship to the Soviet commercial shipping in the area.

The Soviet Navy has a number of weaknesses and vulnerabilities that have particular significance in the Indian Ocean. The lack of seaborne fixed-wing aircraft to provide protection and the lack of aircraft for reconnaissance severely constrain the flexibility of Soviet naval forces in the Indian Ocean. The Soviet Navy does not have a significant seabased intervention capability. The Soviets must support four major fleets in widely separated areas—the Black Sea-Mediterranean Fleets, the Baltic Fleet, the Northern Fleet, and the Pacific Fleet. With Soviet naval resources dispersed over such distant areas, the Indian Ocean is a particularly remote and vulnerable place for Soviet naval ships to be. Western powers control most of the egress and ingress points to the Indian Ocean, and the possibility of wartime reinforcement for Soviet ships in the Indian Ocean seems virtually ruled out. The U.S. Seventh Fleet dominates the western Pacific and western approaches to the Indian Ocean and, as Admiral Thomas Moorer, former chairman of the Joint Chiefs of Staff, has pointed out, "in time of conflict, any waterway such as the Suez Canal is highly vulnerable. Consequently, it would be highly likely that it would be closed by one side or the other."[25] In time of war Soviet ships would be isolated from their bases by U.S. and NATO forces and probably sunk quickly.

The Soviet Navy lacks reliable and secure shore-based support facilities on the Indian Ocean. In fact, Soviet practice has been to rely primarily on its own auxiliaries for fuel, provisions, and repairs. This is one of the reasons the Soviets tend to have more naval ships in the region. The Soviet Union has growing economic and diplomatic relations with local countries, but seems to have no secure base rights along the littoral. The Soviet Navy, as does the U.S. Navy, has access to ports and facilities in a number of countries, but the use of these facilities does not confer base rights or convert them into Soviet naval bases. The instability of even existing base utilization arrangements is demonstrated by Soviet experience with Egypt, where the Soviet Union has lost most of the military advantages it had previously accumulated. The Soviets have aided in harbor development in Iraq, Somalia, Yemen, Aden, India, and Bangladesh, but it is uncertain that this has led to special military base rights.

In June 1975, Secretary Schlesinger revealed new information about Soviet activities at the port of Berbera in Somalia that seemed to indicate an increased Soviet military presence.[26] Two congressional groups visited Berbera at the invitation of the Somalian government and reported findings that supported Secretary Schlesinger's allegations. These revelations played an important role in bringing about final approval by Congress of funding for Diego Garcia. The question of to what extent facilities at Berbera are primarily intended for use by the Soviets or by the Somalis remains uncertain. One measure of the relative support capability of facilities at Berbera, compared to those planned on Diego Garcia, is that the fuel storage capacity on Diego Garcia will be 700,000 barrels, compared with the Defense Department's estimate that facilities at Berbera will have a capacity of about 170,000 barrels.[27]

The desire for a stable and secure base of one's own that can be used without depending on anyone's good will is one of the major factors that has prompted the United States to seek a naval base at Diego Garcia. There are 36 ports in the Indian Ocean where the United States can obtain petroleum supplies for its naval ships, but, as is also the case with the Soviet Navy, access to these ports is partially dependent on political relationships. The United States wants to have a naval support base essentially under its own control, an item that the Soviet Union has not yet achieved.

In terms of capability to support and deploy naval forces overseas without extensive base support, the United States today has a substantial advantage over the Soviet Union. Nuclear-powered naval surface ships are especially useful for extended distant deployments. The Soviet Navy has no nuclear-powered combat surface ships. The United States has in operation or funded a total of 14 nuclear-powered surface combatants, including four nuclear-powered aircraft carriers. The United States also has more oilers, repair ships, and under-way replenishment ships and can sustain a fleet at sea without shore facilities better than the Soviet Union. As Secretary Schlesinger has said, "the ability of the United States fleet to operate at long distances is greater than that of the Soviet Navy."[28]

Senator Stuart Symington brought the former director of the Central Intelligence Agency, William Colby, before his Armed Services Subcommittee in July 1974 for an unprecedented public release of Central Intelligence Agency analyses of Soviet activity in the Indian Ocean.[29] Colby made public some of the conflicting points of view within the U.S. government about the Soviet threat. He described a minimal threat from the Soviet Navy in the Indian Ocean: "The forces the Soviets have deployed in the Indian Ocean . . . have been relatively small and inactive," he stated, adding that the region was relatively low in Soviet priorities, that "Moscow apparently prefers to keep a minimal force in the Ocean," and that their existing facilities were "limited." Colby linked the increase in Soviet naval presence to prior U.S. naval activity and implied that the Diego Garcia build up would prompt a further Soviet response. He expressed doubt that the opening of the Suez Canal would necessarily lead to a Soviet naval expansion in the distant Indian Ocean—"the USSR probably recognizes that the canal is subject to closure in a crisis"—and also argued that the scenario of Soviet blockage of oil shipments was implausible. At nearly every crucial point, the analysis presented by Colby differed from that of Admiral Zumwalt and other military spokesmen. The differences, however, were more in interpretation and emphasis than on the facts.

By way of explanation for an expanded U.S. naval presence in the Indian Ocean, one of the more prominent fears suggested by proponents is that the Soviet Union would attack U.S. and allied merchant ships and oil tankers in the area. This does not appear to be a plausible action on the part of the Soviet Union when one takes into account important factors like relative military power, time and distance factors, and the alternative means of exerting influence and power at the disposal of the Soviet Union. The Soviet Navy is ill-prepared to engage the Western powers in a long-range conventional war. If the Soviets were seriously to attempt to cut off oil shipments to Japan and Western Europe, there are areas outside of the Indian Ocean, closer to Soviet home bases, which would be more suitable for that type of warfare. This is especially true with respect to the use of Soviet submarines. Because of its extensive commercial and shipping interests in the Indian Ocean, the Soviet Union itself would have much to lose in a war at sea or a disruption of shipping. In many ways, the Soviet merchant marine itself serves as a growing hostage to Western military power in the event of a crisis.

A U.S. military buildup in the Indian Ocean does not contribute to an alleviation of or solution to the world energy shortage. Military power does not ensure a supply of oil, as recent events demonstrate. Oil is much more likely to be turned off "at the wellhead" than be stopped by a Soviet naval blockade. U.S. resources and attention could better be concentrated on nonmilitary, more productive means of solving long-term energy needs. Visions of gunboats and convoys could distract attention from more serious, long-term approaches. In terms of the stability and progress of the region, the U.S. money to be spent on a big U.S. naval establishment in the Indian Ocean could perhaps be better spent on assisting in economic development of countries in the area; both the United States and they would benefit.

Secretary Schlesinger has stated that "our concern is first with the stability of the nations of that area."[30] Stability and access to oil may be better served through nonmilitary means, particularly in view of the near-unanimous opposition of the coastal nations to great power military expansion in the region.

There apparently are conflicting assessments within the U.S. government about the ease with which a blockage of oil shipments could be carried out through military means and the probability of that occurring. For example, Admiral Zumwalt and others have alleged that such so-called choke points as the Straits of Hormuz at the mouth of the Persian Gulf could be blocked with ease. The Central

Intelligence Agency, however, in 1973 expressed a different point of
view: "It (the Straits of Hormuz) is too deep and wide to be blocked by
sunken ships and too wide to be effectively controlled by coast artillery. Naval and air power would be required to close the strait, a
serious step since it is considered international waters by the world
community."[31] Scenarists of a war on oil shipments might take heed
of another remark of Secretary Schlesinger: "One can always design
the worst possible case which shows the U.S. military forces at a
decided disadvantage. What one must also do is to estimate the probability of that worst possible case occurring."[32]

REOPENING OF THE SUEZ CANAL

One of the major arguments used to justify expansion of U.S.
military presence in the Indian Ocean and the base at Diego Garcia
is that with the opening of the Suez Canal, the Soviet Union will be
able to increase substantially its number of ships in the Indian Ocean
and the United States needs to be in a position to match any Soviet
buildup. Secretary of State Henry Kissinger has appeared to dissent
from this argument, although in general he has spoken in favor of
Diego Garcia. He has expressed skepticism about the need to engage
in a naval arms race in the Indian Ocean and has stated that there is
no direct relationship between influence and the number of ships there.
He has been particularly outspoken in opposing the view that the
opening of the Suez Canal will be to Soviet advantage: "I have never
fully understood this," he has said. "If it is in our interests, if we
are worried about it, we can follow any Soviet ship through the Suez
Canal with an American ship. We have more ships in the Mediterranean than the Soviet Union does."[33]
It remains to be seen whether the Soviets will utilize the Suez
Canal to increase significantly their naval presence in the Indian
Ocean. The canal reopened in June 1975 and the first foreign military
ship to go through the canal was the flagship, a cruiser, of the U.S.
Sixth Fleet.[34] No Soviet naval ships took part in the reopening cere-
mony. This fact symbolizes the way in which the opening of the Suez
Canal will result in a reassertion of U.S. and Western influence in
this region of the world, probably to the detriment of the Soviet Union.
Soviet influence in countries like Somalia, Yemen, and Iraq was in
part a function of the closing of the canal and the polarized conflict
between Arabs and Israel. The restoration of the Suez link with
Europe and the improvement in Arab-Israeli relations could be an
important contribution to the stability and economic progress of the
region and will help to restore old ties with the West.[35]

DISPUTE OVER DIRECTION OF U.S. POLICY

Within the executive branch and the Congress, there has been extensive debate and controversy about the wisdom of the Diego Garcia proposal. One State Department official describes participating in meetings in which State Department representatives sat on side of the table and navy representatives sat on the other side and "the spirit of Joe Alsop hovered overhead."[36]

Relatively little evidence of the internal policy debate was revealed in public, as officials of the State Department, Defense Department, and even the Arms Control and Disarmament Agency trooped before Congress to defend the expansion of Diego Garcia and increased military presence. At the Defense Department, the then-new secretary, James Schlesinger, was increasingly outspoken in his call for a return to a messianic U.S. role in the world very reminiscent of President Kennedy's New Frontier. The U.S. alleged "burden of responsibility" to preserve world stability was linked to the need for this nation to move into the Indian Ocean to fill a supposed power vacuum and oppose Soviet influence.

Secretary Kissinger's support of the Defense Department on Diego Garcia does not appear to be the result of a strong belief that military power in the Indian Ocean will lead to enhanced U.S. security and influence. The outspoken criticism of Diego Garcia by retiring U.S. ambassador to India Daniel Moynihan in January 1975 may reflect views that Secretary Kissinger himself felt constrained from expressing.[37]

The main opponents of the new military base in the Indian Ocean were members of the Congress, led by Congressman Lee H. Hamilton and Senators Stuart Symington, Mike Mansfield, Clifford Case, Claiborne Pell, Edward Kennedy, and John Culver. Congressman Hamilton's House Foreign Affairs Subcommittee held the most extensive hearings on the subject. Senator Case got the Senate to adopt a stipulation, later dropped, that the new agreement between Britain and the United States for expanding Diego Garcia had to be submitted to the Congress for approval. Senators Pell and Kennedy introduced a resolution calling for arms limitation in the Indian Ocean. Senators Symington and Mansfield, as chairmen of the subcommittees in the Senate that controlled funding for Diego Garcia, were in particularly crucial positions to review and delay the Defense Department's plans. In addition, Senator John Stennis, the chairman of the Senate Armed Services Committee, was influential in stopping the Defense Department from obtaining funding for Diego Garcia early in 1974 in emergency legislation. Senator Stennis maintained that the United States should not act precipitously and should pursue

opportunities for mutual arms restraint in the Indian Ocean with the
Soviet Union. Later in the year, however, Senator Stennis became a
strong supporter of the Defense Department on Diego Garcia, apparently persuaded by the argument about the need to protect oil shipments. He summarized his concern in a Senate speech "in one short,
three-letter word, a very short word, o-i-l, oil."[38] By the end of
1974, there was speculation about the possibility of U.S. military
intervention in the Persian Gulf to secure oil supplies.

A number of Senators urged the executive branch to pursue the
possibility of mutual military restraint in the Indian Ocean. Senator
Stennis asked Secretary Schlesinger: "If we are going to have a big
buildup over there that would call for another fleet, a great augmen-
tation, at least, of what we have, why couldn't that area be the subject
of negotiations or agreements of some kind?"[39]

There had been a minor exchange of views about the possibility
of naval arms control in the Indian Ocean between the U.S. and Soviet
governments in 1971 but no further efforts were made by the United
States.[40] Any potential infringement on the freedom of the seas was
apparently repugnant to both states. Admiral Zumwalt called the
Zone of Peace concept promoted by the littoral states "a very dangerous concept."[41]

POTENTIAL SUPERPOWER CONFLICT

In the absence of serious attempts at naval arms control it is
probable that the United States and the Soviet Union will continue to
increase gradually their military presence in the Indian Ocean. This
does not mean that the United States requires a support base in the
region. In general, occasional patrols from the Atlantic and Mediterranean Sixth Fleets and from the Pacific Seventh Fleet into the Indian
Ocean would suffice to show the U.S. flag and military presence on
those relatively rare occasions when that is warranted. The opening
of the Suez Canal, depending on what controls are placed on military
traffic, facilitates deployments of ships from the Sixth Fleet to the
Indian Ocean and Persian Gulf. The opening of the canal also puts
U.S. naval bases in the Mediterranean closer to the Indian Ocean
than are Soviet bases in the Black Sea.

The U.S. Navy has the capability to move into the Indian Ocean
in force from the Pacific and Atlantic on any necessary occasion. A
support base at Diego Garcia in the western Indian Ocean makes
sense only if significantly increased on-station deployments in
the Indian Ocean are planned. The need for expanded U.S. naval
forces in the Indian Ocean at this time is very doubtful. The marginal

benefits in efficiency that a support base would provide do not compensate for the problems created.

One reason for caution is the risk of a local conflict turning into a confrontation between the two superpowers. Examples would be hostility between India and Pakistan, or between Iran and some of its neighbors like Iraq and Saudi Arabia. An escalation of naval forces would make great-power involvement more likely. Some local countries fear that they will be dragged into superpower conflicts. There will also be temptations for friends of the United States in the region to try to immerse the nation in their local squabbles. The dangers inherent in an abandonment of the low-profile policy by the United States in the Indian Ocean are increased because the search for influence can quickly become a matter of defending established positions and privileges, which soon become national security imperatives as commitment and involvement grow.

NOTES

1. Drew Middleton, "U.S. in Exercise in Indian Ocean," New York Times, November 21, 1974; L. Edgar Prina, "Naval Drill Emphasizes U.S. Interest," San Diego Union, November 17, 1974.

2. U.S. Congress, House, Armed Services Committee, Military Posture Department of Defense Authorization for Appropriations for Fiscal Year 1976 and 197T (Washington, D.C.: Government Printing Office, 1975), Part 1, p. 797.

3. Ronald Spiers, House, Foreign Affairs Committee, The Indian Ocean: Political and Strategic Future (Washington, D.C.: Government Printing Office, 1971), p. 168.

4. Assistant Secretary of State David Abshire, House, Appropriations Committee, Military Construction Appropriations for 1972 (Washington, D.C.: Government Printing Office, 1971), Part 4, p. 571.

5. Congressman Don Fraser, statement on "Congressional Review of Foreign and Military Policies," Congressional Record, March 2, 1972.

6. John Chafee, House, Appropriations Committee, Department of Defense Appropriations for 1973, Part 1, p. 285.

7. Melvin Laird, Senate, Armed Services Committee, Fiscal Year 1973 Authorization for Military Procurement, Research and Development, Construction Authorization for the Safeguard ABM, and Active Duty and Selected Reserve Strengths (Washington, D.C.: Government Printing Office, 1972), Part 2, p. 617.

8. Admiral John McCain, quoted in Colonel Robert D. Heinl, "U.S. Flag over Diego Garcia: Challenging the Soviet Fleet," Armed Forces Journal, February 1, 1971, p. 13.

9. Richard B. Russell, Senate, Armed Services Committee, Selected Material on Diego Garcia (Washington, D.C.: Government Printing Office, 1975), p. 47.

10. James R. Schlesinger, taken from a November 30, 1973 press conference.

11. Seapower, February 1974, p. 5.

12. Senate, Armed Services Committee, Disapprove Construction Projects on the Island of Diego Garcia (Washington, D.C.: Government Printing Office, 1975), p. 9.

13. Senate, Appropriations Committee, Department of Defense Appropriations Fiscal Year 1975 (Washington, D.C.: Government Printing Office, 1974), Part 5, p. 178.

14. Senate, Armed Services Committee, Selected Material on Diego Garcia, op. cit., p. 20.

15. Admiral Elmo Zumwalt, House, Armed Services Committee, Military Posture Department of Defense Authorization for Appropriations for Fiscal Year 1975 (Washington, D.C.: Government Printing Office, 1974), Part 2, p. 1065.

16. Admiral Elmo Zumwalt, House, Appropriations Committee, Department of Defense Appropriations for 1973 (Washington, D.C.: Government Printing Office, 1972), Part 1, p. 224.

17. Admiral Elmo Zumwalt, Senate, Armed Services Committee, Fiscal Year 1973, op. cit., Part 2, p. 981.

18. Admiral Elmo Zumwalt, House, Appropriations Committee, Department of Defense Appropriations for 1975 (Washington, D.C.: Government Printing Office, 1974), Part 2, p. 84.

19. Memorandum prepared by director, Joint Staff of Joint Chiefs of Staff, Defense Department, "Soviet Naval Activity in the Indian Ocean," March 1974.

20. Ibid.

21. George Vest, hearing before House, International Relations Special Subcommittee on Investigations, June 5, 1975, stenographic transcript, p. 3.

22. House, Foreign Affairs Committee, op. cit., p. 16.

23. House, Appropriations Committee, Second Supplemental Appropriations Bill 1974 (Washington, D.C.: Government Printing Office, 1974), Part 2, pp. 85-86.

24. Senate, Armed Services Committee, Selected Material on Diego Garcia, op. cit., p. 16.

25. Admiral Thomas Moorer, House, Appropriations Committee, Department of Defense Appropriations for 1975, op. cit., Part 1, p. 564.

26. James R. Schlesinger, Senate, Armed Services Committee, Disapprove Construction Projects on the Island of Diego Garcia, op. cit., pp. 12-21.

27. Ibid., pp. 9, 18.

28. James R. Schlesinger, House, Appropriations Committee, Department of Defense Appropriations for 1975, op. cit., Part 1, p. 562.

29. William Colby, Senate, Armed Services Committee, Military Construction Authorization Fiscal Year 1975 (Washington, D.C.: Government Printing Office, 1974), Part 1, pp. 161-72.

30. James R. Schlesinger, Senate, Armed Services Committee, Disapprove Construction Projects on the Island of Diego Garcia, op. cit., p. 26.

31. Central Intelligence Agency, Atlas: Issues in the Middle East (Washington, D.C.: Government Printing Office, 1973), p. 39.

32. James R. Schlesinger, Senate, Armed Services Committee, Fiscal Year 1975, Part 1, p. 241.

33. Secretary of State Henry Kissinger, House, Appropriations Committee, Foreign Assistance and Related Agencies Appropriations for 1975 (Washington, D.C.: Government Printing Office, 1974), Part 2, p. 11.

34. Jonathan C. Randal, "U.S. Cruiser Joins Suez Canal Flotilla," the Washington Post, June 6, 1975.

35. On the increase of Western influence and decline of Soviet influence see: Rowland Evans and Robert Novak, "The 'Soviet Naval Base' at Um Qasr," the Washington Post, February 12, 1975; Rowland Evans and Robert Novak, "Solzhenitsyn, Kissinger and Detente" (includes item on Iraq), the Washington Post, July 20, 1975; Henry S. Hayward, "East Africa Watches for Suez Impact on Trade," Christian Science Monitor, May 1, 1975; Reuters, "Aden Looks for Boom," Christian Science Monitor, June 13, 1975; Dusko Doder, "Somalia Offers U.S. Seaport Facilities," the Washington Post, July 4, 1975; William Beecher, "Egypt Ends Soviet Ship Preference," the Washington Post, July 20, 1975; John K. Cooley, "Aden Expects Growth from Suez Canal Trade," Christian Science Monitor, July 30, 1975.

36. Confidential interview by author.

37. United Press International, "Indian Ocean Move—Moynihan Hits U.S. Base Policy," the Washington Star-News, January 7, 1975.

38. Senator John Stennis, Congressional Record, September 11, 1974, p. S16400.

39. Senator John Stennis, Senate, Armed Services Committee, Fiscal Year 1975, op. cit., p. 201.

40. Senate, Armed Services Committee, Disapprove Construction Projects on the Island of Diego Garcia, op. cit., p. 46.

41. Senate, Appropriations Committee, Second Supplemental Appropriations for Fiscal Year 1974 (Washington, D.C.: Government Printing Office, 1974), Part 2, p. 2125.

6

**U.S. ARMS TO
THE PERSIAN GULF**
Robert Berman

U.S. political and military involvement in the Persian Gulf has
been expanding rapidly in recent years. The leading edge of our involvement in this area, as it was in Southeast Asia during the 1950s
and early 1960s, is military assistance and arms sales. As in Southeast Asia, this is likely to lead to additional commitments and trouble
for the United States.

The United States is not the only supplier of arms to the Persian
Gulf, but it is by far the largest. In 1974 the United States sold more
than $6.4 billion worth of arms to Persian Gulf countries. This was
60 percent of all 1974 U.S. arms sales abroad. The Soviet Union
sold $1.5 billion, France sold $1.5 billion, and the United Kingdom
$50 million.[1] In 1975, the United States sold $4.3 billion to Persian
Gulf countries.[2]

Saudi Arabia and Iran have been the chief customers for U.S.
arms. Over FY 1974 and FY 1975, these two countries alone bought
$10.2 billion worth of American weapons. In mid-1975, Iran and the
United States announced a $15 billion, five-year trade deal that is
expected to include the delivery of $5 billion worth of U.S. arms.[3]
U.S. arms are helping to make Iran a major world military power.

The countries of the region are now spending about $18 billion
a year on their military forces. Just five years ago, the total was
$1.6 billion. Kuwait and Saudi Arabia are among the leading countries
of the Middle East and the world in per capita military expenditures,
ranking second and third in the Middle East and 13th and 19th respectively in the world.[4]

Table 6.1 shows how U.S. arms sales to the countries in the
Persian Gulf have increased in recent years.

TABLE 6.1

U.S. Foreign Military Sales and Orders to the Persian Gulf Countries, 1950–75
(thousands of dollars)

	Iran	Iraq	Kuwait	Oman	Saudi Arabia	Total
1950–69	647,497	13,152			161,468	822,117
1970	113,284				14,854	128,138
1971	396,613				95,815	492,428
1972	528,022				342,295	870,317
1973	2,108,787		53		83,984	2,192,824
1974	3,917,121		30,400		2,539,408	6,486,929
1975	2,567,903		370,496	1,613	1,373,862	4,313,874
Total	10,279,227	13,152	400,949	1,613	4,611,686	15,306,627

MAP 6.1

The Persian Gulf Tinderbox

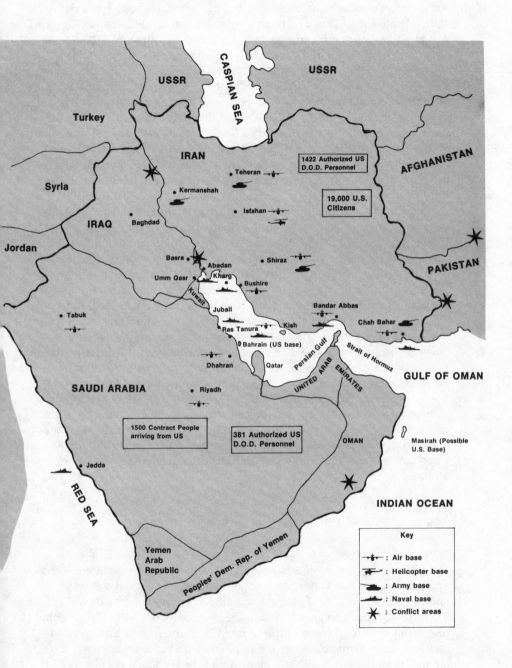

Source: Center for Defense Information.

There are several reasons why the Persian Gulf nations, as well as many other countries, are buying more weapons from the United States than they are from the Soviet Union, France, or Britain. A typical Soviet arms package may include a squadron of MIG 21s at very low prices. Along with these will come air-to-air missiles. But more than likely there will not be an abundance of spare parts that would be needed for major operations. These would come later at high prices or in exchange for political leverage. Weapons from the Soviet Union characteristically are defensive in nature, with the emphasis on quantity over quality. The French typically sell a number of Mirages to a country in a package along with French missiles and bombs. Usually, there are no advisers. A continuing French source of spare parts under renewable contracts is sometimes in doubt after the initial deal is complete. French arms sales have been built around the Mirage fighter-bomber. The French possess a relatively narrow foreign sales supply base that is similar to that of the Soviet Union, but smaller. British arms are not sold as widely as French or Soviet weapons, but that has more to do with economic constraints in Britain than with political inhibitions. British arms are of high quality, but are not as sophisticated as many others, especially when British aircraft designs are compared to those of the United States.

U.S. arms dealers, conversely, offer a complete package to the recipient country. The United States will survey the needs of a country, provide a list of U.S. weapons available to fulfill those needs, send a demonstration team, possibly offer joint production, train pilots as well as others, and provide replacements needed, even, when required, from the active U.S. inventory. Besides being able to provide a wide variety, the United States offers equipment with more military capability. This is so especially in aircraft. It makes a difference to the countries involved whether their frontline airplanes were made in the United States, United Kingdom, Soviet Union, or France.

FIRST-LINE U.S. EQUIPMENT

In recent years, the character of U.S. military assistance and arms transfers has undergone major changes. In the past it was unusual for the United States or any other country to provide or sell its most advanced weapons to foreign governments. With the possible exception of some favored allies, foreign recipients of military aid had to content themselves with older or obsolescent equipment. For example, in the early 1960s, Saudi Arabia's air force consisted of obsolete U.S. B-26s, British Vampires, and some Korean War vintage F-86s.

This pattern has changed quite radically in recent years, particularly in the Middle East and Persian Gulf, where oil-rich governments can afford to pay for the most up-to-date equipment. Beginning
in the mid-1960s Iran began acquiring the F-4 Phantom which was,
and still is, one of the first-line fighter aircraft of the U.S. Air Force.
Iran is buying sophisticated and expensive F-14 fighters from the
United States. It is scheduled to get these aircraft in 1976, only 21
months after the first F-14s were placed in the U.S. Navy's inventory.
Iran will be adding the very large, modern DD-963 destroyers to its
navy soon after the last of these destroyers are introduced into the
U.S. Navy. It will soon receive improved Hawk surface-to-air (SAM)
missiles and has already received TOW antitank missiles, both currently being added to the U.S. inventory. From Britain, Iran has
purchased Chieftain tanks, which are the first-line tank of the British
Army. Kuwait has also announced plans to buy Chieftains. Kuwait will
purchase the Mirage F-1 aircraft from France and will begin adding
it to its inventory at the same time France acquires the Mirage in
large numbers for its own air force. The increasing sophistication
of the weapons available to the countries of the Persian Gulf is significant because it greatly increases the likely destructiveness of any
future wars in the region.

Another consequence of selling sophisticated weapons to foreign
countries is that U.S. technicians and advisers are needed to assist
the purchasing countries for long periods of time. This, of course,
involves the United States even more deeply in the affairs of the
recipient country and tends to create a U.S. "commitment" to its
government.

One justification U.S. officials give for arming the Persian
Gulf countries is that it makes direct U.S. involvement in the area
unnecessary. There are indications, however, that Pentagon officials
have decided that a U.S. presence in the area is necessary in any
case. The navy has begun regular deployment of a carrier task force
to the Indian Ocean and visits to the Persian Gulf. At the same time,
the United States is in the process of expanding its base at Diego
Garcia and there are plans to use the former British base at Masirah.[6]
In addition, the U.S. Navy Middle East Force has a base at Bahrain.
All of these factors point to growing U.S. involvement, directly as
well as indirectly, in the Persian Gulf region.

DISPUTES MAKE GULF A VOLATILE AREA

The Persian Gulf is a highly volatile area. Numerous disputes
among countries in the region make it an area of great instability.

As Senator Edward Kennedy has said, "Passions are deep and distances are short."[7]

The two largest purchasers of U.S. weapons in the Persian Gulf area—Iran and Saudi Arabia—are traditional rivals. At the root of their rivalry are a number of long standing differences. Both are strongly nationalistic and disagree over whether the gulf that separates them is the Persian Gulf or the Arabian Gulf. Saudis are Arab and Iranians are Aryan. Iranians are Shia Muslims and Saudis are Sunni Muslims. Saudi Arabia has been a strong opponent of Israel and a supporter of Israel's Arab enemies, while Iran has quietly supported Israel and continues to sell oil to Israel.

Most important of all, the Shah's ambitions to be the dominant power in the gulf clash with Saudi aspirations and undoubtedly make the Saudis uneasy about their own security. Despite the avowed intention of the United States, massive sales of arms to Iran can only serve further to increase tensions and reduce the chances of peaceful cooperation. Arming one power leads in turn to increased demands for arms by the other. Such a policy may stimulate business for U.S. arms manufacturers, but it could lead to wars—and to U.S. involvement in them. The continuing dispute between Iran and Saudi Arabia is the most prominent among the Persian Gulf countries, but as Table 6.2 shows, it is by no means the only one.

It is worth remembering that the backward and oppressive governments in power in the Persian Gulf—seven of the eight are monarchies and the eighth is a military dictatorship—are constantly faced with the threat of domestic unrest, coups, and rebellion. Saudi Arabia, for example, abolished slavery as recently as 1964. Iran maintains domestic tranquility by means of a powerful and pervasive secret police organization, the Savak. The assassination of King Faisal is rather typical of the kinds of threats that Persian Gulf governments face, especially the conservative monarchies. Iraq, Iran, and Saudi Arabia have all experienced coups, attempted coups, or assassinations in recent years. Thus, while military forces are created to enhance political stability, in developing countries they often produce just the opposite. In sum, political and social change is inevitable in the Persian Gulf, and U.S. programs that create powerful military establishments can repress needed reforms and stimulate political upheavals.

Another result of creating new and powerful military forces in Persian Gulf countries is that once military establishments become powerful domestic political forces,their appetites for weapons grow. They come to absorb larger and larger quantities of resources and aspire to newer and more expensive weapons. Indeed, once they have their appetites whetted for sophisticated modern weapons, we can expect that political and military leaders of the Persian Gulf

TABLE 6.2

Conflicts in the Persian Gulf Region

Opponents	Sources of Conflict	Status
Iran and Iraq	Boundary dispute.	Agreement signed in March 1975 may temporarily resolve conflict.
Iran and Iraq	Iranian support for Kurdish rebels fighting for autonomy from Iraq.	Iran has agreed to cease support in return for settlement of river boundary.
Iran, Saudi Arabia, Iraq, Kuwait, UAE, Oman	Domination of Persian Gulf—Iran has treated Gulf as own lake—has seized islands of Abu Musa and Tunbs—Iraq, Saudi Arabia, and Kuwait resent Iranian domination of Gulf. Conflict also embedded in ancient antagonisms between Iran and the Arabs.	Unresolved—source of tension.
Iraq, Kuwait, Saudi Arabia	Iraq claim to Kuwaiti territory to insure access to harbor at Umm Qasr. Saudis back Kuwait.	Temporarily resolved—Iraq has withdrawn claim to Kuwaiti land.
Oman and Dhofar Rebels, Peoples Republic of Yemen	Rebels in Dhofar province of Oman are fighting for independence—Oman government supported by U.K., Iran, Jordan, and U.S.	Rebellion is in continuing state of ferment.
Afghanistan and Pakistan	Afghanistan has supported aspirations of Pashtu tribes for independence from Pakistan. Iran has supported Pakistan.	Unresolved—in state of ferment.
Pakistan and Baluchi Rebels	Baluchi tribesmen seek independence from Pakistan—Pakistan trying to keep remainder of territory intact—Iran has provided military assistance to Pakistan.	Unresolved—in state of ferment.
India and Pakistan	Long history of Indian and Pakistani hostility—three wars in past 30 years—most recent in 1971. Iran opposes further dismemberment of Pakistan and has expressed support for Pakistan.	Unresolved—source of tension.

countries will begin to think about acquiring nuclear weapons. Iran
has said that it will not unilaterally develop nuclear bombs, [8] but it
has also stated that it will not let another country in the area gain a
monopoly, especially in light of the first Indian nuclear explosion.
Iran has already indicated that planning is under way to build nuclear
air-raid shelters. [9]

IRAN: GROWING REGIONAL DOMINANCE

With American assistance, Iran has become the dominant military power in the Persian Gulf. Iranian military forces are about
twice as large as those of Iraq and five times larger than those of
Saudi Arabia. Iran spends on its military forces ten times what Iraq
spends and almost twice what Saudi Arabia spends. [10]

Iran's arsenal now includes many of the United States' most modern weapons, such as the Phantom, Tiger, and Tomcat fighter-bombers,
the P-3 Orion antisubmarine plane, attack and transport helicopters,
air refueling tankers, jumbo jet and Hercules troop transports. The
improved Hawk surface-to-air missile, which Congress recently said
must not be sold to Jordan, has been purchased by Iran. So have the
Phoenix air-to-air missile to go on the F-14, the TOW antitank
missile, and the Maverick air-to-ground missile. In addition to
DD-963 destroyers, Iran has also ordered Tang-class submarines. [11]

Delivery of these and other weapons is scheduled over the next
several years. Meanwhile, U.S. military advisers are helping to
train Iranian soldiers. There are more than 1,000 American advisers
currently based in Iran. Many more of the 19,000 Americans in Iran, [12]
however, are civilians helping the once-backward country develop its
burgeoning military-industrial complex. Northrop Aviation, for
example, has built facilities for maintaining and overhauling its F-5E
fighter in Iran and perhaps eventually will assemble its new plane,
the F-18, there. Bell Helicopter has a plant in Isfahan. Hughes Aircraft has a missile mainenance facility at Shiraz. Table 6.3 shows
the growth of Iranian military forces.

The United States has been instrumental in providing the weapons
and assistance required for this transformation. But it has done so
on the presumption of a bipolar world—one divided between communism and the free world—in which a country like Iran must find common
cause with the United States against the Soviet Union. Although this
is the reason behind U.S. policies, it is not at all clear that Iranian
officials collaborate in these policies, including arms sales, for the
same reasons.

TABLE 6.3

Iranian Military Growth
(dollars)

	1965	1975	1985*
Defense spending	217 million	10 billion	15-20 billion
Aircraft	90 million	500 million	2,000 million
Ships	32 million	41 million	100 million
Tanks	500 million	1,260 million	3,000 million

*Projected.

Source: International Institute for Strategic Studies, The
Military Balance (London: IISS, 1966-75).

As the Soviet-Iranian detente has moved forward, the deployment of Iranian military forces has been altered to reflect the new
international situation and Iranian ambitions. In the late 1960s Iranian
army units were moved from the northern border area to southwest
of Teheran. The Iranian Navy moved its headquarters to Shiraz in
the south. Three-fourths of the F-14s that Iran has ordered from the
United States will be based in the central and southern parts of the
country.[13] This pattern suggests that Iran is much more concerned
with dominating the politics of the Gulf than it is with the Soviet
threat.
      Consistent with this new policy aimed at dominating the Persian
Gulf, Iran has built several new military bases in the southern part
of the country. Other new bases have been built at Kharg Island,
Tunbs Island, and Abu Musa. A new base is also being built at Chah
Bahar near the Straits of Hormuz on the Indian Ocean, while existing
facilities are being modernized and expanded at Bandar Abbas and
Bushire. The continued growth of Iranian military power and its
southward deployment will make many of the smaller countries of the
Persian Gulf feel increasingly insecure.
      Many of these advanced, long-range weapons, like the F-4,
F-14, and DD-963 destroyers, supplied or about to be supplied to
Iran, also have strategic implications for countries beyond the Persian
Gulf. The Iranian military buildup and Iranian aid to Pakistan could
in the future be seen as a threat by India. At present, Iranian-Indian
relations are cordial, but a continued Iranian buildup and more Iranian

aid to Pakistan could turn the relations between these two countries sour over the next few years and could trigger a regional arms race between them. In similar fashion, Saudi and Kuwaiti arms may soon have an impact on the Arab-Israeli military balance. As Saudi Arabia and Kuwait grow in power, the Israelis may have to begin to weigh them in the total balance. This may make the Israelis less secure and tend to undermine the U.S. policy, which is to insure the survival of Israel. It may also increase Israel's need for further military assistance from the United States.

THE SHAH IS NOT "OUR BOY"

The central figure in the building of modern militarily powerful Iran is the Shah, Mohammed Reza Pahlavi. The Shah is a product of the cold war and was an American creation. Prompted by an obsessive fear of Soviet aggression, the United States raised him from obscurity and kept him propped up as a counterweight to possible Soviet expansion. Until the early 1970s, the Shah had remained a cosmetic figure who photographed well in bright ribbons, but this was not the sort of role suitable to a man of his energy and ambition. It is clear that he dreams of restoring old empires.

To date, the Shah has convinced the leaders of the industrialized nations that he serves their best interests. He has been successful in this respect because of his political skill. He has demonstrated his capacity in maneuvering and operating in the area of power politics with the best. Western leaders have accepted the Shah's assurances, together with his oil policies, because of their alleged fear of the Soviet Union. They have shown little concern for what the Gulf-Indian Ocean region might look like a few years from now.

Although the Shah has made no formal declaration of regional hegemony, there is an expanding concept of Iranian "national security" needs. For now, the Shah's influence is felt throughout the Persian Gulf region. Soon, it may extend beyond.

Indeed, a close look at the Shah should convince U.S. officials that the Shah is not "our boy." He is not looking out for American interests. He represents a separate force following his own "destiny" in a realignment of world power. The Shah may be the recipient of the blessing of current American office holders. He is, however, developing the power to make the Arab-Israeli conflict seem like a minor skirmish.

U.S. officials have recently emphasized that the shared interest between the United States and Iran is safeguarding the flow of oil from the Persian Gulf to the United States, Europe, and Japan. The United

States has an obvious interest in keeping a steady flow of oil—at stable prices—from the Persian Gulf to itself, Western Europe, and Japan. The United States, at present, imports a little more than one-fourth of its oil from the Persian Gulf.[14] A little over 15 percent is from Iran. This is expected to reach a high of 40 to 50 percent by the early 1980s. This dependency is not expected to last far beyond that time, since other sources of oil are expected to become available, but the short-run prospects have caused a great deal of alarm in this country.

Much of this concern has been directed at the possibility that the Soviet Union might use military force to stop oil tankers from Persian Gulf refineries. There has been talk of the Soviets interdicting oil shipments in the Indian Ocean, and thus, a need for a U.S. naval presence there. This argument overlooks the fact that it is easier to interdict oil closer to ports of destination than tens of thousands of miles away from major Soviet bases. Besides, interdiction of oil is imaginable only as part of a long war, which neither the Soviet Navy nor Soviet armed forces are capable of fighting.

A favorite navy scenario is one that involves the Soviets mining the Straits of Hormuz, through which ships must pass to leave the Persian Gulf. The straits are referred to as a "choke point." In fact, the so-called vulnerable Straits of Hormuz are anywhere from 30 to 60 miles wide. The Central Intelligence Agency has stated that, on the contrary, the straits are very difficult to block and it would take a major effort by a major naval power.[15]

The Straits of Hormuz also figure in concerns over internal military threats. Thus, when Dhofar guerrilla forces score moderate success, there is speculation by the Shah of Iran to U.S. officials that if Dhofar falls, then Oman will fall. If that happens then the Straits of Hormuz will be threatened. It is seldom pointed out that the Dhofar rebellion is more than 500 miles away from the straits.

While U.S. officials have occupied themselves with military threats to oil, the fact is that the easiest and most likely method of cutting off the oil supply is at the wellhead—by an embargo—or by extraordinary price increases imposed by the oil producing countries. This can deny the Persian Gulf oil to the United States, Europe, and Japan as effectively as by mines or torpedoes. The Shah has insisted that he will not participate in another embargo under any circumstances.[16] Although there is no reason to doubt the Shah's commitment to this goal—especially given the very high prices he is now getting for his oil—there are some potential dangers. One possibility is that the Shah's ambitions and Iran's growing military power might lead to conflicts in the Persian Gulf area that would disrupt the flow of oil, or might even end with the Shah in control of all Persian Gulf oil.[17]

The future of Iran is dependent on the growth of oil revenues.
If these are ever threatened, whether by inflation or declining markets
in the West, the Shah might be "forced" to go elsewhere in the Gulf
for more oil to make up for his profit deficits. The U.S. policy of
virtually unlimited arms sales to Iran increases this danger.

One rationale for selling arms to the Persian Gulf is that it
will make the oil producing states that receive the arms dependent on
us. This dependence is then supposed to turn itself into actions or
policies by the recipient states that benefit the United States. So far,
this has proved illusory. Billions of dollars in weapons and training
had been promised by 1973 to the Saudis, Kuwaitis, and Iranians.
In "return" the Saudis and other Arab states placed an embargo on
oil directed primarily toward American allies in Western Europe.
Iran, which is not an Arab nation and has no ideological commitment
to the Arab cause, did not participate in the embargo. It even kept
oil flowing to Israel. But as the emotional tide passed, Iran took the
initiative, and along with the other oil producing and exporting countries (OPEC) it succeeded in raising the price of crude oil to five
times the initial cost in a matter of months. Neither Iran nor the
Arab states acted in behalf of U.S. interests, but, as might be expected, in their own. Saudi Arabia and Kuwait embargoed oil and Iran
was instrumental in raising oil prices. This disputes the "leverage
rationale" for continuing massive U.S. aid and U.S. military sales
programs to these countries.

One of the ironies of the energy "crisis" is that Iran is planning
not to use any more oil for lighting cities and running factories. The
Shah feels it is too important a "treasure" to waste in such a way.[18]
Instead of oil, Iran will use nuclear reactors, which were supplied
initially by France, and will eventually come from the United States.
Oil will be used in refineries on the Persian Gulf to make tens of
thousands of petrochemical products. These products will then be
exported in place of crude oil, and at a high cost. Of course, Iran
will also get increased profits from any crude oil it exports.

As time passes in the Persian Gulf area, the United States and
other arms-producing powers are the ones who will remain dependent.
Not only will the arms-selling states be dependent on oil from the
area over the next 10 years, but these arms producers are caught in
a vicious cycle of selling weapons in order to recover some of the
dollars lost to the price of oil. The extensive bribery and hard-sell
techniques of arms sellers threaten to glut these Persian Gulf countries with unneeded weapons. The huge arms bills will further
encourage these oil exporters to keep oil prices high. It is clear that
sales of weapons, in a world of multiple arms sellers, provides a
financial profit, but secure, at best, a very marginal leverage over
the foreign policies of recipient countries. Indeed, once those

countries become military powers in their own right, they may feel
more secure in defying U.S. wishes. We may, indeed, be creating
our own Frankensteins, states in the Persian Gulf that may become
powerful future antagonists to U.S. interests—that wield both economic leverage and military influence adverse to future U.S. interests
or freedom of action.

The expansion of Iranian military power particularly poses
significant risks, both for the United States and for other Persian
Gulf states. By extensively expanding Iranian military capabilities,
the United States may be encouraging Iranian ambitions to dominate
the Persian Gulf. Even if the present regime remains in power, there
are dangers in this policy, as there are in U.S. policies for the entire
region.

U.S. political and military involvement in the Persian Gulf is
growing rapidly, but there is in fact no coherent American foreign
policy for the area.

The increased volume of arms sales, coupled with the high
quality of the weapons being sold, has greatly increased the offensive
military capabilities of several Persian Gulf countries. The countries
in the region are acquiring the capability to make war at ever-
increasing levels of violence and destructiveness. Neighboring countries that previously did not have the means to threaten each other
are now becoming capable of waging full-scale wars and, as we have
seen, such conflicts could lead to U.S. involvement. We may also
be creating military giants that some day could use their new-found
power against us.

NOTES

1. Data derived from World Armaments and Disarmament
SIPRI Yearbook 1975 (Stockholm, Sweden: Stockholm International
Peace Research Institute, 1975).

2. Defense Department figures placed in Congressional Record
by Congressman Lee H. Hamilton, September 18, 1975, p. E4796.

3. "Iran to Buy Nuclear Plants From U.S. in $1.5 Billion Pact,"
the Washington Post, March 3, 1975.

4. U.S. Arms Control and Disarmament Agency, World Military
Expenditures and Arms Trade 1963–1973 (Washington, D.C.: Government Printing Office, 1975).

5. Defense Security Assistance Agency fact sheet, "Foreign
Military Sales Orders," processed July 10, 1975, and data placed in
Congressional Record by Congressman Hamilton, September 18,
1975, p. E4796.

6. "What's Behind New U.S. Aid to Oman," Christian Science Monitor, January 16, 1975.

7. Senator Edward Kennedy, in an interview with Martin Agronsky, Evening Edition, Public Broadcasting Service, March 13, 1975.

8. "Nuclear Weapons for Region 'Ridiculous,'" Kayhan International (Tehran), June 26, 1974; "Government Strongly Denies Nuclear Weapons Report," ibid., June 25, 1974.

9. "Plans for Nuclear Raid Shelters," ibid., June 24, 1974.

10. Information from The Military Balance (London: International Institute for Strategic Studies, 1975).

11. Aviation Week and Space Technology, April 1, 1974, p. 11, and August 26, 1974, p. 22; John Finney, "U.S. Plans to Sell Iran 3 Diesel Submarines," New York Times, June 10, 1975.

12. Senator Charles Percy, report to the Senate Foreign Relations Committee, The Middle East (Washington, D.C.: Government Printing Office, 1975), p. 45.

13. Aviation Week and Space Technology, September 16, 1974, p. 9.

14. George Wilson, "Non-Arab Lands Supply Most U.S. Oil Imports," the Washington Post, October 24, 1974.

15. Central Intelligence Agency, Atlas: Issues in the Middle East (Washington, D.C.: Government Printing Office, 1973), p. 39.

16. "Shah Vows to Keep Oil Flow to West," the Washington Post, January 15, 1975.

17. "Iran Moves to Control Gulf," the Washington Post, January 3, 1975.

18. "A Talk With the Shah of Iran," Time, April 1, 1974, p. 41; "Shah's Iran Moving Unevenly Toward the Persian Renaissance," the New York Times, December 7, 1974.

CHAPTER

7

OVERVIEW OF THE
MILITARY BUDGET
David T. Johnson

Our economy may be on the rocks, the quality of life in America
may be deteriorating for everyone, our foreign policies may be floun-
dering, but the arsenal of democracy is to remain alive and well. The
Defense Department wants the United States to continue to put its faith
in weapons and military power. The United States produces the most
destructive weapons in the world, the most advanced tanks, planes,
submarines, bombers, missiles, and yet we are called upon to try
harder to remain "number one." World demand for the products of
our advanced industrial civilization is insatiable and growing: U.S.
weapons manufacturers took sales orders for a record $10.8 billion
worth of arms overseas in 1974, an increase of more than 100 percent
over 1973. America's dubious world leadership in weaponry may be
the ultimate expression of our philosophy of conspicuous consumption.

In recent years, debate over the defense budget has not produced
change in the overall dimensions or content of the budget, nor much
clarity about the direction that U.S. military policy is taking. Pentagon officials complain about not receiving enough money and about
public misunderstanding, but temporize and put off difficult decisions.
Small, often cosmetic, cost savings are made, but unneeded multi-
billion dollar programs and deployments continue and are expanded.

There are few new, extraordinarily compelling ideas about how
to keep down military spending. The controversy has frequently been
repetitious and stale on all sides. This is not to say that there are
not numerous ways in which savings in the defense budget could be

An earlier version of this chapter appeared in the July 1975
Ramparts. Reprinted with permission.

made. The basic problem is that those who have to make the decisions in the executive branch and in Congress have failed to get serious about demanding a realistic defense budget pruned to the basics.

What is new is that now something has to be done about it. The fact of an era of $100 billion military budgets and growing consciousness of nonmilitary threats to national security may have sufficiently altered attitudes and strengthened motivation so that feasible ways to hold down the military budget will be implemented.

The fiscal 1976 bicentennial federal budget said a great deal about our misplaced priorities. President Ford asked the Congress to appropriate almost $108 billion for military purposes, the highest level of military spending in history. This was an increase of $16 billion over fiscal 1975. At the same time, funding for nondefense programs was projected to decline by more than $25 billion.[1] The Pentagon, according to its five-year plan for 1976 through 1980, plans to spend at least $636 billion over this period.[2]

The military budget contained a bewildering variety of new weapons schemes. The controversy over most of these weapons has continued for at least several years. The air force and Rockwell International want $749 million to continue development of their $21 billion B-1 bomber program so that the United States will possess well into the twenty-first century a bomber that will be able to fly lower, faster, and carry more bombs than any bomber ever built. General Dynamics is working on a submarine for the Navy, the Trident, that will be bigger (two football fields long), quieter, and fire more nuclear weapons than any submarine in history. It will also be the most expensive weapons system in history, at $1.6 billion or more per copy. The army has Chrysler and General Motors competing to produce the "tank of the future," the XM-1 main battle tank.[3] The XM-1, estimated to cost almost $2 million each, will shoot farther, more accurately, have more armor protection, and a smoother ride than any other tank—assuming, of course, that everything goes according to plan, which frequently does not happen.

The 1976 military budget asked for funding of new missiles of every conceivable description: antiship, antiaircraft, antitank, antimissile, surface-to-surface, surface-to-air, air-to-surface, air-to-air, continent-to-continent, laser-guided, radar-guided, electro-optical-guided, television-guided. New military aircraft come in all shapes and sizes and nicknames: Skyhawks, Tomcats, Eagles, Cobras, Prowlers, Hawkeyes, Intruders, Corsairs, Chinooks, Orions, Vikings, Sea Stallions, Sea Cobras, Iroquois, not to mention AWACS and the unpronounceable AABNCPs, which translate into Advanced Warning and Control System and Advanced Airborne Command Post, respectively.

TABLE 7.1

Acquisition Costs of Major Weapons Systems
(in millions of dollars)

Weapon System	Cost
Army	
LANCE (Battalions)	853.6
Imp. HAWK (Btry. Sets)	984.6
SAM-D (Fire Sec.)	5,605.0
HLH (Component Dev.)	218.9
UTTAS	3,323.4
MICV	401.4
AAH	2,835.5
XM-1	4,453.8
ROLAND (Fire Units)	1,119.5
Navy	
A-7E	2,832.8
E-2C	1,329.9
F-14A	8,115.5
P-3C	3,198.7
S-3A	3,324.4
AEGIS (R&D Only)	576.8
CONDOR	423.2
HARPOON	1,590.3
PHOENIX	1,233.8
POSEIDON	4,847.0
SIDEWINDER AIM-9L	181.1
SPARROW III F	789.2
TRIDENT (Sub.) (C-4 Missile)	16,327.7[a]
MX-48 MOD 1	1,844.7
SSN-688	8,623.1
DD-963	3,677.0
DLGN-38	1,605.0
LHA	1,290.2
FFG-7	6,782.2
PRM (DEV/PROC)	1,276.5
CVAH (68 & 69/70)	2,627.2
Air Force	
A-7D	1,584.6
A-10	3,159.7
B-1	20,603.0
F-5E	429.0
F-15	10,820.5
F-111A/D/E/F	7,181.4
AWACS	3,716.2
AABHCP	481.5
MAVERICK	762.5
MINUTEMAN III	7,246.3
SIDEWINDER AIM-9L	241.7
SPARROW III F	531.5
Program Cost Summary	
Army	19,795.7
Navy	72,496.3[b]
Air Force	56,757.9
Grand Total	149,049.9[b]

[a]TRIDENT Current Estimate excludes TRIDENT (C-4)
Backfit Program costs estimated at $2,451.7M as of
June 30, 1975.

[b]POSEIDON costs are included in the Navy total and
Grand Total but are not included in the base year and escalation breakdowns for these totals.

Source: Defense Department estimates for total
equipment costs as of June 30, 1975. Includes R&D and
procurement costs.

117

Every three months the Pentagon is required by Congress to publish the current estimated costs of major weapons systems. The latest cost-overrun status report on 42 big ticket items indicates that these weapons alone will cost $149 billion, $53 billion more than originally expected.[3] See Table 7.1.

The American public has little way of judging whether there is any real need for particular weapons and must rely on the Congress to exercise control over the military budget and the Defense Department. The Congress, however, is barely up to the task of beginning to explore the intricacies of the many complex weapons systems and defense issues buried in the labyrinths of the plus-$100 billion defense budget. Unlike the Defense Department, Congress has little information and even less time. Congressman Michael Harrington of Massachusetts, who has been a member of both the House Armed Services and Foreign Affairs Committees, puts it this way:

> By the time a weapons program reaches the stage at which it becomes a prominent issue for debate in the Congress, the battle is already lost. The Defense Department's near monopoly on relevant information, together with the vested bureaucratic and economic interests which propel the high-budget, high-prestige weapons programs, conspire to give such programs an all but unstoppable momentum.[4]

What the Pentagon wants, the Pentagon gets.

Congress has become increasingly critical of high and escalating levels of military spending. Although there is not yet a consensus on how to reduce the defense budget, there is a new and growing recognition that changed international circumstances and economic pressures make it necessary to choose among competing programs and priorities. Many congressmen are increasingly aware that spending on weapons and forces that contribute to U.S. strength only in a marginal way can no longer be afforded. The American experience in Indochina seems to have taught the lesson that military power is of declining usefulness in coping with the country's problems.

New superweapons are not the answer. Even a hardline conservative like Senator John McClellan, chairman of the Senate Appropriations Committee, has come to admit that any real meaning of national security is far broader than its narrow military component: "Inflation is rapidly becoming as great a danger to our national security and the stability of our society as is the danger from any potential foreign foe."[5]

A number of controversial weapons systems were critically examined by the Congress during hearings and action on the fiscal 1976 defense budget. Questionable strategic weapons include the

B-1 bomber, the Trident submarine, new types of intercontinental
ballistic missiles (ICBMs), strategic cruise missiles, and new Antiballistic Missile Systems. The bulk of the defense budget, about 75
percent, goes to pay for the projection of U.S. military power overseas in Europe and Asia. Controversial conventional weapons include
the AWACS warning and control aircraft, the SAM-D air defense
missile system, the C-5A aircraft, the XM-1 tank, and the expensive
F-14 and F-15 tactical fighter aircraft.

THE WEAPONS SYSTEMS

B-1 Bomber

For the Defense Department, the most vulnerable weapon in the
new budget is the B-1 strategic bomber. The B-1 is a weapon that
may very well be pricing itself out of existence, although Secretary
of the Air Force John McLucas says that he has no "cost breaking
point"[6] for the B-1. Many members of Congress, however, are near
or have already passed their breaking point with the B-1. The cost
of developing and producing 244 B-1s is estimated at $20.6 billion, or
$84 million each. The cost continues to skyrocket and inevitably will
shortly exceed $100 million per plane.

Critics of the B-1 argue that the United States is well ahead of
the Soviet Union in the strategic arms race and point out that the
United States already has 8,500 strategic nuclear weapons and 500
bombers, compared to 2,800 nuclear weapons and 160 bombers for
the Soviet Union. Even a handful of former weapons enthusiasts have
come around to acknowledging that somehow, somewhere a line has
to be drawn. Says Senator John Sparkman of Alabama, the chairman
of the Senate Foreign Relations Committee: "How are we to put a
stop to this dangerous, ruinous rivalry? For a start we can simply
recognize that overkill is overkill, that superfluous weapons are
indeed superfluous, and that many of the new systems being developed,
though technologically fascinating, are redundant and unnecessary."[7]

In an age when missiles can deliver devastating destruction in
less than 30 minutes, a bomber that takes 10 hours to reach its targets can at best have only a minor role. The existing force of B-52
and FB-111 bombers will in any case provide a bomber force with
considerable overkill through the 1980s. The United States spends
about $5 billion a year on its bombers.[8] Including European-based
and aircraft carrier-based planes, the United States today already
has numerous types of aircraft capable of carrying nuclear weapons
in an attack on the Soviet Union.

Through fiscal 1975 $2 billion has already been spent on the
B-1. The fiscal 1976 budget requested another $749 million, including
$77 million to initiate procurement. The $77 million was viewed by
critics as an effort by the air force to get the Congress to commit
itself all the way to ultimate full-production of the B-1. The Defense
Department projects a request for $1.7 billion for fiscal 1977 and
continued funding at $2 billion or more a year through 1983.

As yet, Congress has been unwilling to make a firm decision
for or against the B-1. Alternatives like a B-52 with new engines,
a stretched FB-111, and a wide-body jet like the Boeing 747, armed
with cruise missiles, have been suggested. To counter such specu-
lations, the Defense Department conducted a year-long investigation
called the Joint Strategic Bomber Study that, not surprisingly, concluded that B-1 is best. The official conclusion sounds not unlike a
toothpaste commercial: "Of the equal-cost forces examined, those
containing B-1's performed substantially better. The low-flying,
nuclear-hard B-1, with its high quality ECM, out-performed all other
vehicles by a wide margin."[9] The most egregious flaw of the Defense
Department's study is that it assumed that the United States needs to
spend as much money on bombers as the B-1 costs and compared
only "equal-cost" alternatives. Department analysts neglected to
examine the question of whether the country needs a bomber fleet in
the first place and, if so, whether that capability could be obtained
at much less cost.

A decision on producing the B-1 is scheduled for November 1976
and it seems unlikely that the Congress will stop the B-1 before that
time. Although the plane is viewed with growing skepticism, continued funding of research and development is likely.

Trident Submarine

Next to the B-1, the most expensive weapon program is the
Trident strategic submarine, currently estimated to cost $16.3 billion
for 10 submarines, each armed with 24 4,000-mile-range Trident I
missiles. Each Trident submarine will carry enough nuclear weapons
to destroy any country in the world. The United States already has
41 strategic submarines carrying 656 Polaris and Poseidon missiles
with about 4,000 nuclear weapons. The 1975 defense budget asked for
$2.1 billion for Trident, with a $3.4 billion request expected for
fiscal 1977. The Defense Department hopes to put the first Trident
to sea in 1979.

Existing missile submarines are invulnerable and considered
by liberals and conservatives alike to be the "backbone" of the

deterrent Triad of bombers and land- and sea-based missiles. Because of this "blue water" sentiment and because it was promoted as a bargaining chip in the Strategic Arms Limitation Talks, the Trident program has had relatively smooth sailing through Congress. Although the rate of production has been slowed to three every two years, the momentum has seemed unstoppable.

The "Cadillac of the Sea," or, as Navy Secretary J. William Middendorf calls it, "that great shield for America," is promoted by the navy primarily because of the advantages of having a longer-range missile permitting a submarine to utilize greater expanses of the ocean and escape detection. In the absence of any evidence about how submarines will become vulnerable in the future, critics of the huge Trident believe that it is premature to be putting so many eggs in relatively few baskets. Longer-range missiles could be installed in existing submarines at much less cost, as, in fact, the Navy plans to do. The drive to build the Trident reflects a compulsion toward mindless modernization in the Defense Department, the pursuit of new technologies and superweapons irrespective of any realistic assessments and with ever more marginal returns.

NEW ICBMs

The fiscal 1976 defense budget asked for more than $900 million for continuing procurement of Minuteman missiles and research on a variety of new Intercontinental Ballistic Missile systems. To date, the United States has deployed 1054 ICBMs, including 550 multiple-warhead MIRVed Minuteman III missiles, which can deliver more than 2,000 nuclear weapons. Former Defense Secretary James Schlesinger has stated that the policy of the United States is to increase to the limits of the 1974 Vladivostok SALT agreement, [10] which had stipulated that the United States and the Soviet Union could have as many as 2,400 strategic delivery vehicles, including 1320 MIRVed missiles.

With the expansion of the Soviet nuclear missile force in recent years, U.S. ICBMs have become increasingly vulnerable, at least theoretically, to destruction. Some officials, including Dr. Fred Ikle, director of the U.S. Arms Control and Disarmament Agency, have suggested that the United States should be moving away from reliance on ICBMs. [11] Secretary of State Henry Kissinger has also indicated some differences with Defense Department officials by stating that the much discussed disparity in missile throw-weight between the United States and the Soviet Union is a "phony issue." [12]

The Defense Department's game plan is to keep all options open by investing billions of dollars in exploring almost all of the various schemes for new ICBMs. This is the all too typical pattern of avoiding hard choices by giving everybody what he wants. Options include mobile ICBMs that would be fired from airplanes (a Minuteman missile was dropped from a C-5A plane in the fall of 1974 in a test), mobile ICBMS that would be transported on land by train or truck, and new fixed large ICBMs that would compete with the Russians for the largest missile. Over the next 10 years the United States could spend as much as $50 billion in seeking solutions to the problem of Minuteman vulnerability.

Research is also being conducted on a variety of projects to bring to life Secretary Schlesinger's philosophy of a counterforce strategic policy. These programs to increase the accuracy and destructive power of U.S. missiles cost about $156 million in the fiscal 1976 budget. The most well-known effort involves developing a maneuvering warhead, a MARV (Terminally Guided Maneuverable Reentry Vehicle), which would essentially eliminate all missile inaccuracies. Senator Thomas McIntyre, chairman of the Senate Armed Services Research and Development Subcommittee, fears that counterforce improvements will lead to weapons that could threaten a first strike and make nuclear war more likely. In reporting out of his subcommittee a bill that deleted funds for five counterforce programs, Senator McIntyre argued:

> Secretary Schlesinger is trying to move our basic strategic doctrine from our traditional emphasis on mutual assured destruction to a reliance on U.S. nuclear war fighting capability. We're alarmed that Pentagon preoccupation with exotic technologies and doctrines will distract us from our efforts to meet our prime national security requirement, which is to prevent nuclear war.[13]

Despite Senator McIntyre's opposition, the counterforce programs were approved by Congress.

Strategic Cruise Missiles

A new means of raining death on the Soviet Union and China is being pursued by both the air force and the navy—the strategic cruise missile. Cruise missiles are small, unmanned, electronically-controlled aircraft powered by air-breathing turbofan engines. Strategic cruise missiles with ranges of 1,500 miles or more could be launched from planes, submarines, or surface ships. For fiscal 1976 the navy requested $102 million in the budget to continue work on a sea-launched cruise missile (SLCM) and the air force asked for $51 million for an air-launched cruise missile (ALCM).

Pentagon interest in strategic cruise missiles is a classic case of imitative behavior in the arms race. Lacking aircraft carriers, the Soviet Union has developed relatively primitive and short-range cruise missiles primarily for attacking surface ships. Now, because the SALT agreements do not limit strategic cruise missiles and the Soviets have a weapon that vaguely seems threatening, the Defense Department wants to have them too, although strategic cruise missiles will do virtually nothing for our military capability. However, this may well open up a new channel for the arms race and could severely complicate efforts to control and limit strategic weapons. Any submarine or surface ship could launch such missiles and it would become impossible to verify arms control agreements.

Some members of Congress support the air-launched cruise missiles program as an alternative to the B-1 bomber. A relatively inexpensive stand-off bomber could launch ACLMs from outside of Soviet antibomber defenses.

New ABM Systems

The SALT agreements limit the United States and the Soviet Union to a paltry 100 ABM launchers each. The Safeguard ABM system, the subject of intense Congressional debate in 1969 and 1970, is now completed at Grand Forks, North Dakota, protecting a Minuteman ICBM field. Safeguard cost $5.4 billion, $54 million per ABM launcher. Already, however, the Pentagon is mothballing the Safeguard system and considering deploying something called Site Defense.

The fiscal 1976 budget requested $348 million for ABM systems, more than the previous year. Research is being done on ABMs that would use lasers, and on maneuvering ABMs to shoot down hypothetical Soviet MARVs. Senator McIntyre's subcommittee, recognizing the folly of spending vast amounts of money for such limited protection, cut all $140 million requested for the Site Defense program. Funds were partially restored later.

AWACS (Airborne Warning and Control System)

AWACS is the Air Force's big surveillance, warning, and control aircraft, consisting of special avionics, computers, and large

radar installed in a modified Boeing 707 airframe. The plane is
designed to serve as an airborne command post, warning of Soviet
air attack, and controlling and directing NATO war planes in combat
over Europe. The administration requested $690 million for AWACS
in fiscal 1976. The Air Force hopes to acquire 34 AWACS aircraft.
Congress to date has funded three research and six production aircraft. Estimated program cost is $3.7 billion, $111 million each.

   AWACS was originally developed to serve as an air defense unit
in the United States for protection against Soviet bomber attack, but
because of the decline of the Soviet bomber threat, the AWACS
mission was shifted in 1973 to a tactical role in Europe. Recent
studies by the General Accounting Office indicate that AWACS is vulnerable to jamming by relatively inexpensive ground-based equipment.[14] AWACS would also be highly vulnerable to attack by interceptors and surface-to-air missiles and would likely have to spend
much of its time coordinating its own defense. The other main
criticism raised by opponents is that although it is being built for use
in Europe, U.S. NATO allies have contributed nothing toward the
cost of AWACS. Members of Congress are particularly sensitive
about the continuing disproportionate burden of defense spending
within the NATO alliance and are awaiting burden-sharing arrangements with NATO before purchasing additional AWACSs unilaterally.

SAM-D Missile

   The SAM-D surface-to-air missile system is another weapon
originally conceived for air defense of the United States against a
Soviet bomber threat that never even materialized. To keep the system alive it is now justified for use in Europe to protect allied and
U.S. troops against Soviet air attack. SAM-D is a high altitude (above
40,000 feet) air defense missile designed to replace the Nike Hercules
and Improved Hawk SAMs in the mid-1980s. The current program
cost is estimated at $5.6 billion of which $850 million has already
been spent. The fiscal 1976 defense budget requested $130 million to
continue research and development.

   Congressional critics, notably Senator Birch Bayh, argue that
SAM-D should be canceled because of the absence of a significant
high-altitude threat (Soviet aircraft will have to descend to lower
altitudes to attack targets effectively) and because the great cost of
SAM-D means that it is not worth the money. Each SAM-D fire section
will cost $41.8 million, more than it presumably would cost the
Soviets to destroy it. A General Accounting Office study concludes:
"Cost-effectiveness of the SAM-D or its variants apparently cannot be

proven based on realistic assumptions. It would appear that even if
the SAM-D technology works and even if the threat materializes, the
SAM-D will probably not be necessary if F-15's are available."[15]
As in the case of AWACS, European countries have not come forward
to help pay for a weapons system that will be used theoretically for
their defense.

XM-1 Tank

For fiscal 1976 the army asked for $51 million to continue
research on a new main battle tank. The XM-1 is the latest desig-
nation for the army's cancelled MBT-70 and XM-803 tank programs,
both of which were stopped by Congress because of cost and technical
problems. Estimated program cost for the XM-1 is $6.2 billion, or
$1.9 million each for the planned 3,312 tanks.

The XM-1 is to replace the army's present tank, the M-60, in
Europe. Serious questions have been raised, however, as to whether
it makes any sense for the Defense Department to invest billions in
potentially obsolescent tanks. Recent developments in antitank weapons and the experience of tank losses in the October 1973 Mideast
War indicate that antitank weapons have overcome defenses available
to tanks and that advantage may continue indefinitely. A relatively
inexpensive $4,000 TOW antitank missile can destroy a $500,000 tank.

C-5A Aircraft

The C-5A's troubles never go away. The air force spent $4.5
billion on 81 aircraft built by Lockheed in a $2 billion cost-overrun
scandal. Through 1975, four have been destroyed in accidents, the
latest on April 4, 1975 in Vietnam with a planeful of Vietnamese
children on board. In 1975, the air force indicated that it needed
$900 million to fix the dangerously weak wings on the C-5As.

The C-5A is the world's biggest plane, 248 feet long with a
gross weight of 716,500 pounds. It was developed to implement the
New Frontier concept of the United States as the world's policeman,
the "go everywhere, bear every burden" aircraft to rush American
toops and tanks in an instant to the remotest trouble spot. But even
the C-5A's much heralded successes turn out to be less than meet
the eye. Although it was lauded by the air force for bringing military
supplies to Israel during the October 1973 war in the Middle East,
a subsequent study by the General Accounting Office shows that

60 percent of the C-5A fleet was not operable because of mechanical problems or lack of spare parts. Almost all of the equipment arrived after the cease-fire and, according to the GAO, "had no decisive effect on the war's outcome."[16]

The air force has requested the $900 million program to build new C-5A wings because the life of the current wing is estimated at about 10,000 hours, compared to a planned 30,000 hours. It will cost $11 million for each plane to fix the wings. Air Force Secretary McLucas regretfully admitted that this happened because the Air Force rushed the C-5A into production before it knew whether the plane worked: "We had a large number of aircraft built before we had ever completed the fatigue tests to see whether or not the aircraft was structurally sound."[17]

Tactical Aircraft

The Defense Department's impulse to modernize at any price finds its most profuse flowering in the new generation of tactical fighter aircraft, the air force's F-15 and the navy's F-14. In fiscal 1976 the Defense Department is spending $24 billion on tactical aircraft. The military services have almost always preferred the most complex, technologically sophisticated and thus most expensive weapons. A fully equipped F-14 as of 1975 cost about $24 million. A basic, stripped down F-15 costs $15 million. Although Pentagon officials sometimes try to make it appear that increases in weapons costs are due primarily to inflation, recent studies by analysts at the Brookings Institution in Washington, D.C. indicate that most of the rising cost of tactical aircraft is attributable to the increasing technical complexity of the aircraft themselves and the compulsion to incorporate almost everything that is technologically feasible.[18] The result is weapons that are often overdesigned for their missions.

The air force plans to buy 749 F-15s, at a cost of $10.8 billion and the navy wants an additional 390 F-14s to put on its aircraft carriers at a cost of $8.1 billion. Even these quantities are not enough and both services are also developing "cheap" lightweight fighters in the $7 million per plane range. The air force has selected General Dynamics to build 650 F-16s, but the navy prefers Northrop's F-18. Some congressional and Defense Department officials had hoped that the air force and navy could unify on a common choice to keep down the price.

These are just a few of the more prominent new weapons programs. Others include tactical nuclear weapons ("mininukes"), binary chemical weapons, new nuclear-powered aircraft carriers, killer

satellites, unmanned aircraft, laser cannons, the computerized electronic battlefield, and new airlift and naval programs that could project U.S. military forces around the world. Most of these Defense
Department budget items will be accepted with relatively short attention from the Congress.

It is unfortunate that the world's most powerful country continues
to suffer from exaggerated fears and anxieties that have led our leaders to conclude that, in the words of Deputy Secretary of Defense
William Clements, "In our ever-changing world, strength means
military strength."[19] The militarization of American foreign policy
has been the result. Our real fear should not be that we will be
dominated, but that we will be dominating. If the tragic experience
in Indochina has meant anything it is that the powerful must learn to
control their inclination to excess and arrogance. The consequences
of unrestrained military power can be almost as damaging for our
country as for others.

NOTES

1. See table, Congressional Record, February 3, 1975,
p. H439.
2. The Budget of the United States Government Fiscal Year
1976 (Washington, D.C.: Government Printing Office, 1975), p. 50.
3. U.S. Department of Defense Public Affairs Office fact
sheet, dated September 12, 1975, "Selected Acquisition Reports for
June 30, 1975."
4. Congressman Michael Harrington, "Building Arms Control
Into the National Security Process," Arms Control Today, February
1975, p. 4.
5. Senator John McClellan, Congressional Record, October 10,
1974, p. S18800.
6. Secretary of the Air Force John McLucas, Senate, Armed
Services Committee, Fiscal Year 1976 and July-September Transition
Period Authorization for Military Procurement, Research and Development, and Active Duty, Selected Reserve, and Civilian Personnel
Strengths (Washington, D.C.: Government Printing Office, 1975),
Part 2, p. 852.
7. Senator John Sparkman, Congressional Record, January 28,
1975, pp. S1085-6.
8. Senate, Armed Services Committee, op. cit., p. 505.
9. Dr. Malcolm R. Currie, statement on Program of Research,
Development, Test and Evaluation, FY 1976, February 26, 1975,
p. V-16.

10. James R. Schlesinger, Annual Defense Department Report FY 1976 and FY 197T (Washington, D.C.: Department of Defense, February 5, 1975), p. II-8.

11. Michael Getler, "U.S. Urged to Retire Land-Based ICBMs," the Washington Post, February 2, 1974.

12. Secretary of State Henry Kissinger, from a December 3, 1974 background briefing on the Vladivostok agreement.

13. Senator Thomas McIntyre, in a press release, April 24, 1975.

14. See Richard W. Gutmann, General Accounting Office, statement before Senate, Armed Services Committee, March 6, 1975.

15. General Accounting Office, quoted in "Background and Current Status of the SAM-D Program April 1975," prepared by office of Senator Birch Bayh, p. 2.

16. General Accounting Office, Airlift Operations of the Military Airlift Command During the 1973 Middle East War (Washington, D.C.: Government Printing Office, April 16, 1975), p. II.

17. Senate, Armed Services Committee, op. cit., p. 847.

18. William D. White, U.S. Tactical Air Power (Washington, D.C.: Brookings Institution, 1974).

19. Deputy Defense Secretary William Clements, taken from an April 10, 1975 speech in Dallas, Texas.

8

U.S.-SOVIET STRATEGIC
FORCES: SALT AND THE
SEARCH FOR PARITY

Stefan H. Leader
Barry R. Schneider

By mid-1975 the United States and the Soviet Union had deployed a total of 11,300 strategic nuclear weapons.[*] More than half of these were deployed in the previous five years, that is, after the beginning of the Strategic Arms Limitation Talks in 1969. According to most informed estimates, this vertical proliferation is likely to continue over the next five years. The pace at which U.S. and Soviet strategic nuclear arsenals continue to grow raises serious and troubling questions for military analysts and citizens alike who are concerned about arms limitation and the danger of nuclear war.

This analysis explores the current state of the U.S.-Soviet strategic nuclear balance, and the impact of the Strategic Arms Limitation Talks (SALT) and agreements on the balance. It will deal with three questions:

How is strategic nuclear power measured and who leads or lags in the U.S.-Soviet nuclear arms race?

How does the U.S. doctrine of "essential equivalence" affect the quest for a SALT formula for strategic parity acceptable to both the United States and the Soviet Union?

What impact have SALT I and other strategic arms agreements had upon U.S.-Soviet nuclear weapons proliferation?

---

[*] By mid-1976 it is estimated by Secretary of Defense Rumsfeld that the combined U.S.-Soviet arsenals will total 12,400 strategic nuclear weapons.

This chapter is derived from "United States-Soviet Arms Race, SALT, and Nuclear Proliferation," in Nuclear Proliferation and the Near Nuclear Countries, copyright 1976, Ballinger Publishing Company.

MEASURING STRATEGIC NUCLEAR POWER

The United States and the Soviet Union have longstanding commitments to the maintenance of nuclear forces designed to deter nuclear attacks on their homelands. Both clearly want nuclear forces that at a minimum are able to perform this task at least as well as the other side's forces. At the same time, there are individuals and political groups within each government that would like to deal from positions of military superiority on the assumption that certain political benefits flow from such positions. Other groups, in the United States and the Soviet Union, are concerned about the danger posed by the growing numbers of nuclear weapons on both sides and would prefer to see these reduced or at least their growth slowed. The resulting debate has been complicated by fundamental differences in the composition of the strategic forces of both sides. As a result, comparison is difficult and judgments about the comparative power of U.S. and Soviet nuclear forces vary. There are at least five measures of strategic nuclear power that have been used at one time or another in the recent debate and differing judgments about the importance of each have made comparison of the two forces difficult. The measures that have been used are:*

- Number of nuclear weapons
- Accuracy of nuclear weapons
- Numbers of strategic launchers
- Throw weight of delivery systems
- Megatonnage and equivalent megatonnage of weapons

In fact, assessment of the current nuclear balance between the United States and the Soviet Union requires multiple measures since no single variable by itself is sufficient to describe all dimensions of the U.S.-Soviet balance.

Numbers of Nuclear Weapons

Perhaps the best measure of strategic power is what the Pentagon euphemistically calls "force loadings." These are the total number

---

*Still another measure, reliability, has also been used. However, the absence of reliable data on this measure has forced us to omit this from the discussion.

of nuclear weapons carried by strategic delivery vehicles. The significance of this measure of strategic power was emphasized by Secretary of State Henry Kissinger's statement that "one is hit by warheads, not launchers."[1] General George Brown, chairman of the Joint Chiefs of Staff, has also acknowledged that "the number of strategic warheads and bombs is a very significant measure of the balance."[2] The numbers of strategic nuclear weapons, as of mid-1975, is given by the Department of Defense as United States—8,500, and the Soviet Union—2,800.[3]

This will increase to an estimated 8,900 U.S. strategic nuclear weapons and 3,500 Soviet strategic nuclear weapons by mid-1976 according to Defense Secretary Rumsfeld in his FY 1977 defense posture statement.

The United States has an almost three-to-one advantage in strategic nuclear weapons. This is a function of the fact that by mid-1975 the United States had nearly 1,000 launchers equipped with MIRV warheads, while the Soviets were estimated by the most generous projections to have had only a few MIRV warhead missiles deployed.[4] MIRVS are Multiple Independently-targeted Reentry Vehicles.

Accuracy

Accuracy is one of the most significant measures of the capability of strategic forces available. As John Newhouse puts it, "Although we have fewer ICBMs [Intercontinental Ballistic Missiles] ours are more accurate; and accuracy is a more dominant quality than yield."[5] The standard measure of accuracy is CEP, or circular error probability. CEP is defined as the size of the circle in which 50 percent of the launched warheads land. The ability of a missile to destroy a hard target depends on several factors, such as numbers of warheads, yield, reliability, and most important of all, accuracy. "The better the accuracy, that is, the smaller the CEP, the larger will be the K (the lethality of the warhead to a hard target) and therefore the probability that the warhead can destroy the silo."[6]

More precisely, hard-target kill capability is proportional to the square of accuracy (doubling accuracy increases counterforce capability fourfold); directly proportional to the numbers of warheads (double the number of warheads doubles the counterforce capability); and proportional to the two-thirds power of yield (an increase in megatonnage by a factor of eight will increase counterforce capability only four times).[7]

This can be expressed by the equation $K = Y^{2/3} / CEP^2$ where K equals the ability of a missile to destroy a hard target, Y equals

TABLE 8.1

U.S. and Soviet Missile Accuracy

United States		Soviet Union	
Missile	Reentry Vehicle Accuracy (CEP) nautical miles	Missile	Reentry Vehicle Accuracy (CEP) nautical miles
Minuteman III	0.2	SS-9	1.0
Minuteman II	0.3	SS-11, SS-13	1.0
Titan	0.5	SS-N-6	1.0-2.0
Poseidon	0.3	SS-N-8	1.0-2.0
Polaris	0.5	SS-7, SS-8	1.0-5.0

Sources: Stockholm International Peace Research Institute, Offensive Missiles, Stockholm Paper 5, Uppsalla, Sweden, 1974, p. 20. Also, Clarence Robinson, Jr., "New Propellant Evaluated for Trident Second Stage," Aviation News and Space Technology, October 13, 1975, p. 15; Ian Smart, "Advanced Strategic Missiles: A Short Guide," Adelphi Paper No. 63 (London: International Institute of Strategic Studies, December 1969).

the explosive yield of the warhead, and CEP equals the circular error of probability or the radius in which half of the warheads fired at a given target can be expected to land. As can be seen from the equation, the ability to destroy a hard target, like a missile silo, increases more rapidly with improvement in accuracy than with increases in explosive yield. (See SIPRI, Offensive Missiles, p. 16.) For example, the U.S. Minuteman III ICBM currently has a CEP of about 0.2 miles. It is expected that this will be reduced to 300 feet (.05 miles) in the near future. However, if it is improved to .1 miles its K increases from 22.1 to 148.0—an increase in K of 667 percent for an increase in accuracy of 100 percent. Thus, accuracy increases the efficiency of a missile far more than proportional increases in explosive yields, numbers or warheads, or throw weight.

The significance of all this is that hard target kill capability is more sensitive to the numbers of warheads in a country's arsenal and to their accuracy than to their size or yield. This has been reaffirmed many times by U.S. defense officials. As former chairman of the Joint Chiefs of Staff, Admiral Thomas Moorer pointed out in 1971, ". . . accuracy is much more important than weapon yield."[8] In

1973, then Secretary of Defense Elliot Richardson made the same
point: "Although our warheads are relatively small in terms of megatonnage, with respect to target destruction numbers of warheads and
accuracy are much more sensitive measures of destructive power
than weight."[9] U.S. advantages in these areas give the United States
a significant edge in counterforce capability, although little is gained
in counter-city capability, which can be achieved with several hundred less accurate missiles.

Numbers of Launchers

This is perhaps the oldest, best known measure of nuclear
power and also the one incorporated in both the SALT I and Vladivostok agreements. It is also the least significant in and of itself.

TABLE 8.2

U.S. and Soviet Nuclear Weapon Launchers, 1975

United States		Soviet Union	
Type	Number	Type	Number
ICBM:		ICBM:	
Minuteman II	450	SS-7	190
Minuteman III	550	SS-8	19
Titan II	54	SS-9/18	288
SLBM:		SS-11/19	1,030
Polaris	208	SS-13	60
Poseidon	448	SSN-5	24
		SSN-6	544
		SSN-8	132
Bombers:		Bombers:	
B-52 G&H	498	Bear	100
FB-111	73	Backfire	60
Total	2,182	Total	2,447

Sources: James R. Schlesinger, Annual Defense Department
Report FY 1976-197T (Washington, D.C.: Department of Defense,
1975), pp. II-12-II-16; General George Brown, United States Military
Posture for FY 1976, statement before Senate, Armed Services Committee (Washington, D.C.: Department of Defense, 1975), pp. 7-46.

The Soviets have a slight edge by this measure. The count for the
United States and the Soviet Union for mid-1975 is summarized in
Table 8.2.

Throw Weight

One of the more recent measures of nuclear power and the most
controversial is throw weight. Some have argued that it "is the most
useful verifiable measure of relative missile capability . . ."[10] This
is doubtful. Throw weight is defined as the weight of that part of a
missile above the last boost stage.[11] All things being equal, a missile
with larger throw weight will be able to carry more and larger nuclear
weapons. This is the basis for the Pentagon's argument about the
possibility that increasing numbers of more accurate Soviet nuclear
weapons could expose the United States to an attack in the late 1970s
or early 1980s. Generally, Soviet missiles have greater throw weight
than U.S. missiles. According to General George Brown, chairman
of the Joint Chiefs of Staff, Soviet missiles currently have an advantage of two to one in throw weight.[12] Former Secretary of Defense
James R. Schlesinger has been concerned that if the Soviets are able
to marry accurate MIRV warheads to their larger missiles, the
Soviet force will be able to cover a larger number of targets, including
military ones, and improve their hard-target kill capability.[13]
Schlesinger sees the danger that with this capability the Soviets would
have the ability to launch limited counterforce attacks against U.S.
land-based missiles. Without a comparable capability, it has been
argued, in the event of such an attack the United States would be faced
with a choice of surrender to Soviet blackmail or suicide by attacking
Soviet cities.

Several comments on throw weight and the Pentagon's scenarios
are in order. First, the notion that the Soviets would risk a surprise
nuclear attack on U.S. land-based missiles, leaving the formidable
(4,500 nuclear weapons) U.S. sea-based nuclear forces untouched,
makes little or no sense. As Jeremy Stone has recently pointed out:

> Our sea-based forces could respond against any Soviet
> targets they wish, issuing a counter ultimatum—that
> full-scale attacks on U.S. cities would result in a full-
> scale attack on Soviet cities.
>
> Soviet attacks on our land-based forces would inev-
> itably cause widespread fallout and many millions of
> casualties. No Soviet planner could assume that we
> would carefully and restrainedly calculate after that.

Nor could he be sure that we could distinguish his attack
from an all-out attack. Nor could he be sure that we
could restrain our sea-based forces with suitable communications once the crisis began or our airborne
bombers.

The entire scenario is bizarre, enormous risks for
no point.[14]

A second objection concerns the significance of the Soviet throw
weight advantage. As was pointed out above, all other things being
equal, a missile with a larger throw weight will be able to carry more
and larger warheads. As is usually the case, all other things are not
equal. It is known from what has been seen of Soviet space technology
that Soviet electronics are more primitive than American: the Soviets
still rely heavily on vacuum tubes, and are far behind the United States
in miniaturized solid state circuitry and in computers and minicom-
puters.[15] This means a greater percentage of the space in U.S.
nuclear weapons can be loaded with nuclear explosive material providing the United States significant yield-to-weight advantages over
Soviet nuclear weapons. In short, the Soviets get less explosive
punch to the pound of throw weight than does the United States.[16]

There is a third and final point that needs to be made with
regard to throw weight. It has been acknowledged by Pentagon officials
that by equipping their ICBMs with MIRV warheads, the Soviets will
reduce their yield-to-weight ratios. In testimony before the Senate
Appropriations Committee in 1974, General Harold Collins, air force
assistant deputy chief of staff for research and development, pointed
out that MIRVed Soviet missiles can carry only a fraction of the explosive payload that they could with single warheads. This degradation
of yield-to-weight ratios is due to the added propulsion, hardware,
and electronic components needed to deliver separate warheads on
their targets.[17] All of this raises fundamental and as yet unanswered
questions about the significance of throw weight as a measure of
strategic nuclear power.

MEGATONNAGE AND EQUIVALENT MEGATONNAGE

Still another measure of the state of the U.S.-Soviet strategic
nuclear balance is explosive power measured in megaton equivalents,
that is, millions-of-tons-of-TNT equivalents. In sheer explosive
power, the Soviet Union maintains an edge because the warheads on
its ICBMs and the explosive yields in some of its nuclear bombs are
much greater than those found in U.S. counterparts. Note in Table 8.3

TABLE 8.3

U.S. and Soviet Nuclear Destructive Power
(mid-1974 raw megatonnage)

	World War II Equivalents (2 megatons each)	Hiroshima Equivalents (0.013 megatons each)
United States		
ICBMs	791	121,692
SLBMs	168	25,846
Bombers	1,445	222,231
Total	2,404	369,769
Soviet Union		
ICBMs	3,948	607,308
SLBMs	318	48,923
Bombers	405	62,307
Total	4,671	718,538

Note: The United States from 1941 to 1945 dropped just over 2,000,000 tons of TNT on Germany and Japan—2 megatons (MT). The bomb dropped on Hiroshima in 1945 has been calibrated at 13 kilotons of explosive power. Thus, one Hiroshima equivalent is 0.013 MT. Some calculate the Hiroshima weapon at slightly higher yields, up to 20 kilotons.

Source: Center for Defense Information, Washington, D.C. Numbers of strategic weapons in each category, as well as explosive yields, from SIPRI Yearbook (Stockholm, Sweden: Stockholm International Peace Research Institute, 1974).

the megatonnage of both superpowers expressed in World War II and Hiroshima equivalents.

These raw megatonnage figures are, however, somewhat misleading since beyond a certain point, larger nuclear bombs do proportionately less damage than smaller weapons. Moreover, beyond a certain yield, no more explosive yield is needed to destroy a given target. A better measure of explosive power is "equivalent megatonnage" (EMT). This EMT is the basic ability of a nuclear weapon to destroy a target and is estimated to be proportional to the two-thirds power of its megatonnage if the yield is less than one megaton, and the square root of the megatonnage if the yield is over one megaton.[18]

TABLE 8.4

U.S. Strategic Megatonnage, 1974

Type	Number	Warheads Each	Estimated Raw Megatonnage per Warhead	Total Raw Megatonnage	Total Equivalent Megatonnage
Sea-based strategic missiles					
Polaris A-2	96	1	0.8	76.8	83.0
Polaris A-3	176	3	0.2	105.6	180.0
Poseidon C-3	384	10	0.04	153.6	45.0
Total				336.0	308.0
Intercontinental ballistic missiles					
Titan II	54	1	10.0	540.0	170.0
Minuteman I	100	1	1.0	100.0	100.0
Minuteman II	500	1	1.5	750.0	610.0
Minuteman III	400	3	0.16	192.0	26.0
Total				1,582.0	906.0
Long-range bombers (and ASM)					
B52 A/F	146	4	1.0	584.0	584.0
B52 G/H	274	4	1.0	1,096.0	1,096.0
FB 111	76	2	1.0	152.0	152.0
SRAM	1,140	1	0.2	228.0	390.0
Hound Dog *	510	1	4.0	2,040.0	1,020.0
Total				4,100.0	3,242.0
Summary					
SLBMs				336.0	308.0
ICBMs				1,582.0	906.0
Long-range bombers				4,100.0	3,242.0
Total				6,018.0	4,456.0

* Phased out in fiscal year 1975.

Source: Center for Defense Information, Washington, D.C. Weapons numbers and explosive yields from SIPRI Yearbook (Stockholm, Sweden: Stockholm International Peace Research Institute, 1974). These figures have changed slightly since 1974 so that the Soviet Union now maintains a slight EMT edge over U.S. strategic forces.

TABLE 8.5

Soviet Strategic Megatonnage, 1974

Type	Number	Warheads Each	Estimated Raw Megatonnage per Warhead	Total Raw Megatonnage	Total Equivalent Megatonnage
Sea-launched ballistic missiles					
SS-N-6	528	1	1.0	528	528
SS-N-8	108	1	1.0	108	108
Total	628			636	636
Intercontinental ballistic missiles					
SS-7	139	1	5.0	695	307
SS-8	70	1	5.0	350	158
SS-9	288	1	20.0	5,760	1,282
SS-11 Mod 1	970	1	1.0	970	970
SS-13	60	1	1.0	60	60
SS-11 Mod 3	40	3*	0.5	60	76
Total				7,895	2,853
Long-range bombers					
TU20 "Bear"	90	1	5.0	450	199
Mya 4 "Bison"	36	2	5.0	360	159
Total				810	358
Summary					
SLBMs				636	636
ICBMs				7,895	2,853
Long-range bombers				810	358
Total				9,341	3,847

*MRV.

Source: Center for Defense Information, Washington, D.C. Weapons numbers and explosive yields from SIPRI Yearbook (Stockholm, Sweden: Stockholm International Peace Research Institute, 1974). These figures have changed slightly since 1974 so that the Soviet Union now maintains a slight EMT edge over U.S. strategic forces.

Several smaller nuclear weapons can accomplish the same destruction as one very large weapon. Five one-megaton explosives can inflict damage equivalent to one 25-megaton explosive; four one-megaton bombs equal one 16-megaton bomb, and so on. By this measure (EMT) the U.S. and Soviet arsenals contain roughly the same explosive power.

Using 1974 strategic nuclear weapon figures, U.S. strategic bombers, ballistic-missile submarines, and ICBMs carried 4,456 EMT, whereas the Soviet Union's strategic launchers were capable of hurling 3,847 megaton equivalents. Thus, in equivalent megatonnage, as of mid-1974 the U.S. maintained a slight, if insignificant advantage. This has since shifted slightly in the Soviets' favor. Note the breakdown of megatonnage (MT) and equivalent megatonnage (EMT) by U.S. and Soviet delivery systems, excluding the newly-deployed Soviet SS-16, 17, 18, or 19 series, which are only now being moved beyond the testing phase into operational status.

SUFFICIENCY FOR WHAT?

The essential mission of both U.S. and Soviet strategic forces is to maintain the capability to carry out nuclear attacks against potential enemies and thereby hope to deter nuclear attacks on their homelands. Therefore, the most important question in assessing the nuclear forces of each side is not "who is number one?" but rather, "does each side have sufficient forces to perform this essential mission?" The answer is "yes." As Secretary Schlesinger has stated, "We have a good second strike deterrent, but so does the Soviet Union. Although the two forces differ in a number of respects, no one doubts they are in approximate balance."[19] What is essential is not that the two nuclear forces be in precise balance in terms of every variable by which one measures nuclear power, but that they are in balance in terms of their effect, that is, deterrence.

Furthermore, the mix of nuclear weapons—Intercontinental Ballistic Missiles (ICBMs), Submarine Launched Ballistic Missiles (SLBMs), and bombers—in both the U.S. and Soviet forces, in the view of both U.S. and Soviet military leaders, provide hedges against unforseen failures or technological breakthroughs by the other side that might negate one or two strategic systems and undermine the ability of each side to deter the other.

FUTURE PROSPECTS

Projections of the strategic nuclear balance over the next five years are difficult to determine and are necessarily speculative. However, several observations can be made with a fair degree of confidence. Over the next five years the current U.S. technological lead is likely to continue. The U.S. advantage in numbers of strategic nuclear weapons (SNWs) is also likely to continue. The present 8,500 U.S. SNWs could reach 11,800 by 1980 and 21,000 by 1985 as systems now under development—Trident submarines with MIRVed missiles, the B-1 bomber as well as new MIRV warheads—are deployed. The accuracy and the yield of U.S. nuclear warheads are likely to continue to increase, producing improved hard-target destruction capability for the United States. The Mark 12A reentry vehicle, in advanced stages of development, is expected to improve the yield of the three nuclear weapons carried by Minuteman III from 200 to 300 KT each. It is also expected to reduce the CEP of Minuteman III from the present two-tenths of a mile to 300 feet and give the Trident I missile a CEP of less than 1500 feet compared with Poseidon's 1,800 feet (.3 mile).[20]

Nuclear armed air- and sea-launched cruise missiles, also in the late stages of development, will have very high accuracies and the ability to evade Soviet defenses.[21] In addition, the sea-launched cruise missile could significantly complicate arms control efforts because of the difficulty of identifying delivery vehicles that might carry it. Additionally, the United States is developing two kinds of terminally guided maneuverable reentry vehicles (MARV) with great potential for high accuracy and penetration of Soviet defenses.

Soviet ICBMs are likely to continue to have more throw weight than their U.S. counterparts. The Soviets continue to emphasize land-based ICBMs and are currently testing four new missiles of this type, some with MIRV warheads, and are beginning to deploy at least some of these.[22] Consequently, numbers of warheads in the Soviet arsenal are likely to increase, though the Soviets will probably continue to have significantly fewer nuclear weapons than the United States. The accuracy of Soviet warheads is likely to improve, but will remain significantly inferior to their American counterparts.[23] In addition, the United States will continue to enjoy the advantage of having a "fourth nuclear force" consisting of forward-based fighter-bombers and carrier-based aircraft capable of nuclear attacks on the Soviet Union. Finally, the United States will continue to enjoy the advantage of having only one opponent capable of attacking it with nuclear weapons, while the Soviets will continue to confront growing British, French, and Chinese strategic nuclear capabilities with all the problems this implies.

Soviet emphasis on land-based ICBMs, in contrast to the heavy American reliance on sea-based missiles, could create significant problems for the Soviets as improved accuracy of American missiles makes land-based ICBMs increasingly vulnerable. In short, Soviet strategic forces may be in somewhat greater danger of becoming obsolete than U.S. forces.

FROM "ASSURED DESTRUCTION" TO "ESSENTIAL EQUIVALENCE": A NEGATIVE IMPACT ON SALT

The United States has long maintained a strategic nuclear deterrent force capable of carrying out simultaneous retaliatory attacks on adversary military forces and installations. Thus, for many years the U.S. Strategic Integrated Operations Plan (SIOP) has included both counter-value and counter-force targets with a heavy emphasis on the latter.

What has changed in recent years is the verbal emphasis the Secretary of Defense has given to counterforce targeting and the continued training of forces and deployment of strategic nuclear weapons for use in a counterforce mode.

The difficulty in arriving at mutually agreeable SALT formulas for equating U.S. and Soviet strategic striking forces has been exacerbated by a recent shift in emphasis, led by former Secretary of Defense Schlesinger, in the U.S. rationale for justifying the building of U.S. strategic nuclear weapons. All are agreed that such forces ought to be sufficient to deter any rational adversary from an attack. But the current emphasis on "essential equivalence" rather than simply building forces to accomplish "assured destruction" permits and encourages the building of many additional strategic weapons and delivery systems.

In the 1960s, the United States adopted an announced strategic deterrent doctrine that then Secretary of Defense Robert McNamara called "assured destruction." McNamara argued that the U.S. government could deter any rational Soviet government from launching a military attack on the United States by maintaining a strategic nuclear force capable of riding out a surprise attack and then inflicting "unacceptable" damage on the aggressor. McNamara's operational definition of "unacceptable" damage was damage equivalent to destruction of half the rival's industry and a quarter of its population.[24]

One of the advantages of the "assured destruction" doctrine was that the strategy could be implemented by a finite, limited number of strategic nuclear weapons. Calculations done in the Department of defense indicated that 400 one-megaton nuclear weapons delivered

FIGURE 8.1

Soviet Population and Industrial Capacity Destroyed

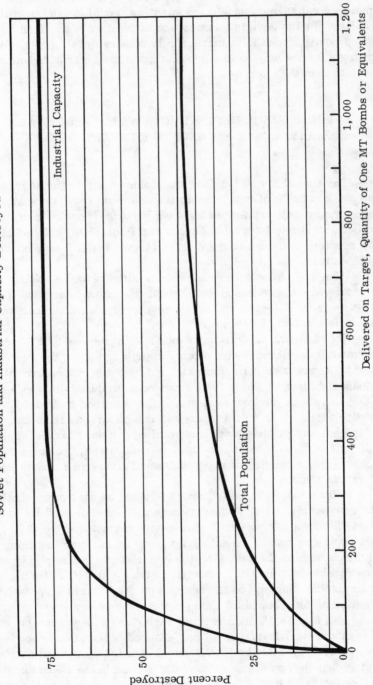

Source: Based on extrapolations from Alain Enthoven and Wayne Smith, How Much is Enough? (New York: Harper and Row, 1974).

142

TABLE 8.6

U.S. and Soviet Strategic Nuclear Weapons, 1970-75
(Defense Department figures)

Year	Soviet Union	United States
1970	1,300	4,000
1971	2,100	4,600
1972	2,200	5,700
1973	2,200	6,800
1974	2,500	7,650
1975	2,800	8,500
1976	—	8,900

Source: Annual reports to Congress by the secretary
of defense, FY 1970-76, Department of Defense.

upon the Soviet Union would inflict 50 to 100 million deaths and would
destroy at least 60 percent of Soviet industry. Beyond 400 such nuclear
weapons, there is a rapid falloff in the amount of further damage that
can be inflicted upon the Soviet Union with additional nuclear weapons.[25]
See Figure 8.1 for an indication of this point of diminishing "utility"
of strategic nuclear forces beyond 400 one-megaton weapons.

The Soviet Union's nuclear capacity from 1970 to 1975 is outlined in Table 8.6. All nuclear weapons could not have "survived"
a first U.S. strike. The United States had 400 strategic nuclear
weapons by the early 1950s. That by 1975 the United States had 8,500
strategic nuclear weapons and the Soviets had 2,800 illustrates the
overkill capability available to each.

In 1974, the Pentagon advanced a new modification of the doctrine
of assured destruction. Secretary Schlesinger stated that an additional
essential element in the U.S. effort to deter nuclear war is that no
perceived asymmetries in levels or capabilities of forces should exist
between the United States and the Soviet Union. This he called the
doctrine of "essential equivalence." Clearly, this new doctrine can
become the rationalization for thousands of new U.S. weapons.
Schlesinger's new doctrine, unlike McNamara's assured destruction
doctrine, would have the United States match or exceed the Soviets
by every measure of strategic nuclear power, including weapons,
launchers, and throw weights, so as not to allow any perceived gap
unfavorable to the United States to develop between the two forces.

The result of this U.S. doctrinal shift is likely to be a continued
nuclear weapons buildup, despite the fact that both the United States

and the Soviet Union have far more nuclear weapons than they now need to destroy each other, even if attacked first by the other.

To critics who point out that both the United States and the Soviets have produced far more strategic nuclear weapons than they need, Schlesinger argued that Soviet perceptions of U.S. strength are perhaps as important as real U.S. strength. The former secretary of defense has argued that decision makers base their policies on perceptions of strengths and weakness, whether they exist or not. Hence, he wants the United States to maintain forces that are perceived by decision makers all over the world as equal or superior in every facet to Soviet forces. Because of the subjective nature of perceptions, this opens the door to virtually endless expansion of the U.S. strategic arsenal. This implies that the United States will match the Soviet Union in arms building, even when those extra weapons outnumber the available targets in the Soviet Union and have passed far beyond the point of diminishing returns in U.S. capability to destroy Soviet industry, forces, or population.

"Essential equivalence" as stated by Schlesinger does not give the Soviet political or military leaders credit for understanding the awesome destructive power of even a few hundred nuclear weapons. Yet, the Soviet leaders for years have given speeches about the terrible consequences of a nuclear war and the awesome capabilities of their own nuclear arsenal, which, until recent years, numbered no more than a few hundred missile warheads and bombs.

Does the United States need more strategic nuclear weapons than it now possesses in order to convince the Soviet leaders that it can inflict vast damage upon them even if they strike first? Surely, they understand the incredible dimensions of such weapons. Labeling the frontrunning or "matching" strategy in the strategic arms race as "essential equivalence" obscures the fact that the only equivalence "essential" to U.S., or Soviet, security is the capacity to inflict unacceptable retaliatory damage upon any aggressor country. Both sides now possess that capacity and have possessed it for more than a decade. Building weapons beyond this level is a wasteful expenditure of funds.

Thus, moving from a strategic doctrine of "assured destruction" to "essential equivalence" is a setback for those who speak for arms restraint, and a victory for those who see more weapons as a means to greater security. Advocates of the "assured destruction" theory of deterrence argue for relatively "small" numbers of U.S. nuclear weapons. Advocates of "essential equivalence" can only promise increased building of nuclear weapons—unless the United States is ahead or even in every category of strategic weapons measurement.

SALT—ACCELERATOR OR BRAKE
ON THE ARMS RACE?

The Strategic Arms Limitation Talks have produced mixed arms control results. They have succeeded in restraining some arms competition—for example, antiballistic missile deployment—but have failed to halt the nuclear arms race overall. Indeed, SALT I has acted to rechannel arms competition and overall has served more as a catalyst for further arms production and deployment than as a force for arms limitation. It froze ICBM launcher numbers, SLBM launch tube numbers, ballistic missile submarine numbers, and the number of ABM missiles per site, as well as the number of ABM sites. The agreement had the virtue of freezing arms building at levels then current and of halting the quantitative arms race in these categories of strategic nuclear weaponry. Unfortunately the agreement left unregulated the numbers of nuclear weapons on each side, perhaps the most important measure of strategic destructive power. Also, two significant loopholes were left in the agreement—strategic long-range bombers and forward-based nuclear systems were not in the agreement. Thus, a significant portion of the nuclear delivery systems was left unregulated and no pact regulated the qualitative arms race whereby new, more efficient, and modern generations of strategic nuclear weapons continue to replace older systems.

Nevertheless the SALT I Treaty was a useful step forward in stabilizing the arms race. The ABM Treaty lessened the chances of either the United States or Soviet Union being able to launch a pre-emptive nuclear strike without being destroyed in return. The treaty thus tended to make nuclear war less likely, although it did nothing to discourage the continued "modernization" of strategic forces. SALT I was a limited victory for those who sought to slow vertical proliferation of nuclear weapons by the Soviet and U.S. governments.

The SALT I agreements were followed by two more summit agreements between the United States and the Soviet Union in the summer and winter of 1974. The Nixon-Brezhnev agreement at Moscow in July accomplished little of substance. It established a threshold of 150 kilotons, which underground test explosions were not to exceed. This was of relatively little importance since less than a half dozen such tests had occurred in the previous five years, and fewer still were scheduled in the projected future. The July 1974 summit also reduced the number of sites where ABMs would be permitted from two to one. This was of little value, as it did not prohibit anything either government planned to do. Both had completed only one ABM site at the time and showed no signs of building another.

These agreements, and the November 1974 Vladivostok accord
reached by President Ford and General Secretary Brezhnev, have led
some analysts to suggest that the SALT negotiations have backfired
on those interested in limiting strategic nuclear weapons. In their
view, SALT has recently been perverted from its initial goals of
arresting the U.S.-Soviet strategic arms race to the point where
strategic arms control negotiations have virtually become a part of
the nuclear weapons acquisition process.

Bargaining-Chip Approach Accelerates
Nuclear Arms Race

SALT has spurred arms competition in three ways. First, the
armed services have gained an argument in the annual budget battles
that helps convince skeptics to fund new nuclear weapons. This is the
"bargaining-chip" approach to SALT. The Pentagon has argued that
we should continue to fund nuclear weapons systems like the B-1
bomber, the Trident submarine, and should continue MIRVing U.S.
strategic missiles—all in order to strengthen our bargaining position
with the Soviets. It is not unreasonable to believe that similar arguments are being presented inside the Kremlin by representatives of
the Soviet military services. As arms control expert Jack Ruina
from the Massachusetts Institute of Technology has put the problem:

> Finding a suitable bargaining chip is a fundamental
> problem. It is hard to think of an arms program that
> simultaneously is good enough to worry an opponent and
> bad enough for the military to be willing to give it up
> in negotiations.[26]

Unfortunately, the previous pattern of arms control agreements
offers few precedents for cutting back nuclear weapons that have
already been produced. Arms control pacts like the Outer Space
Treaty, the Seabeds Treaty, and the Biological Convention of 1972
all prohibited the production of certain weapons of the future. In no
instance has an arms control agreement resulted in arms reduction.
"Bargaining-chip" weaponry, once in place, remains in place, and
serves to induce the other side into further military expenditures to
keep pace with the new development.

Acceleration to Beat SALT Deadlines

Second, the Strategic Arms Limitation Talks have spurred further nuclear weapons production on the part of the military services to get coveted new weapons into production as soon as possible to avoid their prohibition under future arms limitation agreements. This holds true for nuclear weapons testing as well. Soon after the July 1974 Threshold Test Ban Treaty was signed, the Atomic Energy Commission asked for $56 million more to accelerate nuclear testing before the cutoff occurred 21 months later. Congress granted $22 million of this request. Each service is anxious to get its own new nuclear weapons systems under the wire before the negotiators can limit them.

SALT Limits as Magnets

Third, SALT agreements like the November 1974 Vladivostok agreement, allow greater numbers of strategic weapons than exist in current inventories. These high limits on MIRVs and strategic delivery vehicles may serve as "lures" rather than as limits to further arms production. Pentagon spokesmen argue that since the Soviets will build to such limits, the United States must do so. The Soviet military, no doubt, argues in the same manner.

Thus, one might say SALT has been rubbed into the wounds of arms limitation advocates. It has produced the "bargaining-chip" rationale for arms production and spurred the military services to press for new nuclear weapons before they are prohibited. Finally, the SALT limits, because they are higher than existing inventories of strategic weapons, serve as goals to be fulfilled lest the Soviets gain an advantage.

The Ford-Brezhnev SALT II agreement in Vladivostok in late November 1974 was advertised by the parties as the long-awaited "cap on the strategic arms race." In this Vladivostok agreement, both the United States and Soviet Union agreed to limit until 1985: 1) The number of their strategic bombers and missile launchers, either sea- or land-based, to 2,400 for each country; and 2) The number of missile launchers with multiple independently targeted reentry vehicles (MIRV), either sea- or land-based, to 1,320 for each country.

VLADIVOSTOK VIRTUES

Defenders of the Vladivostok "agreement"[*] argue that it helps maintain the atmosphere of detente in U.S.-Soviet relations and keeps the momentum of SALT going in a positive direction. Secretary of State Henry Kissinger has argued immediately after the Vladivostok Summit that the new agreement relieved unfavorable time pressures and the now-or-never quality that the SALT negotiations had taken on in 1974. The new limits established in principle at Vladivostok can be used as starting points for further agreed reductions and as a basis for planning by defense analysts. Some uncertainty about the future is removed for both the military planner and the arms control negotiator.

While the United States agreed to include strategic bombers as a concession to the Soviet Union, it can be plausibly argued that the Soviets have given up more than the United States in this particular agreement. The omission of U.S. forward-based systems, in Europe, Asia, and on aircraft carriers, even though they constitute a substantial nuclear force, was a significant concession in view of the threat that these weapons pose to the Soviet Union. The Vladivostok accord, by stipulating numerical equality in MIRVed missiles and launchers, helped to channel the U.S.-Soviet strategic nuclear arms race in a direction where U.S. military advantages are pronounced. The Soviets will no longer be able to compensate for their technological inferiority by having more missiles. It is likely that the United States will continue to enjoy an advantage in nuclear weapons technology for some time to come and the Soviet Union may have committed itself to a more or less permanent handicap.

However, the Soviet leadership may be realistic about the dubious political utility of nuclear weapons and the significance of nuclear "gaps." It is clear that they believe that forward momentum in overall relations with the United States is more important than putting military considerations above all else.

Lastly, defenders of the Vladivostok SALT accord point out that it "caps" the arms race at some finite point and acts to channel and restrict weapons production at lower future levels than might have been the case with no limits at all.

----

[*] This was not a binding agreement, but rather an agreement in principle. Details and a more formal agreement, as of this writing, are being negotiated.

VLADIVOSTOK VICES

Despite the advantages cited for the 1974 Vladivostok pact, this "cap on the arms race" may well turn out to be a "dunce cap." The limits are so high that the Vladivostok agreement may be seen more as a license to continue the strategic arms race than as an agreement that favors arms restraint.

It is useful to review what President Ford and General Secretary Brezhnev did not accomplish at Vladivostok, in order to put their agreement into proper perspective.

First, the accord imposed no limit on the number of nuclear weapons allowed each side. This is perhaps the most serious defect in the accord. The MIRV limit of 1,320 limits no current weapon or warhead deployment plans of the United States. Before the November 1974 summit, the United States had completed nearly 80 percent of its program to MIRV 550 ICBMs and 496 Poseidon SLBMs. The Vladivostok agreements permitted and encouraged the MIRVing of 274 additional U.S. missiles beyond the 1,046 planned. The result might be an increase in U.S. nuclear weapons beyond numbers initially planned.

Indeed, President Ford has told us that "we do have an obligation to step up to that ceiling" (2,400 strategic delivery vehicles, 1,320 MIRVed missiles), and he promised that "the budgets that I recommend will keep our strategic forces either up to or aimed at that objective."[27] The MIRV limits obviously do not cut into Soviet plans, as the first operational Soviet MIRVed missile had yet to be deployed at the time of the agreement. MIRVing 1,320 missiles may be the work of a decade for the Soviets.

A second weakness of the 1974 Vladivostok agreement is that it did not reduce any U.S. or Soviet nuclear weapon program. Indeed, it has resulted in increased, not reduced, spending for strategic nuclear forces in both countries.

A third major flaw in the Vladivostok accord is that no limits were placed upon the qualitative arms race, that is, on improvements in strategic nuclear weapons. No restrictions were placed on spending for improvements in accuracy and none on the creation of mobile ICBMs, or antisubmarine warfare technology, or on MARV—the logical extension of MIRV technology. These are major loopholes that beg for plugging in future negotiations if real limits are to be imposed on further arms building on both sides.

Finally, there is no indication that the Vladivostok agreement significantly enhanced the national security of either the United States or the Soviet Union. The strategic nuclear forces permitted by Vladivostok until 1985 look as threatening as those promised in the absence of an agreement.

The Ford–Brezhnev agreement at Vladivostok, if not followed by further, more restrictive arms limitation agreements, encourages the building and deployment of as many as three to four times as many deliverable strategic nuclear weapons by each signatory in the next 10 years. Under the 1974 Vladivostok agreement, 29,000 Soviet and American strategic nuclear weapons might well be deployed by 1985 or before.*

As we have indicated, additional strategic weapons are unnecessary for the purposes of either side, since both arsenals are equal in the one measure that really counts, the ability under any conditions to devastate the opposing society.

The Strategic Arms Limitation Talks (SALT) have not, as yet, significantly arrested the strategic nuclear arms building competition. It is true that ABMs have been limited by treaty, and the SALT I agreement rechanneled weapons development away from increased numbers of ICBMs and SLBMs. It is also true that some progress has been made in lowering the size of underground nuclear tests. SALT negotiations have also relaxed the atmosphere of Soviet–American relations.

Nevertheless, a solid case can be made that to date SALT has acted as more of an accelerator than as a brake on the U.S.–Soviet strategic nuclear arms race. Numbers of nuclear weapons in the United States and Soviet Union have dramatically increased during the SALT years. This nuclear proliferation has continued despite, and to some degree because of, the Strategic Arms Limitation Talks. Weapons acquired by governments as "bargaining chips" have been retained. Permissive limits set in negotiations have become production targets—goals to be achieved by the military in both camps.

At the same time, the fundamental objectives that led both the United States and the Soviet Union to begin the SALT talks—a desire by both to reduce tensions and the danger of nuclear war—continue to be of considerable importance for the two countries. This has produced a continuing commitment by both sides to the SALT process

---

*This assumes production and deployment by the United States of the Trident submarine, B-1 bombers up to the Valdivostok limit of 2,400 launchers and MIRV warheads up to the limit of 1,320. This also assumes Soviet deployment of a new family of ICBMs with MIRV warheads. It is conservative in that it assumes no other new qualitative strategic innovations. A conservative estimate has U.S. nuclear weapons growing from 7,650 in mid-1974 to 21,000 by 1985. Soviet weapons are expected to grow to just under 8,000. A worst-case projection of Soviet growth would put Soviet nuclear weapons at 14,500 by 1985.

and it is this basic commitment to the process that provides some basis for hoping that future SALT agreements will be reached and that they will address some of the problems discussed in this chapter.

NOTES

1. Secretary of State Henry Kissinger, taken from an April 26, 1974 news conference.

2. General George Brown, U.S. Military Posture, FY 1976 and FY 197T (Washington, D.C.: Department of Defense, February 1975), p. 37.

3. James R. Schlesinger, Annual Defense Department Report, FY 1976 and FY 197T (Washington, D.C.: Department of Defense, February 1975), pp. II–19.

4. Ibid., pp. 11–12.

5. John Newhouse, counselor of the U.S. Arms Control and Disarmament Agency, from a January 29, 1975 speech at the University of California at Los Angeles in Westwood, California, p. 8.

6. Stockholm International Peace Research Institute, Offensive Missiles, Stockholm Paper 5 (Uppsalla, Sweden: SIPRI, 1974), p. 16.

7. Congressman Robert Leggett, "Two Legs Do Not a Centipede Make," Armed Forces Journal, February 1975, p. 30.

8. Admiral Thomas Moorer, Senate, Armed Services Committee, FY 1972 Defense Department Authorization (Washington, D.C.: Government Printing Office, 1971), Part I, p. 19.

9. Elliot Richardson, House, Armed Services Committee, Department of Defense Authorization, FY 1974 (Washington, D.C.: Government Printing Office, 1973), Part I, p. 482.

10. Paul Nitze, Aviation Week and Space Technology, February 24, 1975, p. 66.

11. General George Brown, op. cit., p. 37.

12. Ibid.

13. Schlesinger, op. cit., p. II–14.

14. Jeremy Stone, Federation of American Scientists, Public Interest Report, February 1975, p. 8.

15. See Aviation Week and Space Technology, October 7, 1974, pp. 12–14, January 27, 1975, p. 61, February 3, 1973, p. 19; see also SIPRI, Offensive Missiles, op. cit., pp. 24n, 25n; also, Dr. Malcolm Currie, Department of Defense Program of RDT and E, Report for FY 1976 (Washington, D.C.: Department of Defense, 1975), p. 11–17.

16. Edgar Ulsamer, "The Soviet Drive for Aerospace Superiority," Air Force Magazine, March 1975, p. 46.

17. U.S. Senate, Committee on Appropriations, Department of Defense Appropriations, FY 1975 (Washington, D.C.: Government Printing Office, 1974), Part 4, p. 704.

18. David Packard, Senate, Foreign Relations Committee, Arms Control Implications of Current Defense Budget FY 1972, June-July 1971 (Washington, D.C.: Government Printing Office, June 1, 1971), p. 179.

19. James R. Schlesinger, House, Armed Services Committee, Department of Defense Authorization, FY 1974 (Washington, D.C.: Government Printing Office, 1973), Part IV, p. 3992.

20. Clarence Robinson, Jr., "New Propellant Evaluated for Trident Second Stage," Aviation Week and Space Technology, October 13, 1975, p. 15.

21. Kosta Tsipis, "The Long Range Cruise Missile," The Bulletin of the Atomic Scientists 31, no. 4 (April 1975): 15-26.

22. Schlesinger, op. cit., pp. II-12-II-17.

23. Secretary Schlesinger testified in September 1974 that the Soviets are expected (by optimistic projections) to achieve accuracies for their ICBMs of 500 to 700 meters, one-third to one-fourth of a mile. U.S. Congress, Senate, Foreign Relations Committee, Briefing of Counterforce Attacks, Hearings before the Subcommittee on Arms Control, International Law and Organization (Washington, D.C.: Government Printing Office, September 11, 1974), p. 10.

24. See testimony of then Secretary of Defense Robert McNamara before U.S. Congress, Senate, Defense Subcommittee of Appropriations Committee, February 24, 1965, Department of Defense Appropriations, 1966 (Washington, D.C.: Government Printing Office, 1965), Part I, pp. 44-45; also McNamara testimony before U.S. Congress, House, Defense Subcommittee of Appropriations Committee, February 14, 1968, Department of Defense Appropriations for 1969 (Washington, D.C.: Government Printing Office, 1968), Part I, pp. 145-47.

25. Alain Enthoven and Wayne Smith, How Much is Enough? (New York: Harper and Row, 1974), pp. 207-10.

26. Jack Ruina, "SALT in a MAD World," the New York Times Magazine, June 30, 1974, p. 42.

27. Transcript of President Gerald Ford's news conference, the New York Times, December 3, 1974.

9

NUCLEAR MISSILE
SUBMARINES AND
NUCLEAR STRATEGY
Phil Stanford

What everyone remembers long afterward is the silence, deeper than the voices or the occasional sounds of machinery. That, and the lack of a sense of motion. If you didn't know better you might imagine that you were sitting in a room somewhere with the shades drawn. Or, perhaps, in a slightly crowded suite of offices. There are overhead fluorescent lights in all the rooms and passageways, and carpets on the floors.

There is no vibration. Nothing but the instruments to indicate how fast you are moving, or where, or that you are moving at all. Sometimes the captain's voice comes over the intercom with a command or an announcement, and sometimes there is music. But usually the only sound is the barely perceptible hush of the air-conditioning as it carries off the carbon monoxide and carbon dioxide and replaces them with oxygen. Sometimes, far off, you can hear sperm whales, which make a sharp cracking sound like a hammer striking a board, or, in more tropical water, the clicking sounds, echolocations, of dolphins talking.

In the control center, men in blue lint-free jump suits sit quietly before panels of instruments, watching dials and colored lights, or, as their work requires it, walk about attending to the machines. When their shift is over they congregate in the recreation areas and pass the time before turning in.

The crew's mess is done in bright colors, with orange Naugahyde booths and posters on the walls, and it has a popcorn machine.

An earlier version of this chapter appeared in the September 21, 1975 New York Times Magazine. Reprinted with permission.

Every 24 hours there is a new movie and the men eat popcorn. Before the patrol is over, the steward says, the men will go through 600 cans of it. There is also a soft ice-cream machine. There is usually a bridge-tournament going on, and every once in a while there is casino night with pizza for everyone. The petty officers' lounge has an oil painting of a bare-breasted Spanish senorita wearing a black mantilla. Some of the men use their off-duty time to read or study correspondence courses.

Then, about once a week, there is a missile drill.

It is necessary to keep in mind that nuclear-missile submarines are unlike other submarines. They do not prowl the sea-lanes looking for enemy ships to send to the bottom, or play cat and mouse with enemy submarines. Their only real similarity with these attack submarines is that they have the same general shape and both travel under water.

Nuclear-missile submarines are, quite simply, underwater missile bases. They have only one purpose, unchanging in peacetime or war. They hide, day in, day out, under millions of square miles of dark sea water. And they wait—for the message that will order them to fire missiles loaded with nuclear bombs into space and back again to earth.

The United States has three kinds of long-range, or strategic, nuclear weapons: bombers, intercontinental ballistic missiles and missile-firing submarines. At the onset of the nuclear age, only airplanes could deliver nuclear bombs. However, with the development of long-range missiles, which could traverse oceans and continents in minutes—as opposed to several hours for an airplane—bombers were relegated to a minor, backup role in strategic war plans. That was in the early 1960s. Now it appears that land-based ICBMs are about to become obsolete. As the new, highly accurate guidance systems, which are now being developed for missiles, find their way into the arsenals of both superpowers, fixed, land-based missiles will become vulnerable to attack. According to most experts, this should take place over the next decade. As a result, both the Soviet Union and the United States are preparing to place more of their nuclear missiles on submarines, or, as the current phrase goes, "move them to sea." It is conceivable that one day virtually all nuclear missiles will be on submarines.

One modern U.S. nuclear-missile submarine carries 16 missiles. Each missile has at least 10 nuclear warheads. Each warhead is three times as powerful as the bomb that was dropped on Hiroshima. Those who study these matters can recite that, or some version of it, as if it were part of a new catechism. Perhaps it is.

The nuclear-missile submarine may well be the most sophisticated weapons system—in the exact meaning of that term—ever built.

It is actually the sum of a number of technologies, and without any one it could not exist. Nuclear power is one. Before small nuclear reactors were developed, submarines had to rely on diesel, air-burning engines in combination with storage batteries. This meant they were able to travel under water for only a few hours at a time before surfacing or coming to snorkel depth to run their diesel engines. With nuclear propulsion it became possible for submarines to cruise under water indefinitely. Nuclear power plants also supply electricity to generate oxygen from sea water. The length of time a nuclear submarine can spend submerged is limited only by the amount of food it can carry and the endurance of the crew. Patrols for U.S. nuclear-missile submarines last about 70 days.

It is not difficult to image the problem of navigating a submarine that must remain always hidden under 100 more more feet of ocean, constantly on the move. It is, however, crucial for nuclear-missile submarines to be able to fix their positions precisely at all times, because it is impossible for a missile to be any more accurate than the error in calculating the position from which it is launched. Therefore, a nuclear-missile submarine depends upon another advanced technology, inertial guidance. Sometimes, at night, nuclear-missile submarines will approach close enough to the surface to put up an antenna to take a fix on a satellite, and occasionally they check their position against charted features on the ocean floor. But for the most part they rely on their inertial guidance systems, self-contained systems of gyroscopes and small weights called accelerometers. As the submarine moves through the water the accelerometers register movement in every direction (the gyroscopes hold the accelerometers in position), and computers translate the signals from the accelerometers into speed, distance and, finally, position. Inertial guidance was originally designed for missiles and then adapted for use by nuclear-missile submarines.

The targets for the missiles are recorded as electrical impulses on electromagnetic discs. These discs are connected to computers that convert the target instructions into trajectories for the missiles. As the submarine moves along under water, computers receiving information from the inertial-guidance system constantly revise the trajectories of the 16 missiles and of each of the warheads on the missiles.

A Poseidon missile is 32 feet long, 6 feet in diameter and weighs 34 tons. It is launched under water and reaches a height of 500 to 800 miles above earth before it begins its descent. Its inertial-guidance system is connected to computers that have been programmed with information about the target's location and instructions on what course the missile must fly to reach it. When the computers determine that the missile has been placed on the proper course, they shut off the rocket engines, and the missile, which is already moving at several times the speed of sound, travels the rest of the way on its momentum. Depending on the distance from which it is fired, it will take 15 to 20 minutes to reach its target.

Of all the technologies that go to make up a nuclear-missile submarine, perhaps the most remarkable is MIRV, which stands for Multiple Independently Targeted Reentry Vehicle. With MIRV technology, which was originally developed to make multiple satellite launches in space, a number of warheads on a single missile can be delivered to targets separated by as much as 100 miles. The MIRV warheads are mounted on a final stage of the missile called the "bus." As the missile begins its descent, the bus, which has its own guidance system and a set of directional jets, begins dropping off warheads according to instructions from its computer. After it releases a warhead, the computer activates the jets that will bring it into position for the next release, and so on until all the warheads have been expended. According to official statistics, the warheads on U.S. submarine missiles can strike within a quarter-mile of a target more than 1,000 miles away. There are indications that the accuracy is actually much greater.

Each Poseidon missile has 10 to 14 warheads; therefore, a single submarine carries anywhere from 160 to 224 warheads. Each warhead is a hydrogen bomb with the explosive power of 50 kilotons (50,000 tons) of TNT. Just one nuclear submarine can destroy any country on earth.

The drill can come at any time, just like the real thing. The Emergency Action Message comes in over the scrambler. If it is an actual order to launch the missiles, it will come from the President. There are contingency plans for someone farther down the chain of command to give the order in the event that Washington, D.C., has been destroyed. Two officers confirm the message's authenticity by comparing it to a format kept on file in one of the submarine's safes, and then they take it to the captain.

While the two officers check the message, the captain or the officer in charge at that time gives the command, "Man battle stations, missile," and the crew begins to prepare the ship. It is only when the message has been authenticated that the captain gives the next command:

"Set condition ISQ," he says. ISQ is the highest state of readiness for a nuclear-missile submarine. From the moment the captain gives the command, it will take about 13 minutes until the missile can be launched. This is the last command he will give until all systems are ISQ. Then it will be a matter of 15 seconds.

The missile tubes must be pressurized to bring the air inside them up to the level of the water outside; otherwise it will be impos-

sible to open the hatches that cover each missile. Flood and drain
valves must be readied for the rush of water into the empty tubes
after the missile has cleared the ship; the water is heavier than the
missile, so if the ship is to continue firing missiles, it is necessary
to compensate for the sudden addition of weight. The hydraulic system
has to be prepared; the missile is actually launched by a blast of
steam and it ignites only as it breaks the surface of the water. Finally,
the missiles' guidance systems must be "spun up."

Before the launch can be made, the submarine must be almost
dead in the water, 100 feet below the surface.

The first nuclear-missile submarine, a Polaris, went to sea
in 1960. Today the United States has 41 of them, 10 Polarises and
31 of the newer Poseidons. The Soviet Union built its first ballistic-
missile submarine in 1963 and now has a fleet of 44, counting just
those that are nuclear-powered. France with three, and Britain,
with four, are the only other nations that have nuclear-missile
submarines.

Over a decade and a half, nuclear-missile submarines have
undergone what the navy describes as an "evolutionary" development.
Generally, this means that while their basic design has stayed the
same, they have grown larger and their equipment, most notably
missiles, has become more advanced. Several times, the United
States and the Soviet Union have replaced missiles on their submarines
with missiles that have a greater range. The chief advantage of
longer-range missiles is that they give the submarine more ocean in
which to hide.

All nuclear missile submarines, Soviet and American, look
very much alike. They are huge black or dark blue steel cylinders,
rounded at the nose and tapered at the tail. (The shape is simply a
concession to the environment, since, next to a sphere, a cylinder is
the shape best able to withstand the pressure at a depth of several
hundred feet beneath the sea.) Living quarters (for approximately 140
men on U.S. submarines) and the various control centers—navigation,
communications, sonar, the torpedo room, launch control, missile
control and the command center—are located in the forward third of
the ship. The engine rooms, with the nuclear reactor, are in the
after third. In the middle are the missiles, vertical in their tubes,
in two rows of eight extending through the hull. A conning tower,
which houses antennas and a periscope, sits atop the hull to the front
of the missile compartment.

A Polaris submarine is 380 feet long, 32 feet in height and
breadth and weighs 7,000 tons. The Poseidon submarine is 435 feet
long, 32 feet high and weighs 8,500 tons. Modern Soviet nuclear-
missile submarines are about the same size as the Poseidon.

Poseidons are basically Polarises that have been refitted with a larger, more advanced missile. The Poseidon missile has from 10 to 14 MIRV warheads. The Polaris missile has just three MRV (for Multiple Reentry Vehicle) warheads, which cannot be independently targeted and are released by the final stage of the missile much like shotgun pellets. The original Polaris missile had a single warhead and a range of 1,500 miles; it was replaced by an 1,800-mile missile. Today, both Polaris and Poseidon missiles have a 2,800-mile range. The navy calculates that this gives a submarine whose assigned target is Moscow a patrol area of 6 million square miles.

In 1979, the United States expects to launch an even larger nuclear-missile submarine, called the Trident. It will be 535 feet long—almost as long as two football fields; 43 feet high—as tall as a four-story office building, and will weigh 18,000 tons. It will carry 24 missiles, each with a range of 4,500 miles. These could eventually be replaced by a later version with a range of 6,000 miles.

The latest Soviet nuclear-missile submarine, the Delta, carries a missile that has a range of 4,000 miles. The Delta has been called the Soviet Trident; however, the Soviets have not yet put MIRV warheads on submarines, so each missile has only one warhead. According to some accounts, each Trident missile will have 17 warheads, for a total of 408 warheads per submarine.

A couple of years ago there was a controversy in Congress over building the Trident. It is, after all, the most expensive weapons system ever to be built. At the price now being quoted, each Trident will cost $1.8 billion. Proponents said that the Trident, with its quieter engines and longer-range missile, was needed as a "hedge" against a Soviet breakthrough in antisubmarine-warfare technology.[1] Another argument for the Trident was that its longer-range missiles would allow the submarine to patrol closer to its bases in the continental United States. Currently, most U.S. nuclear-missile submarines are based at Holy Loch, Scotland; Rota, Spain; and Guam.

Opponents argued that the Trident was an unnecessary extravagance, that it wasn't needed at this time and that furthermore, it could be built for less money. It is clear, however, that there was never any real doubt about the outcome of the debate. The closest vote came in 1973 on an amendment offered by Senator Thomas McIntyre that would only have required the navy to slow production of the Trident. (The amendment lost 49-47, but since then, the navy has decided on its own to build at the slower rate.) Since 1973, there have been no serious attempts in Congress to challenge the Trident program. Through fiscal 1975, Congress has appropriated money for three Tridents, and it is virtually certain by by 1985, the United States will have a fleet of 10 Tridents in addition to its current force of Polarises and Poseidons.

In retrospect, what was most striking about the Trident debate, both in and out of Congress, was the overall agreement that the United States should, sooner or later, get a new nuclear-missile submarine. In fact, those who were most actively opposed to building the Trident, liberals and defense intellectuals for the most part, have always been the biggest promoters of nuclear-missile submarines, or as they would put it, the sea-based deterrent. The only question was how soon a new model should be built (at issue was how soon the submarines now in use would wear out) and how much it should cost. It was not, as Senator McIntyre's aide put it, a doctrinal dispute.[2]

Strategic doctrine is often made to seem more complicated than it really is. Basically, now that both the Soviet Union and the United States have enough nuclear weapons—on bombers, on land-based intercontinental ballistic missiles and on submarines—to blow each other up many times over, the aim of any rational strategy is to keep the weapons from being used. This is called deterrence, and according to accepted doctrine, nuclear deterrence is achieved by having a nuclear strike force that can survive any possible attack by an enemy and still inflict unacceptable damage on the enemy's homeland. The more certain the prospect of a devastating retaliation—"assured destruction," as it is called—the less likely the other side will be to launch an attack in the first place. Or, to put it another way, the more perfect our weapons are—in terms of "survivability" and destructiveness—the less likely it is that they will be used. Anyway, that is the basic article of faith of nuclear deterrence.

Deterrence, that is, preventing the use of nuclear weapons by either side, is a mutual undertaking. Under the doctrine of deterrence, it is, in fact, to the advantage of both superpowers for the other side to have a nuclear strike force that can survive any conceivable attack and still destroy the attacker. It is crucial that the other side should not feel that its nuclear forces are subject to attack. Otherwise, in a crisis it might get nervous and attack first. Therefore, the more perfect the other side's nuclear weapons are, the safer both sides will be.

Under the doctrine, this state of utter vulnerability—of people, not weapons—is called "stability," and the nuclear-missile submarine is a "stable" weapon. Bombers are slow, and because of the threat of enemy air defenses, somewhat uncertain. Fixed land-based missiles—ICBMs—take only 30 minutes to strike their targets, but because they can be located by satellite, they are subject to attack by enemy missiles. Only nuclear-missile submarines are both devastating and, when they are hiding in the ocean, virtually invulnerable for all practical purposes. Therefore, it is logical for each side not only to build up its own nuclear submarine force, but to encourage the other side to do the same. It is, if you have followed the argument this far, the only way they can feel safe.

In front of the captain, attached to an upright girder, is a flat metal box, approximately two feet square and four inches thick. On the face of the box are 16 rows of green lights, lettered with names of each step in the launching process. By watching the lights the captain can follow the progress of each missile as it is prepared for launching. At the bottom center of the box is an opening for a key.

When the Emergency Action Message arrives, the executive officer and one other officer must get the key. The key is kept in a double safe; only they and their two backups have the combinations. One of them has the combination to the outer safe and one has the combination to the inner safe, but neither has the combinations to both. After they have opened the safes, they take the key to the captain.

The key is necessary for firing the missiles, but the captain cannot fire the missiles by himself. The key closes just one of four switches on an electrical circuit, called the firing circuit, which must be closed before the missiles can be launched. The firing circuit is like an old-fashioned string of Christmas-tree lights; if one switch is left open, nothing will work. The captain has a key; launch control has a key; there is a switch in the navigation center; and missile control has the trigger.

The firing circuit with its four switches is the only safeguard against an unauthorized firing of the submarine's nuclear missiles. All other nuclear weapons, on bombers and in silos, have a remote electronic switch, called a Permissive Action Link, that has to be turned before they can be launched. Because of the uncertainties of transmitting an electronic signal to a submerged submarine, nuclear-missile submarines do not have any external controls.

When the captain can see that switches have been turned on in the navigation center and launch control, he inserts his key into the box and turns it. "Weapons control," he says, "you have permission to fire." The executive officer, standing next to the captain, says the same words into a telephone. Now there is just one more switch.

In a background briefing on December 3, 1974, a few days after the Vladivostok strategic-arms agreement was signed, Secretary of State Henry Kissinger told reporters that over the next decade both the United States and the Soviet Union would be moving an increasing percentage of their strategic nuclear-missile forces to sea.* As the secretary presented it, this was ordained by the "essential elements

---

* The transcript of the December 3, 1974 briefing on SALT by Secretary Kissinger is available from the State Department. It was originally classified and was released in response to a Freedom of Information suit brought by Morton Halperin of the Center for National Security Studies.

of the agreement." Under the agreement, each side would be limited to a total of 2,400 missiles and bombers, which it could apportion however it wished—with one exception. Neither side would be allowed to increase the number of its land-based missiles. Thus, both parties were encouraged to pursue alternatives, the most inviting of which, the secretary said, was moving land-based missiles to sea.

Former Secretary of Defense James R. Schlesinger had a similar, though more guarded, interpretation of the agreement.[3] Without further reductions in Soviet arms levels, he said, an increasing share of the United States strategic forces would be forced to move to sea, and he suggested that the United States should increase the size of its nuclear-missile submarine force. One possibility, he said, would be for the United States to expand its Trident program. He also thought it would be good if the Soviet Union would MIRV the missiles on its nuclear-missile submarines. It was time, he said, "to reexamine the basic concepts for our strategic forces."

Some months earlier, in February, Fred Ikle, the chief of the U.S. Arms Control and Disarmament Agency, had been quite outspoken on the subject in an interview with Michael Getler of the Washington Post.[4] Ikle later said that he thought the interview was off the record, so there is perhaps more than usual cause to believe that he was really speaking frankly. The United States, he said, "should move away from reliance on land-based missiles" for nuclear deterrence, and it should do this by actually "getting rid of such obsolete weapons, through negotiations and in our own force planning." The idea of moving our strategic forces to sea, long a favorite idea of defense intellectuals, is now being seriously considered by some of this country's highest ranking officials.

If and when this is accomplished, it will be important to remember the part played by the Vladivostok agreement; however, as Kissinger himself told the reporters in the course of his briefing, that part consists mainly in formalizing something that "is in any case going to happen, with or without this agreement." The reason, as so often in such lofty matters of strategic doctrine, is technology—in this case new, highly accurate guidance systems for missiles. As the accuracy of missiles increases over the next decade, ICBMs will become increasingly vulnerable. The expected improvements in missile accuracy, however, will not threaten submarines, because you cannot hit what you cannot see.

There are, of course, political problems that must be reckoned with before the "move to sea," as the conversion of the missile forces is sometimes called, may be accomplished. The history of the nuclear arms race shows that bureaucratic interests have always been at least as influential as strategic considerations in decisions on what weapons should be produced and deployed. In the United States, the air force will be reluctant to relinquish its ICBMs, no matter how vulnerable they may become. It will no doubt give ground grudgingly and insist on some sort of recompense. This might be either "air-mobile" missiles, which would be launched from huge jet planes, or "land-mobile" missiles, which would be carted around the country in railroad cars. Like nuclear-missile submarines, both would present an enemy with a moving target, and so would seem to avoid the vulnerability problem of fixed land-based missiles. However, both are extremely expensive—according to Defense Department studies, both air-mobile and land-mobile missiles would be considerably less cost-effective in terms of "survivable payload" than nuclear-missile submarines, and they are not favored by many trategic planners outside the Air Force.

In the Soviet Union, the Strategic Rocket Forces have always been under the aegis of the army, whose traditional preference for land-based missiles is another obstacle for those who hope to make the move to sea. However, as Henry Kissinger said, "there is no escaping it."[5] The move to sea has begun.

Down in the missile control center, three floors below the command center, the weapons officer turns to his weapons supervisor, a senior petty officer. "Weapons supervisor, assign missile one."

The weapons supervisor pushes the Assign button and connects missile number one to a computer, which checks out a score or more of the missile's systems. Red lights, moving rapidly up and down a console in front of the weapons officer and the supervisor, indicate that all is in order. The weapons supervisor pushes another button marked Denote and the computer quickly scans the various launching systems.

The captain can follow everything on the green lights: ISQ, ASSIGN, DENOTE. On top of the submarine a hatch, like a giant manhole cover, opens to the sea: PREPARE.

From above the surface of the ocean, it is impossible to see anything beyond the depth of a few feet. Even in the Sargasso Sea, which according to mariners is the clearest of oceans, on the brightest day it is not more than a few fathoms before everything falls off into mystery. Scientists would say that water, especially sea water, does not permit the penetration of electromagnetic energy. That includes not only visible light, but infrared and ultraviolet light, lasers, radar, and magnetic energy. None of these is useful in locating submarines.

The only type of energy that seems to travel well through water is sound. In fact, sound waves actually travel faster and farther under water than they do through the air. Consequently, naval forces have always relied on acoustic devices for locating objects under water. The more familiar type, sonar, which locates objects by bouncing a sound off them, is useful mainly at close range. The kind used to

find nuclear-missile submarines is a system of underwater microphones that listen for engine noises.

Since the 1950s, the United States has been developing a system
called SOSUS, for Sound Surveillance Under Sea. Today it is a vast
network of microphones—on towers set on the continental shelf,
anchored to the ocean floor, on buoys scattered across the oceans—
connected through several relays to huge computers in the United
States that sort the sounds and attempt to plot their origins. Some
of the microphones are capable of listening more than 1,000 miles
out to sea, and according to experts, the computer program for
evaluating the data from the microphones is one of the most elaborate
ever devised.

By all accounts the United States is years ahead of the Soviet
Union in ocean surveillance technology.[6] Yet the SOSUS system does
not begin to give the United States the ability to attack the Soviet
Union's nuclear-missile submarine fleet, especially when by the
logic of mutual assured destruction, an attack could only be considered
successful if it destroyed all the enemy's nuclear-missile submarines
at the same time. (If only one or two survived, they would be able to
annihilate the homeland of the attacker.)

The utter impossibility of this is insured by the physics of the
sea itself. The ocean is actually a structure of many layers of water
at different temperature and pressure—thermoclines as they are
called—and as sound waves pass through the different layers they are
refracted. They bend, they twist and sometimes, when they strike a
particularly dense thermocline, they bounce. To a degree this is
predictable; if you know where all the thermoclines are, it is possible
to program computers to take the bending of sound waves into account.
But the structure of the sea is not only complex, it is also constantly
changing; it changes as the weather changes, day by day and hour by
hour. And as the sea changes, so do the shapes of sound waves in
the sea. Those who understand the problem best, including scientists
who have worked on the SOSUS system, say that this unpredictability
places an absolute limit on what an acoustic-detection system can
accomplish. According to an expert who has access to classified
reports,[7] "on a good day" it might be possible for the United States
to locate several Soviet submarines in the Atlantic, and then only
within an area about 50 miles square. On an ordinary day it might be
possible to locate only one or two. On many days it is impossible to
find anything at all.

But of course, they are out there. At any one time, the United
States has at least 20 nuclear-missile submarines at sea, in the
Atlantic, the Mediterranean, the Pacific and the Indian Ocean. The
Soviet Union usually has about a dozen, most of them in the Barents
Sea, north of Norway in the Arctic Circle.

Even now they are out there, circling and waiting.

The only thing left now is for the weapons officer to pull the trigger. It is set in a revolver handle, like the handle of a Colt .45, but the handle is not attached to a barrel. Instead, there is an electric cord that connects the handle to a computer console. The handle is made of heavy plastic, with cross-hatching for a good grip; the electric cord looks like the kind you might find on a toaster.

There is a black handle for drills and a red one for missile launches. The red handle is kept in a safe in front of the weapons officer, and when the Emergency Action Message arrives he opens the safe and takes it out.

The weapons officer has the black handle in his hand now, and he can squeeze it at any time. However, since this is just a drill, perhaps there is time for a little story. It is a true story, and the person who tells it is a former Polaris captain.[8]

The story takes place some time ago, back in August 1964, at the time of the Gulf of Tonkin incident. At the time, the former captain and his crew were in a nuclear-missile submarine, somewhere in the Pacific.

"Our information was kind of sketchy," said the former captain. "From the news we got we knew something was up, but were weren't sure exactly what. We knew something had happened to American warships on the high seas, and we knew the president was upset about it, but that was about it.

"Then one night we got a message telling us to hold a missile drill. Sometimes you have drills on your own and sometimes headquarters tells you. But this time the officer on duty misread the message and announced over the loudspeaker that this was the real thing.

"If it's the real thing, the officer on duty says, 'Man battle stations, missile.' If it's a drill, the command is, 'Man battle stations, missile. This is a drill.' And this time he didn't say it was a drill.

"Of course, the exec and I went back to double-check. You always would in such a situation. And when we looked at the message, we saw right away that it was a drill. But we decided, what the hell, as long as we've gone this far, let's just keep going and see how the crew does. It is, after all, no small matter to complete the launching procedure. There are any number of complicated operations involved in launching a missile, each one of which must be carried out perfectly before a launching can occur, and if anyone screws up, anyone at all, it won't work.

"Naturally, we told the weapons officer and the officer in launch control so that nothing could happen. But we didn't tell anyone else what was going on. As far as they knew, it was an actual launch.

"And you know," says the former Polaris captain, leaning forward in his chair, "you know, the whole thing went off perfectly. Everyone did his job as if it had been a drill."

The former captain says this was the only time he ever failed to identify a missile drill as a drill. However, he and other officers who have served on nuclear-missile submarines say that the practice is not uncommon on some ships. After all, the purpose of the drill is not just for the crew to attain technical proficiency at their jobs, but according to several commanders, "to get them used to the idea." That is why missile drills are completely realistic until the very last instant.

The trigger makes a solid click when you pull it, not so much a noise as a sensation in the finger. If this is a drill, the computer registers a successful firing, and the drill is over.

If this were not a drill it would take less than a second for the missile to clear the ship. Everyone would feel a slight thump. The submarine would move perhaps a foot and then settle. The submarine can fire one missile every 15 seconds. If this were not a drill, in four minutes all 16 of them would be on their way, climbing over the sea.

NOTES

1. For the best analysis of the arguments for and against Trident see the paper by George W. Rathjens and Jack P. Ruina, "Trident," in The Future of the Sea-Based Deterrent (Cambridge, Mass.: Massachusetts Institute of Technology Press, 1973).

2. Personal interview by author, Washington, D.C., 1975.

3. Michael Getler, "Schlesinger Backs Pact, Sees Some Rise in Arms," the Washington Post, December 7, 1974.

4. Michael Getler, "U.S. Urged to Retire Land-Based ICBMs," the Washington Post, February 2, 1974.

5. Kissinger transcript, op. cit.

6. For a comprehensive discussion see Kosta Tsipis, Tactical and Strategic Antisubmarine Warfare (Stockholm, Sweden: Stockholm International Peace Research Institute, 1974).

7. Personal interview by author, Washington, D.C., 1975.

8. Personal interview by author, Washington, D.C., 1975.

10

THE B-1 BOMBER
Robert Berman

The B-1 bomber, which the air force wants as a "follow-on" to its current strategic bomber, the B-52, is one of the more controversial military budget proposals in recent time.

The air force and the aerospace industry argue that adding the B-1 to our inventory of strategic weapons is necessary for the security of the United States.[1] They say that manned bombers are a vital part of this country's nuclear deterrent force and that the B-1 bomber— often referred to as a "penetrating" bomber because it is designed to fly low and fast in an attempt to get past enemy air defenses—will have important capabilities missing in the B-52.

Critics of the B-1 state that a bomber designed to penetrate enemy air space is an anachronism in the missile age.[2] Even if bombers are still required, they say, it does not necessarily follow that the B-1 should be built. According to some military analysts, the B-1 offers no advantages that justify its cost. The U.S. Air Force plans to build 244 B-1s, and before the program is completed it is likely that each airplane will cost more than $100 million, making the total cost some $25 billion. When associated costs for operations and maintenance, refueling tankers, auxiliary equipment, and armament are added, the life-cycle costs of the B-1 and its supporting systems reach $91.5 billion.

Most of the research and development work on the B-1 has already been done, and Congress is faced with the decision of whether to begin production. As the summaries of the opposing arguments indicate, the debate will center on two principal issues: first, the utility of manned bombers as a strategic weapon today, and second, the relative merits of the B-1 and B-52.

TABLE 10.1

Nuclear Weapons in U.S. Strategic Forces
(in percent)

	1960	1965	1970	1975	1980
On submarines	1	17	36	45	58
On ICBMs	2	17	20	22	19
On bombers	97	66	44	33	23

Sources: James R. Schlesinger, Annual Defense
Department Report FY 1976 and FY 197T (Washington,
D.C.: Department of Defense, 1975), pp. II–19;
also, Strategic Air Command, The Development of
Strategic Air Command, 1946–73: The Military Balance
(London: International Institution for Strategic Studies,
1965–1975).

U.S. strategic nuclear forces consist of bombers, land-based
intercontinental ballistic missiles (ICBMs), and ballistic missiles on
submarines (or SLBMs, for Submarine Launched Ballistic Missiles).
These three forces are commonly referred to by the Defense Department as the "triad." At one time, in the 1940s and 1950s, bombers
provided the only means of delivering nuclear weapons to distant
targets. Since the early 1960s, with the development of missiles
capable of carrying nuclear weapons, the bomber has played a
declining role in U.S. war plans, as Table 10.1 demonstrates.

The main reason for the increasing reliance on missiles, both
land- and sea-based, is clear: missiles are considerably faster than
airplanes. It would take an ICBM 30 minutes to cover the distance
between the United States and the Soviet Union; 15 to 20 minutes for
an SLBM. A bomber would take hours. Flying time for the B-52
would be 11 hours; even the proposed B-1 would take seven hours.[3]

The air force maintains that bombers are still an essential part
of U.S. strategic nuclear forces because they have certain advantages
that neither ICBMs or SLBMs can offer. Bombers can be moved from
one base to another, so they do not present fixed targets as do ICBMs.
They can be dispersed throughout the United States at major airfields
during a crisis, as U.S. bombers were during the Cuban missile
crisis in 1962. Sending manned bombers into the air with nuclear
weapons can be used to signal determination in a confrontation.

Supporters of the manned bomber also say that bombers offer tactical "flexibility" because they can be recalled while on the way to their targets. Once missiles have been launched, they cannot be stopped.

Proponents say that bombers provide diversity to U.S. strategic forces, which makes this country's deterrent forces less likely to be destroyed. Manned bombers increase the number of targets the Soviets must aim at and they increase the size and complexity of an attack against which the Soviets must defend. Bombers, they say, are also an insurance policy against possible technological breakthroughs that could make ICBMs and SLBMs vulnerable to attack.

Manned bombers, however, may be becoming obsolete. Bombers, once the mainstay of the U.S. nuclear force, are being replaced by more reliable and less vulnerable Minuteman ICBMs and Poseidon/Polaris submarine-based missiles.[*] In an era when missiles can reach their targets in 30 minutes or less, bombers can play only a relatively minor role in the first decisive nuclear attacks of a U.S.-Soviet war. A bomber is useless for striking enemy nuclear weapons, because they would all be gone before the bomber would arrive.

In response to the argument that bombers do not present a fixed target to enemy missiles, opponents state that nuclear-missile submarines do not, either. Government experts agree that strategic submarines are virtually invulnerable and will remain so for the foreseeable future. Both ICBMs and SLBMs, they say, are cheaper to operate than bombers, and they can accomplish the same missions faster and better.

Indeed a major drawback of the manned bomber is that existing U.S. wartime tactics require land-based missiles to cut corridors through Soviet defenses for bombers.[4] The bomber is the only strategic weapon system that is dependent on the other parts of the "triad" for its own survival and effectiveness. It is far simpler and cheaper for missiles to be used directly on primary targets than in suppressing defenses for the manned bomber.

It may be argued that bombers do not provide the greater "flexibility" claimed for them. Missiles on submarines or in silos are actually more controllable than manned bombers. It would be easier to keep a nuclear war from escalating by relying on missiles than it would be if bombers were involved. Once a bomber has passed its "fail safe" point and is committed to attacking a target in the Soviet

---

[*] Submarines are obviously less vulnerable when on station than bombers. ICBMs and SLBMs are currently not vulnerable after launch to active air defenses. Bombers, due to their mobility, may be harder to pinpoint than fixed-site ICBMs. Once under direct attack, however, bombers are for "softer" targets than ICBMs. SLBMs are least vulnerable in virtually all situations.

Union, it is out of civilian control for at least two hours. Missiles
fired from land are beyond control for the 30 minutes they are on the
way to their targets.

In sum, there are reasons to question whether manned bombers
have a significant nuclear war role in the 1980s and beyond—whether,
in fact, bombers add anything worth their enormous costs to this
country's large nuclear forces. The Defense Department arguments
for a manned bomber have been based on what they see as a need for
three separate strategic offensive nuclear systems: bombers, SLBMs
and ICBMs. Such justification may prove to be based as much on tradition and an unyielding U.S. Air Force commitment to past roles
and missions as on technological reality and sound strategic policy.
Indeed, one or two delivery systems could be just as devastating as
the present three—and of the three, bombers are the least effective
and most expensive, and, therefore, the most expendable.

The place of manned bombers in nuclear war is one of the
fundamental questions faced by U.S. military planners. The weight
of the evidence seems to indicate that missiles, which reach their
targets quickly and with no opposition, provide a more than adequate
nuclear strike force, especially if most of those missiles are mounted
on invulnerable submarines. It would seem, therefore, that in the
future, there will be a minimal need for the manned bomber in a
nuclear war.

It is possible to accept the need for bombers as one of the three
strategic forces without automatically generating a requirement for
the B-1 bomber. The issue is whether the B-1 will add significantly
to the present U.S. bomber force, composed mainly of B-52s, and
whether the modest increase in capability is worth the cost. Even if
these questions can be answered affirmatively, there is also the
question of whether the B-1 is needed now instead of at some later
date.

The air force contends that it needs the B-1 to replace the
"aging" B-52. The United States has a force of almost 500 long-range
bombers. There are 425 B-52s. The remainder are FB-111s. The
Defense Department spends about $5 billion a year on its bomber
force.[5]

The last B-52 was built in 1962. About 260 B-52s should last
at least until 1990. B-52s are not obsolete. They have been constantly
modernized with improved navigation aids, electronic countermeasures, terrain avoidance equipment, structural rework and numerous
other improvements. Only the 80 D-model B-52s are approaching
the end of their useful lives and the air force plans to spend $272 mil-
lion to modify these planes to keep them operating.[6] The late-model
B-52 Gs and Hs are fully modern and in excellent flying shape. From
the air force's own data, it is clear that the B-1 is an addition to the

late-model B-52 and FB-111 force of more than 300 aircraft that will
exist until the 1990s. Replacements, if indeed they are required, will
not be needed for 15 years.

The air force wishes to have a bomber that is able to penetrate
any possible Soviet air defense system and strike targets anywhere
in the Soviet Union. Between one-third and one-half of the cost of the
proposed B-1 will pay for the capability of flying low and fast and
evading detection in order to get past Soviet defenses. However,
late-model B-52s can also effectively penetrate Soviet air defenses.[7]
More than $3 billion has been spent on electronic jamming devices
and other equipment to give them that capability.

The air force also says that the B-1 is needed because it can
carry more bombs and missiles than the B-52. However, with a projected U.S. inventory of nuclear weapons of at least 9,400 by 1980,[8]
the difference between mission loads of a B-1 and a B-52 is insignificant. Existing bombers can deliver the equivalent of over 220,000
Hiroshima bombs on 1,900 independent targets. The destructive
capability of all U.S. strategic forces, counting bombers, ICBMs
and SLBMs, will increase substantially during the next 10 years,
even without the B-1.

Table 10.2 compares aspects of the B-52 and the B-1.

TABLE 10.2

Performance Characteristics of the B-52 and B-1

Characteristic	B-52	B-1
Speed at high altitude	500 knots[a]	920 knots[b]
Speed at low altitude	390 knots[a]	420 knots[a]
Maximum payload per aircraft:		
Internal	31,000 lbs	75,000 lbs
External (wing racks)	20,000 lbs	
Electro-optical viewing		
system	Yes	Yes
Radar cross section	—	Smaller
Infrared signature	—	Less
Stand-off weapons	Yes	Yes

Sources: John W. R. Taylor and Gordon Swanborough, Military
Aircraft of the World (New York: Charles Scribner's Sons, 1973),
and Jane's All the World's Aircraft (London: McGraw-Hill, 1975).

Finally, some in the U.S. Air Force argue that the B-1 bomber is necessary to the United States because the Soviets are building a similar bomber, the Backfire. This is, however, an irrelevant argument since B-1s and Backfire bombers are not pitted against each other in combat. The B-1 must be measured against Soviet air defenses instead of the Soviet bomber force. One fact about Soviet strategic bombers, however, is worth noting. There are very few of them. There are only 25 Soviet Backfire bombers in the Soviet Air Force, and 100 heavy Bear bombers, all of which are driven by pro- pellers, and 35 Bison jet bombers.[9] Each of these bombers has far less capability than the B-52. The Soviets seem to have learned the lesson so far rejected by the U.S. Air Force that the age of the manned bomber is ending. Soviet near-total reliance on missile forces reflects this fact.

The Soviets have invested heavily in trying to defend themselves against bomber attack. The Defense Department estimates that the Soviets have about 500,000 people in direct support of strategic air defense systems.[10] However, Soviet air defenses can be penetrated now and for the foreseeable future by the present force of B-52s and FB-111s. To see why this is so it is necessary to understand the limitations of the Soviet air defense system.

An air defense, to be effective, must provide warning, identi- fication, interception, and destruction of incoming aircraft. Warning is supplied by ground-based radars, generally limited to line-of- sight ranges that are seriously degraded by low-flying penetrators. A high-flying bomber may be detected at 200 miles, but one at 500 feet will not be seen until it is 25 to 35 miles from the radar.

The Soviet Union has an extensive air defense radar network, but gaps are common. To fill some of these holes, the Soviet Union has a small number of defensive transport aircraft equipped with an airborne radar-detection system, a primitive version of the proposed U.S. AWACS. This radar has a limited capability because it can see bombers below only over a calm sea. Over land or rough ice, the bomber is lost in the ground clutter. The present Soviet warning air- craft can extend radar detection ranges 200 miles over calm seas and later might be able to duplicate this over other types of terrain. The airborne radar, like all other radars when they are operating in Arctic regions, will be subject to auroral effects, the earth's mag- netic energy that disrupts radar reception, and the countermeasures employed by the defending force.

There are other problems in defending against bombers. A fighter interceptor must have ground radar guidance to reach a bomber, must "see" it visually, or with its own radar, and must have weapons capable of destroying it. Even presuming that a Soviet fighter could be directed to a U.S. bomber, the problem of attack is a difficult one because the Soviet Union does not have a fighter with the "look down" fire-control radar essential to separating the bomber from ground clutter for a radar lock-on. Few Soviet interceptors have a low-level dash capability permitting extended pursuit of bombers; such a tactic wastes fuel and therefore reduces range. The bomber can take evasive action or employ countermeasures, complicating the attack yet further. At low levels, bombers and fighters are more evenly matched than at high altitudes because the supersonic interceptor has stricter maneuvering limits in dense air, although retaining a speed advantage.

As former Secretary of Defense James R. Schlesinger pointed out in his February 1975 report to the Congress, [11] the Soviet Union has 2,500 fighter-interceptor aircraft, but the types in service are not especially effective against low-flying bombers such as the B-52 or FB-111. Soviet Foxbat (Mig 25) interceptor aircraft are ineffective against low-flying bombers, be they B-52s, FB-111s, or B-1s. Their radar is intended for a reconnaissance role, not for shooting down bombers.

The Soviet Union has also deployed 1,200 to 1,500 low-altitude surface-to-air missile (SAM) launchers throughout the Soviet Union. [12] There are several thousand others with only a high-altitude capability. The low-level SAMs are SA-3s that are distinctly range-limited—20-30 miles—because they depend on ground-based radar target identification. The Department of Defense has predicted a new SAM, [13] better than the SA-3, that might be deployed in the late 1970s but does not see it as a threat to present U.S. bombers because of penetration refinements already on Strategic Air Command aircraft.

The U.S. Air Force does not forecast any important breakthroughs in Soviet air defense capabilities through 1985. A satellite-based aircraft warning system is not seen as practical, although a radar capable of detecting aircraft beyond the horizon is a proven U.S. development and could be constructed by the Soviets, whose fighters and SAM improvements do not seem a threat to penetrating bombers, even if few changes are made to the current B-52/FB-111 force. Any breakthrough in Soviet air defense technology that would threaten B-52s would likely also threaten B-1s.

Analysis of the B-1 program indicates that the B-1 bomber fleet would provide, at best, a marginal increase in U.S. strategic capability. Present U.S. bomber forces of B-52s and FB-111s will continue to be sufficient. The air force has not been convincing in stating the case for the B-1 bomber, particularly when the extraordinary costs are considered.

In the absence of more Defense Department data, estimates of life-cycle costs remain estimates only, but it is clear that the full cost of the B-1 is far more than the current Defense Department approximation of $21 billion for procurement of the bombers. The

TABLE 10-3

B-1 Life-Cycle Costs
(in billions of dollars)

Procurement of 244 B-1s
    Total   20.6

B-1s will need about 6,700 offensive nuclear weapons
    to maintain "unit equipped" weapons for the active
    bomber force. One-third be SRAMs (Short Range
    Attack Missile). ALCMs (Air Launched Cruise
    Missile) could fill out the remaining two-thirds.
    At least two buys will be needed over the 30-year
    life of the bomber. The cost of the SRAMs are
    about $771,000 and the projected ALCMs are esti-
    mated at about $500,000
    Total   7.9

To operate the bomber for thirty years costs money
    also. There will be 14 B-1 squadrons. There will
    also be at least 14 tanker squadrons. The cost to
    operate one B-1 squadron and one tanker squadron
    is about $150 million annually. This includes
    direct costs (personnel, fuel, spares, base opera-
    tions, and intelligence and communications) and
    indirect costs (depot, overhaul, base support, tuning).
    Total   63.0

Total life-cycle cost of B-1s   91.5

Source: Center for Defense Information calculations.

cost of developing and producing the bomber itself has reached $84
million per plane, in 1975, and is rising. These estimates do not
include the costs of armament needed to perform the B-1 missions,
or of tanker aircraft needed to refuel the B-1s. The costs of operating
and maintaining both the bombers and the tankers will also be significant. Combined, these components of the B-1 life cycle could add
up to $91.5 billion, or $375 million for each B-1. A new tanker,
which may be required, would, of course, increase the cost.
    Table 10-3 gives a breakdown of the life-cycle costs of the B-1.

To counter criticisms that the B-1 may be an extravagant waste of money and that other ways to bomb the Soviet Union might be cheaper, the Defense Department conducted a year-long investigation called the Joint Strategic Bomber Study, which, not surprisingly, concluded that the B-1 was best.

The major conclusion of this study was the following: "Of the equal-cost forces examined, those containing B-1s performed substantially better. The low-flying, nuclear-hard B-1, with its high quality ECM (electronic counter-measures), outperformed all other vehicles by a wide margin."[14] Critical to the department's study was the assumption that the United States needs to spend as much money on bombers as the B-1 costs and in its methodology the study compared only "equal-cost" alternatives. The Defense Department analysts did not examine the essential question of whether the country needs a bomber fleet at all, and they made no determination whether an adequate U.S. deterrent capability could be obtained at much less cost.

Senator Thomas McIntyre, chairman of the Senate Armed Services Research and Development Subcommittee, has commented on the Joint Strategic Bomber Study: "This study, like other incidents in the history of the B-1 program, has led me to fear that there is little or no real consideration within the [Defense Department] and air force that we may not need the B-1 and that, therefore, we should prudently examine other alternatives for our future bomber force."[15]

The clear conclusion to be drawn from this examination is that a new manned bomber force is not now necessary. The B-1 bomber is not needed for a credible U.S. deterrent. It is not needed to fight a nuclear war if one should break out. It provides only a marginally greater capability for breeching Soviet air defenses, which can be easily penetrated by the present U.S. strategic bomber force. The case for the B-1 bomber force has not been made and it is, moreover, an inordinately expensive program.

NOTES

1. For the Defense Department's position on the B-1, see statement by Dr. Malcolm R. Currie, director of defense research and engineering, The Department of Defense Program of Research, Development, Test and Evaluation, FY 1976, February 26, 1976 (Washington, D.C.: Government Printing Office, 1975), pp. V-14-V-21; and Senate, Armed Services Committee, Fiscal Year 1976 and July-September 1976 Transition Period Authorization for Military Procurement, Research and Development, and Active Duty, Selected

Reserve, and Civilian Personnel Strengths (Washington, D.C.:
Government Printing Office, 1975), Part 10, pp. 5517-5619.

2. For a critique of the B-1, see paper by Senator George
McGovern and Congressman John F. Seiberling, Report on the B-1
Bomber Program, prepared for Members of Congress for Peace
Through Law, May 1974, Congressional Record, May 20, 1974; and
Senator McGovern's comment on the Joint Strategic Bomber Study in
Congressional Record, June 4, 1975, pp. S9662-S9665.

3. John W. R. Taylor and Gordon Swanborough, Military Aircraft of the World (New York: Charles Scribner's Sons, 1973),
pp. 20, 106.

4. James R. Schlesinger, Annual Defense Department Report
FY 1976 and 197T, February 5, 1975 (Washington, D.C.: Department
of Defense, 1975), p. II-20.

5. Senate, Armed Services Committee, op. cit., Part 2, p. 505.

6. U.S. Department of Defense, Program Acquisition Costs by
Weapon System Department of Defense Budget for Fiscal Year 1976
(Washington, D.C.: Government Printing Office, 1975), p. 103.

7. Michael Getler, "U.S. Air Force Is 'Stronger' Than Soviets',
Chief Claims," the Washington Post, March 23, 1974.

8. Senate, Armed Services Committee, op. cit., Part 5,
p. 2508.

9. James R. Schlesinger, op. cit., p. II-19, and The Military
Balance, 1975-1976 (London: Institute for Strategic Studies, 1975).
The total number of Backfires is about 50-60, but only half today are
with the Soviet Air Force. The rest are with the Soviet Navy.

10. Senate, Armed Services Committee, op. cit., Part 2, p. 505.

11. Schlesinger, op. cit., p. II-19.

12. Senate, Appropriations Committee, Department of Defense
Appropriations Fiscal Year 1973 (Washington, D.C.: Government
Printing Office, 1972), Part 4, p. 805.

13. Ibid.

14. Currie, op. cit., p. V-16.

15. Senate, Armed Services Committee, op. cit., Part 10,
p. 5565.

11

U.S. TACTICAL
NUCLEAR WEAPONS: A
CONTROVERSIAL ARSENAL
Barry R. Schneider

The widespread dispersion of 22,000 U.S. tactical or theater[*] nuclear weapons across Europe, Asia, and the United States, as well as aboard more than half the ships in the U.S. Navy, poses many questions about the wisdom of current U.S. policies concerning theater nuclear weapons. The size of the U.S. nuclear arsenal is large, more than 30,000 strategic and theater nuclear weapons. This raises the question of why the United States needs so many weapons.

These weapons, even the theater nuclear weapons, are more destructive than any other weapons ever deployed. It is difficult to comprehend how much of a quantum leap they represent in destructive capability over conventional high explosive weapons. The magnitude of destruction they can cause prompts speculation about the utility of employing them on a battlefield.

First, it would seem to make little sense to use theater nuclear weapons extensively to defend an ally if, in the process, the use of such weapons destroyed the people, the cities, and countryside of that ally. Second, it appears quite likely that the first use of nuclear weapons against a nuclear adversary like the Soviet Union will provoke escalation to all-out nuclear exchanges. The result would be catastrophic beyond imagination.

The rationale for the production and widespread dispersion of such large numbers of U.S. theater nuclear weapons is that they are

---

[*] The words theater and tactical nuclear weapons will be used interchangeably in this chapter. TNW stands for either and is distinguished from strategic nuclear weapons, SNWs.

thought to deter attacks upon the United States and its allies, but once this deterrent has failed, the United States forward deployment of theater nuclear weapons draws us into the nuclear fire and likely would consume the country and its allies.

Not only is the dispersion of such quantities of theater nuclear weapons extremely dangerous to the United States and its allies in wartime, it is also extremely dangerous in peacetime. The existence of such weapons dispersed to many locations and handled by many people creates extreme dangers. Terrorists may seize nuclear weapons and blackmail entire countries or cities. U.S. allies may seize theater nuclear weapons in their territory and use them on their own opponents. One or more of the hundreds of thousands of persons who handle, train with, and have access to nuclear weapons may steal or detonate such weapons without authority to do so. The great number and dispersion of theater nuclear weapons increases the risks of dangerous nuclear accidents.

The curtain of secrecy surrounding U.S. nuclear weapons has hindered discussion of the numbers of theater nuclear weapons the United States possesses; where these U.S. nuclear weapons are deployed; the implications of warfighting with theater nuclear weapons; and the dangers from terrorists, accidents, allied seizures, and unauthorized use of the so widely dispersed and numerous U.S. theater nuclear weapons.

THE U.S. NUCLEAR STOCKPILE

When the United States dropped atomic bombs on Hiroshima and Nagasaki in August 1945, it temporarily expended the entire existing U.S. nuclear stockpile. Yet, 30 years after the beginning of the atomic age, the United States has assembled a nuclear arsenal of incredible proportions.

As of mid-1975 the United States had nearly 30,500 nuclear weapons at home, at sea, in Europe and in Asia. Eight thousand five hundred of these are considered strategic nuclear weapons (SNWs).[1] Twenty-two thousand are considered tactical and theater nuclear weapons (TNWs).[2] The three main differences between strategic nuclear weapons and tactical or theater nuclear weapons are: TNWs are shorter range than SNWs; TNWs are capable of hitting local targets and are not normally targeted upon the adversary homeland, [*]

---

[*]Some of the 22,000 "tactical" or "theater" nuclear weapons fall in a gray area between TNWs and SNWs—for example, the Pershing

while SNWs are primarily targeted upon targets in the enemy homeland; the large majority of TNWs are smaller in explosive yield than
SNWs, although this distinction does not always hold true. For
example, the Pershing missile carries a theater nuclear weapon equal
in explosive yield of up to 28 "Hiroshimas" and has a greater yield
than that of the Polaris or Poseidon missile reentry vehicles. Data
on the U.S. stockpile of tactical nuclear weapons are presented as
follows.

U.S. Army Tactical Nuclear Weapons

- Lance Surface-to-Surface Missile: Located in Europe and the United
  States. Warhead yield up to 50 kilotons. Its range is 70 miles.
- Pershing Surface-to-Surface Missile: Located in Europe with
  U.S. Army and German units. Warhead of missile has explosive
  yields up to 400 kilotons. Range is 450 miles. Pershings are
  capable of hitting the Soviet Union from Germany and are put on
  Quick Reaction Alert status.
- Honest John Surface-to-Surface Missile: Located in Korea and in
  Europe with U.S. and North Atlantic Treaty Organization units.
  Warhead has an estimated yield of up to 100 kilotons. Range is
  25 miles. These are being phased out of Europe and replaced by
  Lance SSMs.
- Sergeant Surface-to-Surface Missile: Located in Europe with U.S.
  and NATO units. Warhead has estimated yield of up to 100 kilotons.
  Range is 85 miles. Sergeants are now being phased out by the
  U.S. Army.
- Nuclear Artillery: 155mm and 203mm nuclear howitzers are
  located in Europe with U.S. Army and NATO forces. These are
  also found in Korea, in the United States, and perhaps elsewhere.
  Range is 10 miles.
- Atomic Demolition Munitions: These explosives are needed to
  destroy bridges, to seal mountain passes, to destroy roads and
  transportation links, and to create impediments. ADMs have an
  explosive yield of one kiloton or less.
- Nike-Hercules Surface-to-Air Missiles: These SAMs have an
  explosive yield of up to five kilotons and will be phased out to be
  replaced by the new SAM-D under development. Located with U.S.
  NATO forces in Europe and in Korea. The range of these SAMs
  is 80 miles.

Missile and forward-based aircraft carrying nuclear bombs and air-
to-surface missiles.

U.S. Navy Tactical Nuclear Weapons

- U.S. Attack Aircraft Carriers: All 13 U.S. carriers carry fighter-bombers configured for attack roles and capable of launching nuclear air-to-surface missiles or dropping nuclear bombs. An estimated 100 nuclear weapons are aboard each U.S. carrier.
- Carrier-based Aircraft: Nuclear-capable aircraft have ranges of 400 to 1,100 miles and can carry nuclear bombs (see air-to-surface bombs) and nuclear air-to-surface missiles (see Walleye) with maximum yields of one megaton and 10 kilotons, respectively. Carrier aircraft include F-4s, F-14s, A-4s, A-6s, and A-7s.
- Terrier Surface-to-Air Missile: Yield of warhead is about one kiloton. Found aboard U.S. destroyers and cruisers to defend against air attack. The range is 25 miles.
- Talos Surface-to-Air Missile: The yield of a Talos warhead is five kilotons. Found aboard U.S. cruisers to defend against air attack. The range is 70 miles.
- SUBROC Missile: Antisubmarine rockets, fired below water by submarines, travel in the air before reentering water. SUBROC has a yield of one kiloton. The range is 30 miles.
- Antisubmarine Rocket: ASROC weapons carry an explosive of one kiloton and are aboard U.S. cruisers, destroyers, and destroyer escorts. ASROCs are fired by eight-celled "Pepperbox" launchers. The range is 6 miles.
- Mark 57 and Mark 101 Nuclear Depth Bombs: Used in antisubmarine warfare (ASW) and delivered by P-3 and S-3 aircraft and ASW helicopters. The estimated yield is from under one kiloton to up to five kilotons.

U.S. Air Force Tactical Nuclear Weapons

- Forward-based aircraft: USAF fighter-bombers, nuclear capable, are deployed at bases in Europe and Asia. Combat radiuses vary between 400 and 1,100 miles. U.S. aircraft include F-4s, F-111s, A-4s, A-7s, F-8s, F-14s, and many others.
- Nuclear Air-to-Surface Bombs: Carried by U.S. and NATO fighter-bombers. Bombs such as the B-28, B-43, B-57, B-61, and W-72 have yields from five kilotons to more than one megaton.
- Walleye Air-to-Surface Missile: Carried by fighter-bombers like the F-4, F-111, A-4, A-6, or A-7. Warhead has a yield of 5 to 10 kilotons. Range is up to 35 miles.

In 1975, the United States had 8,500 strategic nuclear weapons in its inventory poised for combat should the occasion arise. The United States has been producing strategic weapons at about the rate

TABLE 11.1

U.S. Tactical Nuclear Weapons Widely Dispersed

Region	Number
Europe	7,000
Atlantic (U.S. Navy)	1,000
Asia	1,700
Pacific (U.S. Navy)	1,500
United States	10,800
Total	22,000

Source: Interviews.

of four per day and retiring strategic nuclear weapons at about the rate of one per day, a net gain of three per day. This rapid increase in U.S. strategic nuclear weapons has received a great deal of critical attention by other countries, the press, and critics of nuclear proliferation.

Less publicized and understood is the fact that about 22,000 U.S. tactical nuclear weapons are in position worldwide (see Table 11.1). There are 7,000 U.S. tactical nuclear weapons on land in Europe.[3] Approximately 1,700 are located on land in Asia. Twenty-five hundred tactical nuclear weapons, as well as 4,500 strategic nuclear weapons, are estimated to be aboard U.S. Navy ships and submarines. The remainder, approximately 10,800 tactical nuclear weapons, are assigned to bases and forces in the United States.[4]

U.S. Tactical Nuclear Weapons in Europe

In Europe as of mid-1975, the United States and its NATO allies had 2,250 aircraft, missile launchers, and cannons and land mines that can deliver 7,000 U.S. tactical weapons.[5] These weapons carry a combined explosive capability calculated at 460 million tons of TNT—roughly 35,000 times greater than the nuclear weapon that destroyed Hiroshima in 1945. These U.S. tactical nuclear weapons are ready for offensive and defensive use in Germany, England, Italy, Turkey, Greece, and the Netherlands.

France maintains its own tactical nuclear weapons in France.
U.S. nuclear forces in Europe are most heavily concentrated in West
Germany, where more than 200,000 U.S. military personnel are
based.

U.S. tactical nuclear weapons in Europe include at least four
different kinds of surface-to-surface missiles (Lance, Sergeant,
Honest John, and Pershing), two sizes of nuclear artillery shells
(155mm and 203mm), and more than 500 aircraft with nuclear missles,
and nuclear ground mines. The aircraft can attack with air-to-surface
nuclear missiles or four different sizes of nuclear bombs, or a combination of nuclear missiles and bombs. The largest tactical nuclear
missile, the Pershing, has more than 400 kilotons in explosive power,
equivalent to over 30 "Hiroshimas." Forward-based systems like the
Pershing surface-to-surface missile or the nuclear-loaded aircraft,
are capable of attacking targets inside the Soviet Union from bases
in Europe.

The first U.S. nuclear weapons were introduced in Europe in
1954, three years before the Soviet Union introduced similar weapons
in that area. Since that time, the U.S. nuclear weapons in Europe
have multiplied in numbers with extensive weapon turnover, and
newer tactical nuclear designs have replaced older ones. Soviet
tactical nuclear deployment has been later, slower, and shows little
weapon turnover. Soviet nuclear weapons in Europe have accumulated
without much retirement of earlier weapons.

The United States is believed to hold a decisive numerical edge
in numbers of theater nuclear weapons in Europe, perhaps as high
as two-to-one. However, published information on Soviet TNW deployments, numbers, and warhead yields is incomplete.[6]

Soviet forces deploy a wide range of tactical nuclear weapons,
although there is no public knowledge of their possessing nuclear
artillery such as is found widely in North Atlantic Treaty Organization
forces. Nor is there anything in public print that indicates that they
possess nuclear mines known as Atomic Demolition Munitions. The
lack of these "defensive" nuclear weapons in the Soviet arsenal reflects
the offensive emphasis given to nuclear weapons in the Soviet military
doctrine. Soviet tactical nuclear forces are thought capable of inflicting over 100 million casualties in Central Europe by themselves, and
their employment could destroy most of the towns and cities in the
battle area without answering NATO nuclear volleys.

The U.S. armed forces deployed nuclear weapons to Europe in
the 1950s as soon as the technology became available. The rationale
for their deployment by the Department of Defense was that these
weapons would offset what was considered to be the Soviet conventional
force advantage in Central Europe. At the time, the Eisenhower

administration was seeking to check the Soviet Union with a strategy of "massive retaliation" both at the strategic and tactical levels. The U.S. tactical nuclear weapons monopoly in Europe was rapidly broken by the introduction of Soviet TNWs in the late 1950s, making this policy of nuclear first use less and less viable as the risks of the policy, if implemented, mounted.

Facing the 7,000 U.S. tactical nuclear weapons are an estimated 3,500 Soviet tactical nuclear weapons.[7] These arms, in Soviet military doctrine, are to blow large holes in NATO lines to be followed by an avalanche of Soviet tanks to exploit the openings afforded.[8]

Soviet doctrine emphasizes the importance of surprise and of taking the offensive. Nuclear weapons have reinforced this emphasis. As Colonel A.A. Sidorenko, once of the Soviet Army's leading strategists, has written:

> To attain the greatest effectiveness, it is recommended
> that the nuclear strike be launched at the start of the
> firepower preparation unexpectedly for the enemy.
> Preemption in launching a nuclear strike is expected
> to be the decisive condition for the attainment of
> superiority over him and the seizure and retention of
> the initiative.[9]

The NATO reliance on nuclear artillery, air-delivered TNWs and nuclear mines is one strategy for destroying the large masses of tanks grouped for just such a nuclear breakthrough. Thus, U.S. and NATO tactical nuclear weapons tend somewhat to offset Soviet and Warsaw Pact advantages in tanks. This fact has been recognized at the Mutual Balanced Force Reductions negotiations and NATO has offered cuts in TNWs for Soviet tank force cuts. The recent introduction of extremely accurate, light, inexpensive TOW antitank conventional weapons may make reliance on these theater nuclear weapons less necessary in defending against tank advances.

U.S. Tactical Nuclear Weapons in Asia

Far less information has been released to the public by the Pentagon about the estimated 1,700 tactical nuclear weapons that the United States maintains on land in Asia. U.S. tactical nuclear weapons in 1975 were in Korea, Taiwan, and the Philippines as well as at U.S. installations on Guam and Midway. Possibly, they remain in Thailand where they reportedly existed as late as 1973. Most of these weapons are air-delivered air-to-surface missiles and nuclear bombs. The situation is different in Korea, where several hundred U.S. Army weapons are based (see Chapter 3). U.S. tactical nuclear weapons numbers in the Asian-Pacific area are declining and pressure has been developing within the United States and some of the countries where the United States now keeps TNWs to withdraw the weapons. Pressure has been brought by the government of Thailand to reduce the American presence, and with it the reduction of any remaining TNWs on Thai soil. The Philippine government has considered limiting and perhaps closing U.S. operations at Subic Bay and Clark Air Base. The Republic of Korea government on the other hand has pushed for retention of the estimated 600 to 700 tactical nuclear weapons stationed south of the demilitarized zone.[10] These nuclear weapons located near the Korean DMZ are for use against the North Koreans in time of war and are deployed in hopes that they will deter North Korean leaders from carrying out any attack upon South Korea. This deployment of U.S. nuclear forces close to a potential battleline in a high-tension area thus risks a U.S. first use of nuclear weapons, which, in turn, could bring a physical disaster to the people of both North and South Korea, and might well be an enormous blow to U.S. prestige worldwide. Removal or redeployment, or both, of these Korean-based TNWs have been steps urged by critics of current U.S. deployment. They argue that such steps will extract the United States from an unwanted risk of involvement of nuclear weapons in Korea. Such a removal, they argue, will leave the U.S. president and Congress with greater flexibility and more options in dealing with any new Korean conflict.

U.S. Nuclear Weapons at Sea and in the United States

In mid-1975, the United States had approximately 7,000 strategic and tactical nuclear weapons at sea. There are 284 ships and submarines in the U.S. Navy that can carry nuclear weapons. In 1965, only 38 percent of U.S. ships could carry nuclear weapons. In 1975, 56 percent of the ships carried weapons that were nuclear-capable, and the percentage is increasing each year.[11]

The U.S. Navy is capable of delivering up to 12,000 tactical nuclear weapons in bombs, depth charges, torpedoes, and missiles. Many of these naval weapons systems fire weapons capable of carrying both conventional and nuclear warheads. An estimated 2,500 U.S. tactical nuclear weapons are at sea.[12] This is a conservative estimate. The maximum loading of nuclear weapons would result in a number four times larger.

This number of weapons carries an estimated explosive punch equivalent to 150 million tons of TNT, more than 75 times the amount of explosives dropped from 1941 to 1945 on Germany and Japan by U.S. bombers. More than 90 percent of this nuclear destructive power is estimated to be in the 1,300 tactical weapons aboard 13 U.S. attack aircraft carriers.[13]

Nuclear Weapons in the United States

As of mid-1975, an estimated 14,800 U.S. nuclear weapons were kept in the United States. Four thousand strategic nuclear weapons were deployed at U.S. Minuteman and Titan missile sites and at Strategic Air Command bomber bases.[14] An additional 10,800 U.S. tactical nuclear weapons were estimated to be in the custody of U.S. forces in the United States.[15] The seven army divisions on active duty in the United States have the full spectrum of tactical nuclear weapons. Stateside navy and air force units also are armed with theater nuclear weapons. Thousands more are stockpiled at U.S. storage facilities.

TACTICAL NUCLEAR WEAPONS
IN SEARCH OF A DOCTRINE

According to former Secretary of Defense James R. Schlesinger, the United States deploys nuclear weapons to Europe to deter Soviet use of tactical nuclear weapons and Warsaw Pact attacks, and to provide a nuclear option short of all-out war should deterrence fail and our conventional defenses collapse.[16] As Morton Halperin, former deputy assistant secretary of defense, recently put it, "The NATO doctrine is that we will fight with conventional forces until we are losing, then we fight with tactical nuclear weapons until we are losing, and then we will blow up the world."[17]

No one yet has been able to devise any reasonable set of scenarios for the use of our European-based tactical nuclear weapons. Secretary Schlesinger has admitted to continuing to search unsuccessfully for a doctrine whereby tactical nuclear weapons could be confidently used without triggering total war. That is likely to be a fruitless search, since there is no present or foreseeable coherent or rational doctrine for the use of the U.S. land-based tactical nuclear weapons in Europe and Asia.

Defending Allies by Destroying Them

It is obvious that something is wrong with a strategy that, if implemented, would destroy the country it is designed to defend. The use of 10 percent of the 7,000 U.S. tactical nuclear weapons in Europe might well destroy the entire area where such massive nuclear exchanges occurred. War games practiced by NATO troops indicate the tremendous collateral damage that would be inflicted upon cities and people bordering the battle area. A 1955 NATO war game, named Carte Blanche, was run for 48 hours during which 335 tactical nuclear weapon explosions were simulated, 268 on German territory. A conservative estimate placed German dead at between 1.5 and 1.7 million, plus an additional 3.5 million wounded.[18] In comparison, in the six years of World War II, 305,000 German civilians were killed and 780,000 were wounded by aerial bombardment. Thus, a very limited tactical nuclear war would produce more than five times as many German casualties in two days as occurred in all World War II through massive allied air attacks.[19]

A similar 1955 NATO war game, Operation Sagebrush, simulated the use of 275 tactical nuclear weapons that ranged in yield from 2 to 40 kilotons. According to the evaluation of the exercise, "the destruction was so great that no such thing as limited nuclear war was possible in such an area."[20] Former Assistant Secretary of Defense Alain Enthoven, in testimony before the Senate Foreign Relations Committee, quoted a Defense Department report on war games conducted in Europe in the 1960s as saying that:

Even under the most favorable assumptions about restraint and limitations in yields and targets, between 2 and 20 million Europeans would be killed in a limited tactical nuclear war . . . and a high risk of 100 million dead if the war escalated to attacks on cities.[21]

Not all analysts believe that casualties would be this high. A far more conservative figure has been estimated by Defense Department officials in the event of a counterforce nuclear exchange with the Soviet Union, although independent analysts estimate far higher casualty figures.[22] Some weapons analysts have indicated that they believe the new modern subkiloton weapons, which comprise the bulk of the U.S. nuclear force today in Europe, to be far less lethal to surrounding civilians than their older, "dirtier," and larger counterparts.[23]

Nuclear War Likely to be Total

It is unlikely that nuclear war, once begun, can be kept controlled. Herman Kahn, for example, has argued that there are 29 levels of nuclear conflict—rungs in the escalation ladder—at which decision makers can stay short of all-out "spasm" nuclear war, even after nuclear weapons have been introduced into battle.[24] Kahn's escalation ladders may be useful to decision makers under stress in such a situation to remind them of the logically possible more limited options they might elect, but Kahn's analysis has grave flaws, for he fails to indicate how rival states can climb down from such a ladder. Warfare is easy to escalate, but incredibly difficult to end.[25] One nation can start a nuclear war, but it requires two nations to stop it.

Former Secretary of Defense Schlesinger has also voiced the opinion that nuclear wars, once started, can be limited and terminated short of Armageddon. He has argued that

> should there be a breakdown of deterrence, there will be
> very powerful incentives on both sides to restrain the
> destructiveness of the use of nuclear weapons, and to
> come as rapidly as possible to the termination of not
> only the war but also the causes of war that led to that
> hopefully small-scale use of weapons. Those are very
> powerful forces because they relate to the very survival
> of the societies that have placed themselves at risk.
> . . .[26]

The arguments of Kahn and Schlesinger are, however, contradicted by a more powerful set of arguments that explain why the idea of being able to fight a limited nuclear war against the Soviet Union or Warsaw Pact is an illusion. Escalation is far more likely to occur than is limitation in nuclear war.

First, once the nuclear threshold has been broken, there is no easy stopping point on the way to the top of the escalation ladder. The line between conventional warfare and nuclear warfare is clear and unambiguous. Once nuclear weapons are fired in battle the clearest perceived "firebreak" on the path towards complete nuclear holocaust will have been crossed. Decision makers have long been conditioned to think in distinctions between nuclear and nonnuclear weapons. Once this nuclear taboo is violated, there is no similar consensus as to where a conflict should stop. Indeed, pressures to launch more escalatory and preemptive attacks would be enormous. Political decision makers and battlefield commanders would realize that it is kill-or-be-killed in nuclear war and the side that hits first and hardest within the battle area stands the greatest chance for at least temporary survival of its forces.

Second, a nuclear war is likely to grow simply because command and control procedures will break down in battle. Political leaders are likely to lose control of their nuclear forces in the field. Approximately 10,000 theater nuclear weapons are in the hands of the NATO and Warsaw Pact forces that confront each other in Europe. With so many fingers on nuclear triggers it would be wishful thinking to suppose that some unauthorized use of TNWs would not occur, especially when units possessing nuclear weapons are locked in combat, cut off, surrounded, or perceive themselves about to be overwhelmed and annihilated. The pressures to use the weapons by frontline units would become intense. Moreover, communications in "the fog of war" are likely to be disrupted or cut, especially once the first nuclear exchanges occurred on the battlefield. Frontline commanders would be put in a position where they might feel compelled to make such decisions when cut off from higher authority. The longer nuclear exchanges went on, the more difficult command and control problems would become.

Third, once nuclear weapons are detonated over the battle area, radars and electronics equipment may become useless because of the electromagnetic pulse caused by such explosions.[27] Moreover, the lessons of recent conventional wars like the Yom Kippur War indicate a very rapid destruction of aircraft equipment due to increased accuracies of SAMs. The loss of radar and reconnaissance aircraft means that military forces might rapidly lose their target acquisition capability. The logical next step in such a kill-or-be-killed environment would be the launching of "blind" volleys of longer-range, higher-yield TNWs such as the Lance, Pershing, Frog, or Scud surface-to-surface missiles into large areas where adversary forces might be gathered. Large areas would be designated for destruction since precision targeting would no longer be possible. Thus, the loss of target acquisition capabilities, radars, and reconnaissance aircraft would result in escalatory saturation strikes blanketing entire areas.

Fourth, the introduction of nuclear weapons into battle would create enormous confusion and stress at all decision-making levels, destroying the subtle peacetime distinctions between lower-level tactical nuclear war and higher-level nuclear war and all-out spasm nuclear war. Whole companies of troops could be annihilated by one tactical nuclear weapon. Whole armies might disappear in a matter of minutes. Entire cities in the area might disappear in a moment or two. Decision makers could not be immediately sure whether these were "selective" enemy strikes or the first of many now imminent nuclear attacks. The enormous stress upon U.S. and Soviet decision makers could easily trigger irrational and emotional responses at a time when it would be most crucial for leaders to remain rational and cool.[28]

Finally, escalation of a limited nuclear exchange would seem inevitable because Soviet military forces apparently emphasize high-yield theater nuclear weapons that would spread lethal radioactive fallout to cover large areas. Further, Soviet military doctrine emphasizes all-out use of nuclear weapons in any war with NATO and makes no fine distinctions between limited and unlimited nuclear war-fighting.[29] Thus, it would seem impossible to limit any nuclear war, even if the United States developed a new generation of smaller-yield, "cleaner," and more accurate TNWs based on a battle doctrine of limited and selective use of TNWs. It takes two sides with better-than-present command and control, with doctrines of limited nuclear use, with forces trained in implementing such doctrine, with much smaller and more accurate nuclear weapons, and with many fewer nuclear weapons present in the likely battle area before anyone should expect that any nuclear exchange can be kept limited. Even then, the possibility is remote.

Nuclear first-use by the U.S. and NATO forces would trigger massive Soviet and Warsaw Pact nuclear responses leading to further escalation. Whatever the sequence of exchange, the result of a U.S.-Soviet nuclear exchange on the battlefield is likely to mean an unlimited rather than a limited nuclear war.

One risk of developing tactical nuclear weapons, especially those now euphemistically called "mininukes," is that they may create the illusion that a limited nuclear war can be fought. Small weapons, like the 155mm nuclear artillery projectiles, have already been introduced. The trend is toward more of the same. As smaller, "cleaner," and more accurate tactical nuclear weapons are added to the U.S. arsenal, they will add to the dangerous misconception that tactical nuclear weapons can be used without very great risks of escalation.

In summary, the idea of a limited nuclear war is an illusion. To embrace it and to prepare for it may unfortunately encourage policy makers to be more reckless and make nuclear war, especially during acute crises, more likely.

TOWARD A MORE RATIONAL POLICY

The implications of the current numbers of U.S. nuclear weapons (8,500, strategic; 22,000, tactical or theater), their wide dispersion throughout the United State, at sea, and in a dozen or more foreign states, and their potential for misuse in either war or peace make it imperative that a thorough reexamination of U.S. nuclear weapons policy be conducted.

The secrecy surrounding U.S. nuclear weapons has hitherto made it nearly impossible for the Congress and the public to understand clearly how many U.S. tactical nuclear weapons exist, where they are, how they would be used, and what the effects of their use would be. Adequate congressional surveillance and broad public understanding are necessary and secrecy should be lifted to the extent necessary to guarantee it.

Many, possibly most, of the U.S. tactical nuclear weapons overseas can be brought home at no detriment to our national defense. Indeed, there should be a net gain in security for our citizens as the chances decrease for accidents, for theft, and for unauthorized use of the weapons.

Upon analysis of our present nuclear weapons deployment, it is reasonable to conclude that U.S. national security would be increased as a result of adoption of the following changes.

First, remove all nuclear weapons from the Republic of Korea, the Philippines, and other Asian states where they exist. Such U.S. weapons pose dangers of theft, unauthorized use, allied seizures, and accidents. They threaten to involve the United States in areas where we would be forced to intervene. Such situations not only make our foreign policy hostage to our weapons policy but might force the United States to create another precedent of nuclear first-use 30 years after Hiroshima and Nagasaki.

The greatest dangers from such weapons occur in the Republic of Korea, where the U.S. TNWs are deployed close to the DMZ that separates the two mutually hostile Koreas. Reason dictates that these weapons, at the very least, ought to be removed from forward areas so as to give the U.S. president and Congress an option as to whether the United States has to use nuclear weapons in any second Korean War. Removal of all TNWs from Korea would be preferable.

Second, substantially cut the number of U.S. nuclear weapons in Europe. Phase-downs of perhaps 1,000 per year could occur over the next several years. The remaining U.S. TNWs, perhaps half of our current 7,000, or less, would still be sufficient to guarantee the participation of U.S. strategic deterrent forces in a general European war. Yet substantial cuts in TNW numbers would substantially reduce the safety problems and costs of maintaining the force. U.S. phase-downs could be gradual and might serve to produce similar Soviet phase-downs as the danger to them somewhat receded. Preferably, mutual phase-downs might occur simultaneously as a result of agreements reached at the Mutual Balanced Force Reduction Talks in Vienna, although U.S. TNWs should not be endlessly counted as bargaining chips to be held in place in Europe in hopes of a substantial MBFR agreement that is unlikely to occur in the first place. Unnecessary weapons should be removed within a reasonable time of perhaps several years either by negotiation or by independent U.S. action.

Third, restructure the remaining tactical nuclear weapons in Europe so that they are under the continuous operational control of the supreme commander of NATO (SACEUR). Weapons should be taken away from frontline field commanders of local units and deployed in the rear. This will improve security and control of these weapons.

Given the current forward deployment and large number of U.S. theater nuclear weapons in Europe, command and control problems are likely to become impossible in wartime.

Forward deployed atomic artillery is subject to unauthorized use if forward units become surrounded or come under attack. They might be captured, if not used or destroyed, and turned against the NATO army they were designed to serve. Their forward deployment makes it likely that any war in Europe will be nuclear.

Nuclear artillery, "atomic demolition" munitions, nuclear surface-to-surface missiles, and nuclear ordnance aboard U.S. and NATO aircraft ought to be deployed far from hostile borders and should constitute a second line of defense to be activated only if conventional defenses completely fail or if nuclear attacks are launched by adversary forces.

A far more selective and pruned U.S. and NATO theater nuclear force should be retained in this clearly defensive mode, capable of destroying large conventional forces, including tank forces, whenever massed within their range and when these are threatening breakthroughs.

The present TNW doctrine certainly is contradictory. Secretary Schlesinger has admitted as much.[30] Like Topsy, the U.S. 7,000 TNW arsenal in Europe "just grew." Several hundred U.S. TNWs, carefully selected and tied to a coherent doctrine, would make far more sense than the current potpourri of thousands. The U.S. and NATO strategy of flexible response envisions NATO forces using theater nuclear weapons only if being overwhelmed at the conventional level of conflict. Yet forward deployment of U.S. theater nuclear weapons promises a breakdown in command and control of these forces. Forward deployment of U.S. TNWs also invites early Soviet and Warsaw Pact nuclear preemption in any conflict. Forward deployment for both reasons thus would shorten the time a purely conventional defense can be tried against a purely conventional attack. A first-line conventional defense backed by a second-line theater nuclear weapon defensive force makes more sense.

While mainly useful as deterrents to Soviet nuclear first use, the presence of such second-line defensive TNWs would be designed to act in wartime mainly as a force to plug gaps, by breaking up large tank forces moving through holes in the forward defense lines.

Four, remove aircraft and surface-to-surface missiles capable of hitting targets in the Soviet Union or deploy them to the rear, out of range of the Soviet Union, where their status as tactical weapons is clear to their officials. This also reduces the danger of unauthorized launching of bombs and missiles by U.S. forces directly against the Soviet Union. Such an unauthorized attack could otherwise trigger a Soviet response directly on U.S. cities and people.

Five, remove all Quick Reaction Alert aircraft (QRA). Such systems are vulnerable to a surprise attack and lend themselves to the danger of hair-trigger reactions and unauthorized use by U.S. and NATO pilots. Their missions can be taken over and performed more effectively by the ballistic missile submarine fleet.

Six, nuclear-capable missiles, and long- or medium-range missile launchers should not be sold or given to countries that have a near-nuclear capability. To do so increases the risks of new countries "going nuclear" and increases the dangers to the security of neighboring states and to the United States thereafter.

Seven, remove all nuclear weapons from U.S. aircraft carriers. Carrier aircraft have no strategic nuclear role that cannot be better carried out by other systems. Carriers are unlikely to exist for long in a nuclear war and their primary remaining useful mission is as mobile launching platforms for aircraft engaged in conventional attacks in limited wars. Nuclear weapons aboard would degrade the capability of the carriers to perform that role.

And eight, substantially increase the security precautions around U.S. nuclear weapons compounds and more intensively screen U.S. personnel who handle tactical nuclear weapons. Improvement in this area has been reported by the Defense Department and should be insured by continued vigorous congressional supervision of nuclear weapons security systems.

NOTES

1. U.S. Department of Defense, Annual Defense Department Report, FY 1976 and FY 197T (Washington, D.C.: Department of Defense, February 1975), p. II-19.

2. This figure was the calculated result of numerous interviews with U.S. officials and nuclear weapons experts as well as the evidence of congressional testimony and other public sources. It should be treated as a "round-figure" estimate and not an exact total.

3. James R. Schlesinger, U.S. Congress, Senate, Foreign Relations Committee, Nuclear Weapons and Foreign Policy

(Washington, D.C.: Government Printing Office, April 4, 1974), p. 163.

4. This TNW breakdown was the calculated result of numerous interviews with U.S. officials and experts and should be treated as an approximation.

5. The aircraft figure was derived from the numerous standard works on U.S. and NATO aircraft including the International Institute for Strategic Studies annual report, The Military Balance. The 7,000 TNW figure for Europe is well known. Secretary of Defense Robert McNamara first revealed it in 1966. Secretary of Defense Clark Clifford in 1968 quoted it at 7,200. Secretary of Defense Schlesinger has publicly put it back at 7,000. See Senate Foreign Relations Committee, op. cit., p. 163.

6. William Lyons and Sam Cohen, "A Comparison of U.S.-Allied and Soviet Tactical Nuclear Forces Capabilities and Policies," Orbis, Spring 1975.

7. Senate, Foreign Relations Committee, op. cit., p. 163. Jeffrey Record cites a lower number, 2,250, in a recent study. See Sizing Up the Soviet Army (Washington, D.C.: Brookings Institution, 1975).

8. Lyons and Cohen, op. cit. The original source is P. A. Rotminstrov, Nauka i Zhizn' (Moscow), April 1968.

9. A. S. Sidorenko, The Offensive, A Soviet View (Moscow: U.S. Air Force Translations, 1970), p. 115. See also, Lyons and Cohen, op. cit.

10. This estimate was calculated by first identifying U.S. nuclear-capable delivery systems in Korea; then, based on European load and reload experience, a total for each system was computed.

11. Barry R. Schneider, "The Nuclear Navy" (Washington, D.C.: Center for Defense Information, January 1975), unpublished research paper, pp. 108. The findings are the composite of information on nuclear-capable navy weapons extracted from congressional hearings, professional journals, and interviews, as well as Jane's Fighting Ships and the CHINFO, Chief of Naval Information, at the Pentagon.

12. An approximation based on interviews conducted in Washington, D.C. during Fall and Winter, 1974.

13. Ibid.

14. The Military Balance, op. cit. See also SIPRI Yearbook, 1975 (Stockholm, Sweden: Stockholm International Peace Research Institute, 1975); available also from Department of Defense, Public Information Service.

15. Based on interviews and on assumptions of the number of weapons per nuclear-capable aircraft, and nuclear-capable units—all multiplied by these numbers of aircraft and units. Calculations were

done in unpublished research at the Center for Defense Information.
A very approximate figure.

16. Senate, Foreign Relations Committee, op. cit., pp. 155-58.

17. Ibid., p. 44. Morton Halperin testified to the Senate Foreign
Relations Committee that "we have never been able to develop any
doctrine whereby after the first two hours anybody has any idea what
happens next. We deploy a lot of different kinds of nuclear weapons
and we design them and build them but in the end nobody has any
notion how to use them in any way other than to say we will use them
and see what happens."

18. See opening statement by Senator Stuart Symington, Senate,
Foreign Relations Committee, op. cit., p. 50. The original source
for the statistics came to light in a book written by Helmut Schmidt,
Defense or Retaliation, A German View, trans. Edward Thomas
(New York: Praeger Publishers, 1962).

19. Ibid., p. 50.

20. Ibid.

21. Alain Enthoven, in ibid., p. 74.

22. Senate, Foreign Relations Committee, Analyses of Effects
of Limited Nuclear Warfare (Washington, D.C.: Government Printing
Office, 1975).

23. Lyons and Cohen, op. cit. Also based on private conversations.

24. Herman Kahn, On Escalation: Metaphors and Scenarios,
2d ed. rev. (Baltimore, Maryland: Penguin Books, 1968), p. 39.

25. Fred Ikle, in Every War Must End (New York: Columbia
University Press, 1971), makes the point based on case studies that
wars are easy to begin, but difficult in the extreme to bring to an
end. Herman Kahn's escalation ladder is limited by the fact that he
traces no deescalation ladders from the rungs of his ladder. This
indicates his preoccupation with the uses of force and games of
nuclear "chicken" and his inattention to the means of "climbing down"
during crisis and wartime confrontations. Secretary Schlesinger also
has exhibited a tendency to emphasize what he perceives as the political utilities of military forces. He stresses the supposed utilities
of selective uses of force rather than emphasizing the limits of
coercive diplomacy and risks of escalation.

26. Schlesinger, Senate, Foreign Relations Committee, op. cit.,
p. 177.

27. Fred C. Ikle, "Nuclear Disarmament Without Secrecy,"
speech delivered to Council on Foreign Relations, September 5, 1975
(Washington, D.C.: U.S. Arms Control and Disarmament Agency
Press Release), p. 5.

28. For a discussion of the impact of stress on crisis decision
makers, see Ole R. Holsti, Crisis/Escalation/War (Montreal:

McGill-Queens University Press, 1972). See also Barry R. Schneider, "Danger and Opportunity: Decision-Making, Bargaining, and Management in Three United States and Six Simulated Crises" (Ph.D. diss., Columbia University, 1974).

29. This is based on the prevailing literature that assumes Soviet TNWs to be larger, dirtier, and based on a massive-use military doctrine rather than a selective-use doctrine. Lyons and Cohen, two Los Alamos Laboratory consultants, question U.S. knowledge of current Soviet TNWs and TNW doctrine. See Lyons and Cohen, op. cit.

30. James R. Schlesinger, The Theater Nuclear Force Posture in Europe, a report to the U.S. Congress in compliance with public law 93-365 (Washington, D.C.: U.S. Department of Defense, Spring 1975), pp. 25-30.

TACTICAL NUCLEAR WEAPONS: FOUR PEACETIME SAFETY DILEMMAS
Barry R. Schneider

The worldwide dispersion of U.S. tactical nuclear weapons (TNWs) creates many unacceptable dangers to the physical security of the United States and to American citizens should war break out between the United States and other country.[*] Tactical nuclear weapons create, even in peacetime, at least four extreme nuclear safety dilemmas for the United States. First, the widespread dispersion of TNWs increases the dangers of nuclear weapons theft and violence by terrorists. Second, dispersion increases the dangers of the seizure of U.S. tactical nuclear weapons by allies. Third, widespread dispersion of U.S. TNWs increases the chances of unauthorized use of nuclear weapons. And finally, the great dispersion of U.S. TNWs increases the chance for nuclear accidents. Each of these nuclear safety dilemmas, caused by the large number and widespread dispersion of these weapons, merits a reevaluation of current policies, procedures, and force levels.

NUCLEAR SAFETY DILEMMAS

Dilemma 1: Danger from Nuclear Terrorists

The risk of war with the Soviet Union has long been regarded as the primary threat to the security of the United States. In the hope

---

[*] See Chapter 11, Barry Schneider, "U.S. Tactical Nuclear Weapons: A Controversial Arsenal."

of averting such a catastrophe, thousands of man-years have been spent by analysts exploring how such a war is likely to erupt.

The research and contingency plans designed to control escalation of crises and limited wars, to prevent accidental war or unauthorized attacks, and to deter a surprise attack, may be ignoring a likelier danger to U.S. national security—the nuclear terrorist.

A half-dozen terrorists with a homemade or hijacked nuclear weapon could cause thousands of deaths in a city like New York. Yet, thousands of nuclear weapons are deployed by the U.S., Soviet, French, and British forces in many different locations, some with questionable security precautions. If a terrorist group stole and detonated one "small" 10-kiloton nuclear weapon in New York City, the explosion could cause nearly 100,000 deaths[1]—more than all the U.S. battle deaths incurred in the Vietnam and Korean Wars.[2]

One of the hundreds of U.S. tactical nuclear bombs in the one-megaton range, if exploded on Manhattan Island, would inflict casualties exceeding the combined totals of the war dead from the American Revolution, the War of 1812, the Mexican War, the U.S. Civil War, the Spanish-American War, World War I, World War II, the Korean War, and the Vietnam War. Nearly 1.5 million people would perish.[3]

More than 40 major terrorist groups are reported to exist worldwide.[4] Urban guerrilla activities, Olympic murders, airplane hijackings, terror bombings, and airport massacres are all well-known.

How safe are nuclear weapons from theft by terrorist groups? Not very, according to the few indicators available in this highly classified area. U.S. Army Special Forces exercises have shown that nuclear weapons storage areas can be penetrated successfully without detection, despite guards, fences, and sensors.[5] Their example could obviously be followed by a daring and well organized terrorist organization.

The United States, its allies, and the Soviet Union have now deployed thousands of tactical nuclear weapons across the world, each in an effort to bolster its own national security. In doing so, these governments have made their societies more vulnerable to the nuclear terrorist. Our cities, as a result, are more likely to become casualties from nuclear terrorist attacks than from attacks by other countries.

Dilemma 2: Seizure by Allies

More than half of all U.S. nuclear weapons are stationed in foreign countries or on the high seas. Countries where U.S. nuclear weapons are reportedly stationed include: Federal Republic of Germany, Greece, United Kingdom, Turkey, the Netherlands, Spain, Belgium, Portugal, Italy, Philippines, Iceland, Republic of Korea, and Taiwan.*

Once the U.S. deploys nuclear weapons to an allied country, we put in jeopardy our control of those weapons if that nation ever becomes unfriendly to the United States. Allied seizures of U.S. weapons could result in the United States having to fight its way into an allied country to rescue its own weapons.

This scenario takes on more plausibility in the light of the recent Greek and Turkish fighting on Cyprus. Greece and Turkey are host countries for U.S. tactical nuclear weapons and U.S. security forces were put on maximum alert guarding the weapons compounds during the short war between these two North Atlantic Treaty Organization allies.

Many of the allied host countries that permit U.S. nuclear bases are dictatorships with oppressive regimes that spark dissent. Some allies that permit U.S. nuclear weapons already have domestic insurrections on their hands. The Philippines and the United Kingdom are current examples. In Greece and Portugal recent government overthrows have changed the complexion of the ruling groups. In countries plagued by civil wars and coups, U.S. tactical nuclear bases may not be safe from our "allies." During internal political disruptions in allied countries, U.S. bases might find themselves caught in the middle of a firefight. One side or the other might find it advantageous, or even necessary, to seize U.S. tactical nuclear weapons to gain the upper hand in the local struggle. Nor can we discount the possibility that an ally like the Republic of Korea might seize U.S. weapons to defend itself from—or possibly to attack—its antagonists.

---

*This is not an exhaustive list of countries that house U.S. nuclear weapons abroad. For example, research indicates that U.S. TNWs have been in Taiwan and Thailand in recent years, although they are believed removed by 1975. There are numerous sources that indicate U.S. TNWs are installed everywhere listed except in Iceland and the Philippines. These are extremely logical choices, however. Iceland serves as home base for P-3s, which are assigned ASW work in the vital Norwegian Sea. If any P-3 is nuclear-loaded, these will be. The U.S. Navy use of Subic Bay as a port for nuclear-capable forces at Clark Air Base makes the Philippines an almost certain "host" for U.S. TNWs.

Dilemma 3: Unauthorized Use of Nuclear Weapons

The danger of misuse of U.S. nuclear weapons increases dramatically with the number of persons who are involved in their production, transportation, storage, security, and wartime use. Yet, the 30,000 U.S. nuclear weapons are handled by many thousands of people, including U.S. military personnel, NATO allies, security guards, scientists at weapons labs, and shipyard and arsenal workers. Overall, it is estimated that nearly 120,000 persons have access to U.S. nuclear weapons and weapons-grade fissionable material.[6] Although these positions are carefully screened by the Human Reliability Programs set up by the United States, there have been problems with the people who handle and would fight with nuclear weapons. An average of three persons per 1,000 in the U.S. armed services have been identified as suffering from mental illness serious enough for professional care.[7] Congressional testimony indicates that 3,647 persons with access to nuclear weapons were removed from their jobs during a single year because of mental illness, alcoholism, drug abuse, or discipline problems.[8] Twenty percent of the discharges from the U.S. armed forces that occurred in 1972 and 1973 were for drug abuse. This problem is unlikely to be foreign to those who handle U.S. nuclear weapons.

Dilemma 4: Nuclear Accidents

The dispersion of 30,000 U.S. nuclear weapons across the world's oceans, in dozens of ports, in numerous countries in Europe and Asia, and in the United States creates risks of accidents of unprecedented magnitude.

The Department of Defense has provided information on at least 11 of what it calls "Broken Arrows," or major nuclear accidents.[9] The Atomic Energy Commission reports at least four other accidents involving various components of nuclear weapons while under the AEC's control. There is evidence that many other unreported and unconfirmed nuclear accidents have occurred since World War II. Serious students of the problem estimate that an average of one U.S. nuclear accident has occurred every year since 1945, with some estimating as many as 30 major nuclear accidents and 250 "minor" nuclear accidental incidents during that time.[10] Following are five such examples of "broken arrows."[11]

1) The best known U.S. nuclear accident occurred on January 17, 1966, when an American B-52 bomber collided with a KC-135 refueling

tanker over Palomeres, Spain, causing the deaths of five crewmen
and the dropping of four hydrogen bombs, which were recovered after
an intensive ground and sea search. Radioactive leakage and conventional explosions occurred in the area.

2) Another nuclear near-miss occurred on March 11, 1958,
when a B-47 bomber accidentally dropped a nuclear weapon, in the
megaton range, over Mars Bluff, South Carolina. The conventional
explosive "trigger" of the nuclear bomb detonated, leaving a crater
75 feet wide and 35 feet deep. One farmhouse was obliterated. For-
tunately, no nuclear radiation leakage was detected, no nuclear
explosion occurred, and no one was killed.

3) Another "broken arrow" occurred on June 7, 1969, when a
fire at McGuire Air Force Base in New Jersey led to a series of
shattering explosions and the destruction of one of 56 nuclear-armed
Bomarc missiles. Although no nuclear explosion occurred, there
was a small amount of radioactive leakage creating a temporary
health hazard.

4) Perhaps the most dangerous U.S. nuclear accident occurred
in 1961, when there was a near-catastrophe at Goldsboro, North
Carolina. A B-52 bomber had to jettison a 24-megaton bomb. Five
of the six interlocking safety devices were set off by the fall. A
single switch prevented the bomb from exploding. The explosion
would have been more than 1,800 times more powerful than the
Hiroshima bomb.

5) Another potentially lethal nuclear "broken arrow" happened
on January 21, 1968, when a B-52 attempting an emergency landing
at Thule Air Force Base, Greenland, crashed and burned on the ice
of North Star Bay. The high explosive components of all four nuclear
weapons aboard detonated producing a plutonium-contaminated area
a minimum of 300 to 400 feet wide and 2,200 feet long.

CONCLUSIONS

For years, analysts and policy makers have worried about the
dangers of nuclear violence, triggered either by a surprise attack on
the United States or the escalation of a limited war or acute international crisis.

While these possibilities should remain our concern, the dangers
of such action in an age of nuclear overkill and detente may be less
than the new peacetime dangers of nuclear violence initiated by
nuclear theft, or by terrorists, or by "allies," who seize and use our
weapons stored abroad, and by nuclear accidents, as well as by
unauthorized use of the weapons by U.S. troops. These latter four

peacetime dangers may pose likelier risks to Americans than any war
with another country, whose leaders could be assured that they would
be destroyed in retaliation if they attack the United States. Terrorists,
accidents, and unauthorized use of nuclear weapons are a new set of
nuclear dilemmas that require the most serious and responsible
attention to prevent peacetime nuclear catastrophes.

NOTES

1. Unpublished research done at the Center for Defense Information by Barry R. Schneider and Tom Weber. Calculations were
done on the GE Missile Effectiveness Calculator and cross-checked
on a nuclear explosion damage calculator produced by the RAND
Corporation.

2. U.S. Department of Defense, Office of Public Information,
provided casualty figures on the Vietnam and Korean Wars.

3. Conclusion was reached by comparing DOD figures for
previous U.S. wars with results of CDI calculations done by Barry R.
Schneider and Tom Weber.

4. Jack Anderson, "Will Nuclear Weapons Fall Into the Hands
of Terrorists?" Parade, the Washington Post, September 29, 1974,
p. 12. Original source: National Bomb Data Center, Federal Bureau
of Investigation.

5. Ibid.

6. Testimony of Dr. Carl Walske, Assistant Secretary of
Defense for Atomic Energy, before the Subcommittee on Military
Applications, Joint Committee on Atomic Energy, U.S. Congress,
May 27, 1973, Military Applications of Nuclear Technology (Wash-
ington, D.C.: Government Printing Office, 1973), Part 2, p. 6.

7. Jerome Frank, Sanity and Survival (New York: Vintage
Books, 1967), pp. 80, 84.

8. Walske, op. cit., p. 6. See also the Associated Press,
"Missileman Used Drug on Duty, Ex-GI Recalls," the Washington
Star, December 17, 1974.

9. Joel Larus, Nuclear Weapons Safety and the Common Defense
(Columbus, Ohio: Ohio State University Press, 1967).

10. Milton Leitenberg, "Accidents of Nuclear Weapons and
Nuclear Weapons Delivery Systems," SIPRI Yearbook, 1968-69
(Stockholm, Sweden: Stockholm International Peace Research Insti-
tute, 1969), pp. 259-70.

11. Larus, op. cit.

13

THE GLOBAL
AUTOMATED
BATTLEFIELD
Phil Stanford

It was in 1969, in a speech to the Association of the United States Army, that General William C. Westmoreland offered his vision of the future. "I foresee," he said, "a new battlefield array."[1] On the "battlefield of the future," as he called it, the enemy would be located and tracked by remote electronic sensors and targeted instantaneously by computers. Bombs and missiles with new precision guidance systems would "destroy anything we can locate." He compared the new battlefield to a modern factory where "machines and technology are permitting economy of manpower." Wherever possible on the new battlefield, he said, machines would replace men. General Westmoreland called his vision the Automated Battlefield and, although he spoke in the future, the United States was already operating one in Southeast Asia.

A good deal has been written about the Automated Battlefield in the Vietnam War:[2] Battery-operated sensors, dropped behind enemy lines, able to detect the vibrations of marching troops or trucks on the move, sensitive to metal, heat, sound, even the smell of urine; drones circling high above the battlefield, relaying the signals broadcast by the sensors to a distant control center—Igloo White—where giant computers analyzed the data and presented probable targets to military technicians in attendance; fighter-bombers piloted by their own computers; bombs dropped by computer.

Perhaps the best description of the Automated Battlefield comes from one of the officers who worked on it. "We got the Ho Chi Minh

An earlier version of this chapter appeared in the February 23, 1975 New York Times Magazine. Reprinted with permission.

Trail wired like a pinball machine," he told a reporter, "and we plug
it in every night."[3]

The only real problem with the Automated Battlefield in Southeast Asia, as the press has reported in full, was that it didn't work
very well. It was frequently in error, almost haphazard at times,
and, despite the expenditure of $3 billion or more, it never more
than slowed down traffic on the Ho Chi Minh Trail. Igloo White was
quietly dismantled even before United States forces began to withdraw. However, those who wish to take heart should remember that
Westmoreland, at least, never expected the Automated Battlefield
to work in Southeast Asia. He compared it to the "slow, clumsy,
underarmed, largely ineffective tanks of World War I," tanks that
revolutionized ground combat in World War II.[4] Vietnam was a proving
ground. "With cooperative effort," he said, "no more than 10 years
separate us from the Automated Battlefield." Today, it appears that
his vision may have been modest.

Dr. Malcolm R. Currie is the Pentagon's director of defense
research and engineering. In 1974, when he testified before Congress
he proclaimed the coming of still another age of weaponry. "A remarkable series of technical developments," he said, "has brought us to
the threshold of what I believe will become a true revolution in conventional warfare."[5] The outlines of this revolution are apparent from
his testimony and from other official and semiofficial sources: wars
fought by planes without pilots, between armies that may never see
each other except as blips on an oscilloscope; artillery able to hit
moving tanks 10 miles away; guns that select their own targets;
missiles that read maps; self-operated torpedoes on the ocean floor;
laser cannons capable of knocking airplanes out of the sky; satellite
battles on the other side of the moon.

It is Westmoreland's automated battlefield, but on a much
grander scale. Although Currie didn't say so—perhaps because it
didn't occur to him—he was describing a global, even universal, automated battlefield.

The following is a catalogue of some of the weapons listed by
Currie and others that will be used on that new battlefield. Some of
them are now in the early stages of development and won't be ready,
even if all goes as planned, for several years. Some are ready now.

SMART BOMBS AND MISSILES

Some of the new weapons, in their "Model T stages"[6] as Currie
puts it, have already been used in combat in Vietnam and the last
Mideast war. One example is what the military calls Precision Guided

Munitions. "Smart bombs" is their more common name. These are bombs—or missiles—that have their own sensors and guidance systems and can be directed all the way to their targets.

The United States has two kinds of smart bombs. One is laser-guided—able to home in on the reflection of a low-energy laser beam. In Vietnam it was used against targets such as bridges; one plane dropped the bomb while another pointed what is called the laser designator. The other kind of smart bomb has a miniature television camera in its nose and the camera transmits pictures back to the airplane that dropped it. A technician in the airplane watches the picture and adjusts the trajectory of the bomb as it falls to earth. The United States has a television-guided air-to-surface missile called the Maverick, and is developing a laser-guided version. The laser- and television-guided bombs and missiles used in Vietnam and the Mideast are called line-of-sight weapons. That is, they work as long as the laser designator holds on target or as long as the airplane is not out of TV range.

The Tow (tube-launched, optically-tracked, wire-guided) anti-tank missile, used in Vietnam and the Mideast, and now being mass produced for export to other countries, is guided by signals sent along a thin, almost filamentlike wire that plays out behind the missile as it flies toward its target. The operator simply keeps his sights trained on the target, and, as he moves, electrical impulses sent over the wire adjust the course of the missile. In the last Mideast war the Tow was deadly accurate at ranges of two kilometers. Anti-aircraft missiles, with infrared sensors, desinged to seek the heat of jet engines, are now standard equipment for all armies. Over the years, as heat-seeking missiles have become smaller and more accurate—the Soviets' Stella is small enough for one man to hold—they have made air warfare almost unacceptably hazardous.

Now the U.S. Army has a laser-guided artillery shell. It is for its 155mm cannon and is in "advanced development," which, according to a Department of Defense spokesman, means it should be ready in a few years. One way of using laser-guided artillery will be for a spotter on the ground, known as the forward observer, to shine a laser beam on targets that come into view and radio his position to the rear. A shell, or for that matter, a missile, fired into the area will pick up the reflection of the laser beam and home in on it. It doesn't make any difference whether the target is stationary or moving. All the forward observer has to do is keep it in his sights.

The army is already producing prototypes of the laser designators that will be used. They weigh 30 pounds and are small and compact enough to be carried by a soldier in the field. The army is also working on small unmanned aircraft with laser designators that will eventually take the place of human forward observers.

The revolution in smart weapons has begun. "Given an average day," says Army magazine,[7]"you can expect more than 50 percent of the bomb impacts to be direct hits." And these are just the Model Ts. The more advanced models are only a short way down the assembly line. "Essentially," says Currie, "we would like for every missile, bomb or shell, when properly employed, to kill its target."[8]

STAND-OFF BOMBERS

It doesn't take much imagination to see how the new highly accurate shells and missiles will alter the make-up of armed forces. Tanks and fighter planes may become obsolete. It simply isn't cost-effective, to use a favorite expression of military planners, to use $20-million airplanes or $1-million tanks when they can be destroyed by a soldier with a $10,000 missile. Of course, it will always be possible to use these weapons for wars against underdeveloped nations that haven't been supplied with the latest antitank and anti-aircraft weapons. However, to judge from the carcasses of tanks and jet fighters in the Sinai Desert, their usefulness in wars between modern armies is already somewhat diminished. Besides being unacceptably vulnerable, weapons like supersonic bombers, once needed to swoop in low under enemy radar and deposit bombs on target, may simply be superfluous.

As some weapons become obsolete, others will take their place. One of these, according to William Graham, RAND's director of engineering sciences,[9] is something known in the trade as a stand-off bomber. "All I need is a blimp or a DC-10 sitting back a few miles, and lobbing shells," says Graham. "As long as each one hits, that's all anyone needs. The goddamn 747," he says excitedly, "is a perfectly good combat airplane." These "bombers" will no longer drop bombs. They will stand back out of range of enemy antiaircraft defenses—maybe ten miles, maybe hundreds—and fire missiles.

However, the point of this item is not so much to describe a new weapon—since there is really nothing new about large lumbering jet transports except the notion of using them for weapons platforms—as it is to offer a tip of the wing to "Terry and the Pirates" before combat pilots pass forever from the scene.

BATTLEFIELD SENSORS

Battlefield sensors were first used in 1967 on the McNamara Line, named for the secretary of defense. It was to be a barrier of

sensors stretching across the northern part of South Vietnam to
monitor invasion from the north. However, it was so unsatisfactory
that it was abandoned before it was completed. Later, sensors were
used with only partial success along the Ho Chi Minh Trail. Many of
the problems must be blamed on the relative newness of the technology,
the "state of the art," as they say in the trade. As soon as a new
sensor emerged from a laboratory, it was produced and rushed to the
battlefield. Since the war, the private research group Defense Marketing Service says, progress has been more "orderly."[10]

Certainly the military has not been discouraged by its experience
with sensors in Southeast Asia. Commanders Digest, an official publication, reports that the "success achieved with the present surveillance systems has led to the exploration of sensor uses at many levels
of warfare. The Army, Navy, and Air Force have set up organizations
responsible for exploiting the existing technology."[11]

The navy's sensor system is called SOSUS, which stands for
Sound Surveillance Under Sea. It is a vast network of microphones—
on buoys, on planes and on the ocean floor—designed to detect passing
submarines. The microphones broadcast the sounds, via relay stations in Norway, Iceland and Canada, to a control center in Norfolk,
Virginia, where they are analyzed to determine the type of vessel that
made them and to plot its location and course. Although it does not
provide instantaneous information, it does permit the United States
to monitor submarine movements in a general way.

The army's next generation of battlefield sensors will be something called REMBASS (for Remotely Monitored Battlefield Sensor
System)—a self-contained all-purpose system of sensors and trans-
mitters that can be dropped from an airplane. The military is also
developing mobile computer centers. When these projects are completed, the United States will be able to set up an Automated Battlefield anywhere in the world on a few hours' notice.

There is also interest in permanent sensor systems. In Iran,
the American military is currently installing a sensor barrier—a
modern version of the old McNamara Line—along the Iraqi border.[12]

UNMANNED AIRCRAFT

Unmanned aircraft, also called drones and RPVs (for Remotely
Piloted Vehicles) have long been used for target practice. In Vietnam,
the United States used them for surveillance and jamming enemy
radars as well as for more unusual jobs. As reported in Armed
Forces Journal, pilotless airplanes were used on Christmas Day of
1969 to drop leaflets with former President Nixon's picture and a

plea for peace over North Vietnam.[13] High-flying drones, equipped with electronic gear, have already assumed the sort of reconnaissance missions that Gary Powers once flew in a U-2.

The Pentagon is currently developing "mini-RPVs"—small unmanned airplanes, with a wing-span of perhaps no more than six to eight feet and weighing no more than 200 pounds. They could be used in swarms to confuse enemy radars and overload antiaircraft defenses. According to Aviation Week, the United States has agreed to send some of these to Israel. Another mini-RPV is to have a television camera and a laser designator for spotting enemy targets. As the aircraft circles above enemy lines, the camera scans the scene below and transmits pictures to a distant control center. When the operator at the center sees a target, he activates the laser beam, locks it on the target and holds it there while someone else launches a laser-guided artillery round.

The next step is combat missions. Ordnance (now National Defense) magazine reports that in 1971 a remotely guided plane without a pilot "in a test over the California coast demonstrated it could out-fight a manned fighter." The same article says that some military planners "envision fleets of unmanned bombers in the not-too-distant future. . . . It is clear that the 'robot era' in air weaponry is just around the corner."[14]

"Actually, it has already begun," says Dr. Francis Niedenfuhr, who is one of the assistant directors of the Defense Department's in-house think tank, the Advance Research Projects Agency. Planes like the F-111 fighter bomber, he explains, already come equipped with something called terrain-following radar, which comes into play when the aircraft is flying at extremely low altitudes, as it might to slip in below enemy radar on a bombing run. "It actually takes con-trol of the plane away from the pilot. I don't think the pilots like it very much," he says.

"It's true that there are certain things that a human pilot is able to do that a RPV can't. There are certain penalties. An RPV is just not as versatile," says Niedenfuhr. "On the other hand, when the mission is fairly straightforward, there is not reason why it can't be done by electronic means."[15]

In the end, the battle between scientists and pilots may be decided by cost. Manned fighter planes may simply be becoming too expensive. At last look, the navy's new F-14 was $23 million a copy, the air force's F-15 was $15 million, and the new supersonic bomber, the B-1, was $84 million. Unmanned aircraft are considerably cheaper because they do not require expensive life-support systems, such as oxygen, ejection systems, even cockpits, needed for a human crew.

The air force says that unmanned aircraft should be ready for combat missions by the early 1980s.

AUTOMATIC GUNS

When former ARPA director Dr. Stephen J. Lukasik appeared before Congress in 1974, he gave his own assessment of the battle-field of the future. His "time horizon" was for the next 10 to 30 years. "The tactical world," he said, "will be dominated by systems that are cheap and widely distributed: man-portable antitank and anti-aircraft weapons, unmanned remotely piloted vehicles, and"—this is the point here—"unattended ground sensors directly coupled to weapon systems."[16] That means automatic guns.

The agency's scientists are developing a missile that picks its own targets and launches itself. "Things just move too fast these days," says a project officer. "We've got to get man out of the loop."[17] "Loop" is computer talk, so popular at ARPA these days, short for control loop. The name of the missile is SIAM, which stands for Self-Initiating Antiaircraft Munition.

The SIAM project is secret, so it is impossible to get a clear idea of what the missile will look like or how it will work. The only hint to date is a vague, somewhat opaque description in ARPA's budget presentation to Congress. "For enemy airfield interdiction," it says, "a self-contained SIAM is air-delivered to the vicinity of an enemy airfield. It implants in the ground, essentially hidden from view, in a dormant state except for a target detector-launch initiator which activates the attack missile subsystem. Launch occurs when the threat is within range of the missile acquisition sensor. The missile then acquires and homes in on the aircraft. . . ."[18] There will be a navy version, which will be released from a submerged submarine. The SIAM will rise to the surface of the ocean and, when a target comes within range, launch its missile. Another project is a system of microphones hooked to computers that will be designed to pinpoint distant artillery, distinguish between different kinds of guns by their sounds and direct return fire.

The self-launching missile and the microphone arrays are still in the early stages of development. However, there are other auto-matic guns that are about to be deployed. The latest development in antisubmarine warfare is a combination torpedo-mine called Captor, a sort of "smart" torpedo for the ocean depths. Captor, which stands for Encapsulated Torpedo, will be moored to the ocean floor and when enemy submarines pass within range it will attack by releasing a homing torpedo. Sensors will be able to distinguish between ships and submarines by their sounds. Captor mines, which are large enough to carry nuclear explosives, would be used in time of war to seal off the straits between Iceland and northern Europe through which Soviet submarines must pass to reach the open sea. The navy intends to start purchasing Captor mines this year.

The navy is also testing an automatic gun called Phalanx, so named, presumably, because it is intended to be the last-ditch defense against missiles. When testing is finished the navy hopes to put one aboard every ship. There is no human in the Phalanx loop either. A radar picks up the incoming missile and a computer does the rest—plots the course of the missile, points the gun and fires it. The Phalanx recently gained some notoriety when, during a test off the coast of California, it identified Santa Barbara Islands as an incoming missile. To some observers this points up an inherent problem with smart guns. The navy says it can work the bugs out, and plans to start putting Phalanxes on ships in 1976.

CRUISE MISSILES

Before World War II naval battles were fought by battleships blasting away at each other at 20 paces. What changed all this was the aircraft carrier, which was able, with its floating air force, to strike from greater distances at greater speed. As the carrier became the dominant fact of our naval policy, other ships of the line were reduced to supporting roles, defending or supplying the carriers. Now, according to Robert Berman of the Center for Defense Information and the Brookings Institution in Washington, D.C., as a result of new technologies in naval weapons, we may go full circle again.[19]

One reason is hovercraft, or Surface Effects Ships, as the U.S. Navy calls them. Hovercraft are a totally new kind of naval vessel that rides across the water on a cushion of air. They are extremely fast, and because they ride on air they can travel over practically any surface. Hovercraft are already in commercial use in many parts of the world, and according to Jane's Surface Skimmers,[20] the Soviet Navy has one that carries 900 men and will travel 220 miles an hour. The United States plans to build a fleet of 2,000-ton Surface Effects Ships. Eventually, if this works out, 10,000-ton Surface Effects Ships, as big as cruisers, will be built.

The other reason is cruise missiles. It was a Soviet-built cruise missile that sank the Israeli destroyer Elath in 1967 four months after the Six-Day War. Besides electronic jamming, the only defense ships have against cruise missiles is to scatter bits of aluminum in the air in hopes of confusing the missile's radar. In 1975, the United States got its first tactical cruise missile, a 15-foot, 1,400-pound weapon named the Harpoon. The Soviet Navy has a number of cruise missiles, which it has built over the years instead of airplanes for aircraft carriers. The Soviet Union has never had a strike aircraft carrier. The threat of cruise missiles has already forced some changes in naval strategy. Hovercraft armed with cruise missiles, darting about on the high seas, could, as Berman suggests, very well upset all calculations.

Actually, cruise missiles, like unmanned aircraft, have been around a long time. They used to be called "buzz bombs," and the V-1s that the Germans used against Britain in World War II were an early example. However, until a few years ago when the new precision guidance systems began to appear, they were generally considered too inaccurate to use against targets much smaller than the British Isles. Now, a cruise missile on a ship can be counted on to hit anything visible above the horizon.

It is probably time for a definition or two. Ballistic missiles, as in Intercontinental Ballistic Missiles (ICBMs) are powered by rocket engines. When they are fired they rise up through the earth's atmosphere into space and then fall back to earth toward their targets. Cruise missiles are slower, have small wings and are powered by air-breathing turbofan jet engines. They travel more or less the path an airplane flies. It is, in fact, possible to think of cruise missiles as one-way unmanned jet planes: kamikaze planes, but without pilots. Even kamikaze pilots are faced with technological obsolescence.

A few years ago the first generation of precision guidance systems made it possible to use cruise missiles with great accuracy over distances up to about 30 miles, about as far as a man can see. Even newer guidance technologies now under development will extend that range to thousands of miles.

MISSILES THAT READ MAPS

Dr. Kosta Tsipis, a physics professor at the Massachusetts Institute of Technology who specializes in arms control, explains it this way: "Until recently available electronics technology did not provide for long-range missile guidance. Deployed guided weapons, such as the Soviet surface-to-surface naval cruise missiles, have ranges generally under 50 kilometers and are usually of the remotely guided type requiring line-of-sight contact between the target and the human operator or the guidance radar."[21] (An exception of course is the ICBMs, which are guided by inertial guidance systems during the powered first few minutes of their flight and then follow a ballistic trajectory completely determined by the local gravitational field and the initial powered portion of their flight.)

There are two kinds of missile guidance—remote guidance and self-guidance. Remotely guided missiles need to be able to communicate with a distant operator. That is, as Tsipis describes it,

they need a data link—"a device that can gather and transmit over
large distances and in real time visual information about the terrain
the vehicle overflies, and, in addition, can receive and execute com-
mands to launch and subsequently guide the missiles on target." Self-
guided missiles need an elaborate computer on board to correlate
information from sensors with the course that has been programmed
for the missiles. "Both correlators and data links," says Tsipis,
"are complex, elaborate electronic devices; until recently they have
been too bulky to carry on a missile or even a remotely piloted vehicle.

"Recent advances in large-array microcircuitry, however,
have made possible an entirely new set of microminiaturized electronic
devices, and sensors of electromagnetic radiation that in turn make
possible the construction of guidance systems for long-range self-
guided missiles. . . ."

What this means is that missiles can now read maps. The military calls it Terrain Contour Matching. "Terrain matching and
terminal guidance based on pattern recognition," explains Tsipis,
"utilizes the fact that the numerical values of certain measurable
time-independent terrain variables, such as altitude above sea level
or ground reflectivity at a given wave length, vary as a function of
location on the earth." If you don't understand that, that's O.K.,
because the missile does. The map is translated into the mathematical
language of computers. Topographical features are given numerical
values according to their altitude, and before the missile is launched
its computer memory is given a digital map of its flight path. While
the missile is in flight, altimeters scan the ground below and feed
information to the computer. The computer compares this information
with the programmed course and makes any necessary course adjustments. National Defense magazine reports that the Boeing Company
successfully tested missiles with Terrain Contour Matching in 1973.
"The new system checked out on two 600-mile flights that originated
in Seattle, Washington."[22]

In a recent interview with Currie, Air Force Magazine asked
about the cost of "digitizing the world." Currie, it was reported,
"dismissed these reservations," saying that the area considered is
relatively small and the cost appears reasonable.[23]

LASER CANNONS

The following is from the December 6, 1974 issue of Aerospace
Daily, which is sort of the Variety of the defense industry.

A significant acceleration of interest in high-powered
lasers as destructive weapons—not merely range finders

and communications systems—is quietly occurring at
the very highest levels of the Defense Department.

Although the program is hidden under tight security,
the Daily has learned that fiscal year 1975 funds have
been increased from $123 million to $150 million, a
newly created High Energy Laser Review Group is
reporting directly to D.O.D.R.&E. chief Dr. Malcolm
Currie, and an accelerated development program has
been launched to prepare for a decision on whether to
begin prototype fabrication of tactical laser weapons
around 1978. . . . Top R.&D. officials briefed industry
representatives at a secret meeting in San Diego in
October and told them the laser weapons program was
entering a transition period between previous technological exploration and demonstration and a decision
on prototype weapons due in the 1978-79 period.

When the laser was developed in 1960, one of its inventors described it as a "solution looking for a problem."[24] The military, which
is never at a loss about the problem, began work immediately. Security precautions at Kirtland Air Force Base outside Albuquerque,
New Mexico, where laser research was conducted under the code
name Eighth Card, have been described as comparable to those taken
on the Manhattan Project.[25] Low-energy lasers have been used in
guidance systems, but now Aerospace Daily reports that high-energy
laser guns—the kind Buck Rogers might have used—are about to go
into production.[26]

High-energy lasers—beams traveling at the speed of light—able
to melt metal armor in a fraction of a second should be in the American arsenal by the early 1980s. The air force has plans to put a
laser gun on the new B-1 bomber to shoot down enemy missiles and
interceptors. It is also considering a laser gun for the F-15 fighter
plane; Aerospace Daily says that laser cannons have already shot down
drones in experiments at Kirtland AFB.[27] The navy can use laser
cannons against enemy ships, and, perhaps more important, for defense against cruise missiles. The army and the marines are currently
testing a huge tank that is armed with a laser cannon. Laser weapons
could also be used in space, perhaps on killer satellites. The Defense
Department has also done work on a space-based laser antiballistic-
missile system.

NAVSTAR

"Space," the military is fond of saying, "is a medium, not a
mission." Since 1957 when the Soviets put Sputnik I into orbit, more

than 1,700 satellites have been placed in space. All but about 50 of these have been launched by the Soviet Union and the United States, about 870 by the Soviet Union and 800 by the United States. At least half of these have been military.[28]

Since the mid-1960s, satellites have been used as communications relays—data links, as the military technicians say. It is already possible, using satellites, for the Pentagon to communicate instantly with ships or planes anywhere on the planet. Surveillance and warning satellites are the sensors of the Global Automated Battlefield. A satellite system launched in 1972, equipped with infrared sensors that are capable of detecting the hot plumes of ballistic missiles the moment they are fired, is part of our early-warning system—an elaborate network of detection devices on earth and in space connected to great banks of computers in a hollowed-out mountain in Colorado. These computers are a part of something called the World Wide Military Command and Control System, which Air Force Magazine describes as "a sprawling computer-based network of command centers"[29] linked to the National Command Center in the Pentagon.

Recently, as a result of a Defense Department directive to expand and upgrade the system, it received 35 new Honeywell computers, weighing a total of 57 tons.

One of the United States' newer surveillance satellites is an 11-ton camera called Big Bird. It ejects film cartridges that are then caught by air force airplanes and processed in a few hours. A successor to Big Bird, yet unnamed, will be able to deliver "near real-time" pictures by satellite relay.

The choice will probably be a satellite system called Navstar. Once Navstar is ready, satellites will also be used to guide missiles. According to Air Force Magazine,[30] which is the official magazine of the Air Force Association and can always be counted on for inside information, the "leading candidate" for a high-accuracy guidance system on long-range missiles is computerized map reading.

Navstar, also called the Global Positioning System, will consist of 24 satellites circling the earth in synchronous orbit at an altitude of about 11,000 miles. The satellites will send out signals that will, as Air Force Magazine describes it, "permit an unlimited number of properly equipped users to determine their position and velocity in three dimensions anywhere in the world, day or night, under all weather conditions, with an estimated accuracy of about 30 feet."[31] "Users" with the proper receiving equipment will be able to tune in the signals from four satellites, and by a simple process, for a computer, of triangulation know instantly where they are.

There are plans to equip soldiers in the field with sets that will be small enough to be carried in a backpack. Ships and aircraft will have receiving equipment. And, of course, many of the users will be missiles, both tactical and strategic, equipped with their own receivers and computers and programmed to fly a path defined by Navstar signals. Navstar is simply a space-based version of the loran navigational radio used to guide bombers over the Automated Battlefield in Southeast Asia.

"This program, just under way," says a Defense budget document,[32] "could revolutionize world navigation and weapon delivery." The first three Navstar satellites are scheduled to be launched in 1977. All 24 should be in place by 1984.

KILLER SATELLITES

Predictably, as satellites become an essential part of military operations they will become, as the Defense Department's Stephen Lukasik puts it, "high-value targets," and space will become "an increasingly contested area."[33]

The Pentagon is now developing special antisatellite satellites—killer satellites, as they are sometimes known—that will be able to hunt down and destroy enemy satellites. Until last year the United States had another kind of antisatellite system—a battery of long-range missiles based on an island in the Pacific, which, presumably, could have been used to shoot down enemy satellites. However, it was never used, and now it has been dismantled. Basically, it was an unworkable plan. It takes too long for a rocket fired from earth to reach a target 10,000 to 20,000 miles in space. Antisatellite satellites do not have this disadvantage; they can be put into space at any time and kept there until needed.

According to one plan, killer satellites will be launched into deep space, about 60,000 miles from earth, and hidden there until they are called. On a signal from earth, one of them will leave its refuge and move toward earth, to an altitude where it will encounter an alien satellite deemed dangerous or suspicious by observers on earth. It will slip into orbit with the alien satellite, inspect it with various sensors and transmit its findings to the control station. Then, on command, it can destroy the satellite, using conventional or nuclear explosives, or perhaps laser beams. If the inspection proves that the alien satellite is on a friendly mission, the killer satellite will switch orbits and move away. In 1972, Jane's All the World's Aircraft, a military encyclopedia with close ties to the Department of Defense, reported that the Soviets were testing a killer satellite of their own.[34]

Aviation Week reports that the United States is working on ways to protect satellites from attack: "Most of the measures rely on deception, including reducing radar and optical signature"[35]—

fairly standard electronic warfare countermeasures practiced on earth—"or disguising a military spacecraft as a scientific space telescope." One plan calls for a satellite to switch orbits. The article also alludes to unspecified "active defense mechanisms."

Very soon, if all goes according to plan, it will be possible to think of the entire world as one big pinball machine. And when that day arrives it will be possible for someone to think about plugging it in.

NOTES

1. General William C. Westmoreland, taken from a speech given in Washington, D.C., October 14, 1969.

2. See, for example: William Haseltine, "The Automated Air War," The New Republic, October 16, 1971; "Components and Contractors of the Automated Air War," published by NARMIC (American Friends Service Committee), December 1972; George Weiss, "Battle for Control of the Ho Chi Minh Trail," Armed Forces Journal, February 15, 1971, p. 21.

3. Quoted in Weiss, op. cit.

4. General Westmoreland, op. cit.

5. U.S. Congress, House, Appropriations Committee, Department of Defense Appropriations for 1975 (Washington, D.C.: Government Printing Office, 1974), Part 4, p. 450.

6. Ibid.

7. "What Every Ground Commander Should Know About Guided Bombs," Army, June 1973.

8. House, Appropriations Committee, op. cit., p. 450.

9. William Graham, in a telephone interview by the author in 1974. Graham at RAND in Santa Monica, California.

10. Defense Marketing Service, DMS Market Intelligence Report, October 1974, p. 4.

11. Commanders Digest, September 20, 1973, p. 7.

12. "Projects Providing ESO Impetus," Aviation Week, July 15, 1974, p. 165.

13. Armed Forces Journal, November 1974, p. 24.

14. Ordnance, July–August 1973, p. 16.

15. Dr. Francis Niedenfuhr, in a personal interview by the author in Rosslyn, Virginia, 1974.

16. House, Appropriations Committee, op. cit., p. 636.

17. Personal interview by author.

18. U.S. Congress, Senate, Armed Services Committee, Fiscal Year 1975 Military Procurement Authorization (Washington, D.C.: Government Printing Office, 1974), Part 6, p. 3079.

19. Robert Berman, in a personal interview by the author in Washington, D.C., 1974.

20. Jane's Surface Skimmers, 1971-72 (London: McGraw-Hill, 1971).

21. Kosta Tsipis, "The Long-Range Cruise Missile," Bulletin of the Atomic Scientists, April 1975, p. 17.

22. National Defense, September–October 1973, p. 108.

23. Edgar Ulsamer, "Urgent U.S. R&D Requirements," Air Force, April 1974, p. 38.

24. Robert Barkan, "Buck Rogers and the Deadly Laser," The New Republic, April 8, 1972, p. 11.

25. Ibid., p. 10.

26. "Laser Weapons Interest on Rise at Pentagon," Aerospace Daily, December 6, 1974, p. 8.

27. Ibid.

28. "Satellite Count Reaches 1718," Air Force Times, December 11, 1974.

29. Edgar Ulsamer, "USAF's R&D Riddle," Air Force, November 1974, p. 40.

30. Ulsamer, "Urgent U.S. R&D Requirements," op. cit., p. 40.

31. Ulsamer, "USAF's R&D Riddle," op. cit., p. 40.

32. Unclassified portion of Defense Department "budget justification" to congressional committees. Not available to public.

33. House, Appropriations Committee, op. cit., p. 637.

34. John W. R. Taylor, ed., Jane's All the World's Aircraft, 1971-72 (London: McGraw-Hill, 1971), p. 614.

35. Aviation Week, February 4, 1974, p. 11.

14

U.S. TACTICAL
AIR FORCES: TECHNOLOGY
OUTPACES MANAGEMENT
Robert W. Whitaker

However the United States chooses to define its commitments abroad—including those having a military component—the economical management of military programs remains a persistent problem. In the post-Vietnam period, high military budgets appear to be relatively insensitive to changes in national commitments. The expected "peace dividend" has not materialized, in part because of inflation, but more to the point, because of a reexpansion of U.S. general purpose forces and a substantial boost in tactical air capabilities.

The army is to be increased from 13 to 16 active divisions, and its air complement—already the largest in the United States—increased also. The air force will go from 22 to 26 tactical wings with modernized fighter and support aircraft, while the navy—mired in the high costs of its ship and aircraft programs—will operate at least 13 attack carriers and fly their decks with a new generation of high-performance fighters. Only the marine corps will stay at present strength, but it too is looking for a new inventory of tactical aircraft.

These developments are largely keyed to Pentagon perceptions of Soviet military threat capabilities, the North Atlantic Treaty Organization's nonnuclear defenses against Warsaw Pact attack, the problem of controlling vital sea lanes, and the U.S. need to project military power on a global scale. How the United States responds to these perceptions—in terms of force size and kinds of equipment—sets the parameters of our defense spending.

COSTS AND RETURNS

Former Secretary of Defense James R. Schlesinger estimates
that "more than 70 percent of our defense expenditures is attributable
to the general purpose forces"[1]—or $74 billion out of this year's
record $105 billion military budget. He has also called the four sepa-
rate tactical air forces in the services "the most expensive components of the general purpose force in terms of investment costs."[2]
This year alone the services will spend over $9 billion for new tactical
aircraft and for their advanced missiles and other air weapons. The
Pentagon places the annual procurement and operating costs of these
tactical air forces at approximately $24 billion—roughly one-quarter
of all military expenditures. This figure is understated by at least
$3 billion because Pentagon estimates do not include apportioned costs
of a carrier's support ships, the full costs of the army's aviation, or
those of mobility forces providing logistical support.

In ready parlance, the air components of our conventional forces
are called TACAIR. Except for some 500 strategic bombers, TACAIR
contains all U.S. combat aircraft and most of their supporting air
fleet*—or more than 20,000 airplanes and helicopters. Despite uncertainties about total TACAIR costs, two facts are apparent: we spend
more on our combat aircraft than anyone else in the world, and the
bill is rising. At the present rate of spending, the United States will
have to budget nearly $300 billion (in 1975 dollars) in the next ten
years for TACAIR programs, and possibly more if costs are not
brought under control.

Will the United States get its money's worth? A qualified "no"
must be given. Former Deputy Secretary of Defense David Packard
has said the military services "think more in terms of getting what
was effective in the last war rather than thinking ahead in an imaginative way about what might be needed for the future."[3] Their choice
after the Vietnam War was either to make major adjustments in their
programs to reflect changed requirements, or to press along old
paths with higher levels of spending for TACAIR. We are now on the
second road: by bits and pieces, Congress is being asked to approve
a $42 billion purchase of new tactical aircraft. (See Figure 14.1.)
It has something for everybody in the way of hardware, but few
promises of new directions.

------

*The 628 air refueling tankers and 902 cargo transports support
both strategic and conventional forces.

FIGURE 14.1

$42 Billion in New Aircraft Up Over 40 Percent from Estimates

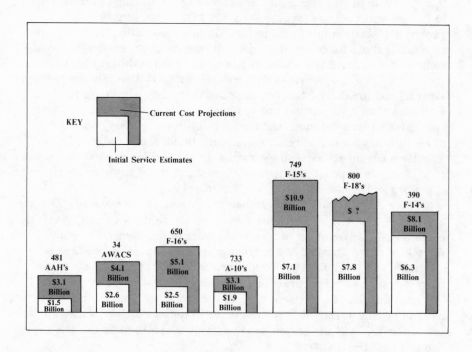

Source: SAR Program Acquisition Cost Summary (as of June 30, 1975). Department of Defense Fact Sheet, September 12, 1975.

Supersonic Costs

In the last three decades the unit price of fighter aircraft, inflation not included, has doubled every four years, followed by rising operational and support costs. These aircraft have grown pro- gressively bigger, heavier, faster, and incredibly complex to build and maintain. Pacing this growth is the military drive for techno- logical superiority and a desire to incorporate "state-of-the-art" advances in each aircraft.

Supersonic cost escalation has not been caused by inflation, but rather by open-ended design philosophies leading to extraordinarily sophisticated aircraft. For example, during World War II the army and navy bought 43,000 fighter aircraft for slightly over $12 billion (in 1975 dollars).[4] The average unit cost was less than $300,000. By contrast, the Pentagon's $42 billion TACAIR program will net about 3,800 new aircraft whose average unit price will be more than $10 million.

The acquisition cost of these aircraft, however, is augmented by the average costs of operating them over their useful service life—

FIGURE 14.2

15-Year Life-Cycle Costs Per Aircraft
(in 1975 dollars)

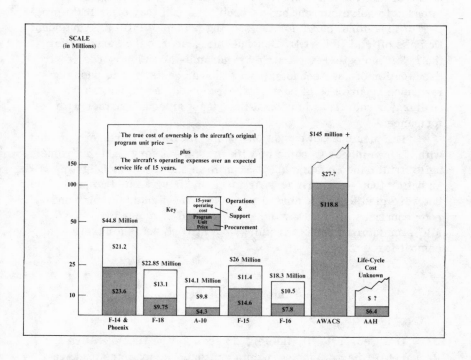

Sources: Hearings on Lightweight Fighter Aircraft Program, FY 1976. Appropriations Committee, U.S. Senate, 94th Congress, 1st session. Hearings on Air Combat Fighter Programs, Part 1. Government Operations Committee, U.S. Senate, 94th Congress, 1st session. Hearings on Tactical Air Power, Parts 8 and 9. Armed Services Committee, U.S. Senate, 94th Congress, 1st session. Hearings on Lightweight Fighter Aircraft Program, Part 9. Appropriations Committee, U.S. House, 94th Congress, 1st session.

typically, 15 years. In most cases, these operating costs equal or exceed the original purchase price. (See Figure 14.2.)

A prime example of technological cost escalation—and high life-cycle expense—is in the navy's $20.8 million F-14 fighter. Just one of its $500,000 Phoenix missiles costs more than a World War II fighter, and because the missile can be used only on the F-14 the true acquisition cost of the aircraft and its armament is $23.6 million. This is more than 60 times what the navy paid for its F-4U fighter in 1944. And although the air force's F-15 fighter is being procured for "only" $14.6 million each, this is 77 times the cost of the highly successful P-51 of the 1940s.[5]

Many Defense Department managers are known to be highly concerned over "affordability" and its causes. The "high-low" cost mixes of tactical fighters directed by Secretary Schlesinger were intended to solve current budget problems, but they offer little prospect of long-term cures for the soaring prices of military equipment. Defense official Robert E. Donohue, Jr., scores the services for their "technological imperative" syndrome—or in his words, their "application of new technology not to lower costs, but to push performance regardless of cost." What we need, he thinks, is "a 'cultural revolution' where cost is at least an equal partner with performance."[6]

The idea has not caught on yet. In the 1960s Northrop gambled with its own money to come up with the F-5—a very light, extremely agile fighter then costing about $1 million and capable of fighting MIGs on better than even terms.[7] Air force and navy wanted no part of it, but were glad to sell it abroad as a first-line fighter for rich and poor countries alike. Now the air force and navy use the F-5 as a MIG simulator in combat training, but still reject it for their own combat forces.

Diminishing Returns

Dr. George H. Heilmeier, director of the Defense Advanced Research Projects Agency, points out that "the avionics package costs in current tactical combat aircraft are running at 20-25 percent of the aircraft flyaway costs."[*] Why, he asks, "must each (aircraft)

---

[*] Avionics—a contraction of the words "aviation electronics"—refers to the various flight guidance, defensive and fire control systems in military aircraft. It includes radars, computers, cockpit control panels and displays, navigation and other flight aids, and communications equipment.

radar have a new tube and power supply design . . . When are we
going to start using standardized (integrated circuits) instead of cus-
tom designs?" And he says "we should push for common navy/air
force avionics" to cut back on costs.[8] To a lesser extent, but with
significant savings, common airframes and engines among aircraft
are practical propositions—but more talked about than achieved. In
fact, of all the new aircraft in development, only two share as much
as the same engine.

The tough truth is that military reliance on technological advantage, regardless of costs, is a policy flawed by constantly diminishing
returns: it can be maintained only by increasing military budgets or
by diverting funds from force structure into technology. Both of these
approaches are at work in TACAIR programs: neither can be continued
very much longer.

Cost overruns in major procurement programs are major problems. "It is clear," says Assistant Secretary of Defense Leonard
Sullivan, "that the military departments are either unwilling or unable
to make the hard decisions to keep program costs down." Citing a
review of eight "design-to-cost" programs in the Pentagon, he found
"the results are not encouraging," with program costs about $2 billion
more than expected.[9] The new A-10 close support fighter program is
already up 20 percent over air force estimates, and F-16 fighter up
a sizable 47 percent on the first 300 aircraft. Higher engine and development costs of the F-16, according to Sullivan, "have caused the
(Light Weight Fighter) cost target to be forgotten in the search for
more performance." Without harsh controls over aircraft costs he
sees no way "to obtain the force modernization we need within the budgets we are likely to obtain."[10]

Like war, perhaps procurement is too important to leave to the
generals. Comptroller General Elmer B. Staats is one official who
thinks so: "Under current Defense Department policy . . . the military
services determine their own needs for major acquisitions and they
start acquisition programs several years before the Secretary of
Defense is asked to approve the program." By then, he says, it is
"all too late to do much about the program, except to question imple-
mentation details."[11]

To remedy these kinds of problems, the Office of Federal Procurement Policy and the Office of Management and Budget recently
proposed a policy directive that would shift control over major weapon
system acquisitions from the services to the secretary of defense.
Under it, the services would retain control over basic and exploratory
research programs, but the secretary of defense would be required
to determine mission needs—or, in other words, to establish service
equipment requirements.[12] While this would be a signal improvement
over current practices, it hinges on the secretary's willingness and
ability to carry out the function, and to follow it through in the

acquisition programs themselves. For it has not been the lack of
legal authority that has prevented the secretary from acting decisively
in these matters, but the strange complexion of the Department of
Defense's bureaucracies and politics. Without strong congressional
and White House backing, no secretary of defense is really master of
his own house, and new policy directives are not likely to change
that.

TOO MANY AIR FORCES?

Each service has developed its air force independently of the
others, emphasizing its own operating environment and supposedly
unique capabilities. The tactical air effort is divided because of the
common desire of the services to equip themselves for independent,
instead of mutually supporting missions. At the extreme is the
Marine Corps, with its own TACAIR in a self-contained combat force.
The army's large number of helicopter gunships is justified under the
rubric of "direct fire support" instead of close air support—an air
force mission. And the navy's case for its TACAIR assumes independent carrier operations without assistance from other forces.
    On this score, Senator Barry Goldwater has an informed view-
point. "Today," he says, "all the forces are developing tactical
aircraft specifically designed [for] close air support. In my opinion

TABLE 14.1

Four U.S. Air Forces

Service	Aircraft*
Army	11,000
Air Force	9,400
Navy	5,100
Marine Corps	1,300
Total Aircraft	26,800

*
  Includes both active and reserve aircraft, figures
rounded to nearest hundreds as of 1975.
    Sources: Report on Department of Defense Appropri-
ations Bill, 1976, 94th Cong., 1st sess; U.S. Bureau
of the Census, Statistical Abstract of the United States,
1974, Washington, D.C., 1974.

it is costing us . . . more than it should and it is causing a lot of
confusion in command in the field. . . ." In this and other mission
areas, both savings and improved efficiency are possible. He concludes: "I have long had the feeling that maintaining four tactical air
forces is one of those avenues we could shoot at" to correct unnecessary overlap and duplication of effort.[13]

One encouraging move has been made by the Pentagon. All
tactical airlift assets among the services are to be transferred and
consolidated into one air force command, centrally-run for the benefit of all. Not so encouraging is the Marine Corps refusal to relinquish
control of its C-130 medium air transports, and the Defense Department's reluctance to force the issue. It needs to be done, and it
needs to be extended to the rest of TACAIR.

CHANGING TASKS

Long-standing conventional wisdom has held that defeating
opposing air forces is the priority air mission. Only when that job
is well in hand, and air superiority assured, could TACAIR turn to
battlefield strikes and attacks deep into enemy territory. Most U.S.
tactical fighters are still designed with these considerations in mind,
and for offensive operations rather than air defense.

But the 1973 war in the Middle East showed the tactical fighter
and the tank—the two mainstays of combat—to be extremely vulnerable
to cheap defensive missiles. Less than 5 percent of Israeli fighter
losses resulted from air-to-air combat; 95 percent were credited to
the array of Soviet-made ground-to-air missiles in the hands of
Egyptian and Syrian troops.[14]

Despite their overwhelming numerical superiority, air force
and navy fighters over North Vietnam achieved only a 2.5-to-1 kill
advantage in air-to-air combat compared to the 14-to-1 ratio achieved
in the Korean War. The bulk of U.S. air losses, as in the Mideast,
came from relatively cheap ground-fired missiles.[15]

These air lessons raise questions on the kind of air power needed
for the future, particularly in Europe. Soviet, and Warsaw Pact, integrated air defenses are now seen as formidable barriers to theater-
wide air superiority and to strikes against targets deep behind the
battlefield, as is their ability to inflict very high losses on penetrating
fighters. In net terms, Soviet-style air defenses are more efficient
than our offensive aircraft and contain them very close to the battlefield.

"Tactical air power," concludes RAND strategist Steven L.
Canby, "retains two major missions: battlefield interdiction . . . and

the derived mission of local air superiority."[16] The recent air commander in Europe, General John W. Vogt, Jr., also acknowledges that the classic goal of theater-wide air superiority is no longer possible for NATO forces. Like others, he sees the air situation near the battle line "pretty much determining the outcome of what's happening on the ground."[17]

Air strikes deep into enemy-controlled territory, except in lightly defended areas, may also belong to the air sagas of the past. Secretary Schlesinger has conceded that such missions would be very costly in fighter losses to Warsaw Pact defenses, and ineffective in stemming the flow of manpower and military supplies to the forward edge of the battle line.[18] And given a short conventional conflict in Europe, the effects of such strikes might not be felt before the war ended—or crossed the nuclear threshold.

Despite these developments, TACAIR continues to be tilted towards missions of questionable priority. Two-thirds of the new fighters—the F-15 and F-16 in the air force and the F-14 and F-18 in the navy—are designed for deep penetration missions. Though they will have good performance over the battlefield itself, they will carry into combat more sophisticated and expensive capabilities than are needed, or usable.

THE BLUE SKY NAVY

The Navy's tactical air problems are the most serious among the services, and can be solved only through larger compromises between aspirations and resources. At their base is the oft-heard view: "We simply can't afford the navy anymore!" The reason? Billion-dollar aircraft carriers plus multi-million dollar fighter plus "go-everywhere, do-everything" concepts.

Naval TACAIR has two basic missions—sea control including antisubmarine warfare and projecting air power ashore. To do these, it must be able to help defend the carrier task force in conjunction with ship-borne missiles. Keeping the sea lanes open is the recognized first-level objective, but if striking land targets is given the same priority, as is now the case, both missions will suffer from lack of resources. Moreover both the cost and the kind of TACAIR required for each of the two missions are quite different—only the fleet air defense requirement stays relatively unchanged. The navy's dilemma is compounded by attaching virtually the same geographical spread to both missions, although equipment needs ought to be determined by mission and area of intended operations. Keeping the sea lanes open, for example, requires ship and aircraft characteristics relatively the same regardless of area. By contrast, what might be required in attack fighters to strike Soviet naval bases is materially different from what was needed to bomb Hanoi. Aircraft capable of attacking Soviet land targets naturally will have more than enough capability to strike elsewhere, but this represents surplus performance that may not have to be provided.

The carrier itself is the Achilles heel of naval TACAIR. The last one was sunk by enemy action in 1945. Since then, carriers have been involved in operations against countries that could offer no real opposition to them, and where land-based TACAIR provided an ample margin of air defense. Carriers probably will remain suitable for such operations in the future. But in a major U.S.-Soviet conflict where intense air and surface opposition would be mounted, the attack carrier could be a serious liability: more aircraft would have to go into just defending the carrier than could be used for other TACAIR missions.

There is good evidence that the navy, in continuing to emphasize carriers and fighters for strike missions on land, is less and less able to perform its priority task of keeping the sea lanes open. Its plea for more ships is not likely to be heeded for cost reasons alone, and it seems to be compounding its money problems through uncoordinated planning and management. The Navy has too many different kinds of aircraft in carriers, and virtually no cost-saving interchange of components among them. While the new Phoenix missile is probably needed for fleet defense, the only plane that can carry it—the F-14—was intended to counter a bomber threat that could come only from Soviet shore-based aircraft. For lesser contingencies in which the carriers have normally operated, the F-14 is needlessly over-designed and unnecessarily costly.

In a controversial move, the Navy recently chose the F-18 as its Naval Air Combat Fighter (NACF). Vice Admiral William P. Houser told a Senate committee that except for differences in their weaponry and avionics, "all Navy tactical missions should be conducted by either the F-14 or the NACF."[19]

On another occasion Admiral Houser promised House members that the Navy will "take, say, at least four airplanes (now in use) on board (its carriers) and reduce those down to two."[20] In justifying the F-18 selection, Chief of Naval Operations James L. Holloway pointed to its ability to replace F-4's and A-7's in limited space aboard aircraft carriers: "The cascade effect of this simplification," he wrote Congressman George H. Mahon, "will be felt throughout the Naval establishment, in terms of reduced cost for personnel, training, support equipment, intermediate and depot facilities, overhaul, spares and repair parts."[21] But shortly thereafter his deputy, Vice Admiral K. L. Lee, told a Senate Subcommittee on Appropriations that "the

F-18 will replace only the A-7's."[22] More belatedly, the Navy
revealed a third aircraft—an A-18 attack version of the F-18 fighter—
would have to be developed to make the NACF program cost-effective,
and by implication, to provide an attack aircraft for a mission the
F-18 would not be able to do after all.

The already deep confusion in navy's TACAIR programs is complicated by still another aircraft—the A-8 now under study in the
Pentagon. This is to be a new attack aircraft but its performance
and its place in the navy's inventory are presently unknown. Whatever
comes of the A-8 concept, the navy is moving neither toward fewer
types of aircraft nor greater common use of components among them.
Even the F-18, criticized because it is not derived from the air force
F-16, apparently has little in common with its own attack version,
the A-18.

In response to criticisms of navy programs, Admiral Houser
replies, "We can't do everything at once."[23] But navy TACAIR programs are seemingly not in control, attempting to do more than
is needed with too much of the wrong kind of air power. TACAIR is
discussed in a vacuum, with little or no mention of carrier issues
and strategic utility. Other naval aircraft, like the A-6, will soon
come up for replacement. If the navy is to resolve its mission problems the planning time remaining is very short. We must come to
grips with the navy's first task—controlling vital sea lanes—and decide
what kind of secondary land-strike capability will be necessary and
feasible.

WHAT TO DO WITH THE MARINES

The endurance of the Marine Corps is legendary, but nowhere
as much as for its ability to withstand outside criticism and attempted
changes in its mission and structure. Fixed by law at three divisions
and three air wings, the Marine Corps budget of about $4 billion is
modest compared to that of the other services, but offers large poten-
tials for savings if the corps were reoriented to new tasks.

Indications are that alternatives are being looked at in the
Pentagon. Joint Chiefs of Staff Chairman General George S. Brown
has stressed "broadening the Marine Corps scope of employment
beyond the amphibious mode." Instead of taking it for granted that
the Marines would go in over the beach, "What we really ought to do,"
he says, "is find the most effective way of using these forces flexibly
and in context with other capabilities.[24]

Several options are open. As presently structured and positioned,
the marines are a light infantry backed by its own air force. Since

World War II the Marine Corps has been oriented primarily toward the Pacific. Its new commandant, General Louis H. Wilson, states candidly that he is "not wedded to the concept that all Marine divisions should be mirror images of the others,"[25] as is now the case. And he suggests that they could be equipped according to the regions in which they would likely fight.

The most plausible alternatives are for the marines to replace the army in Asia, to join it in Europe, or some combination of both that would maintain the projected total ground force of 19 divisions (16 army, three marine). Whichever path is chosen, marine TACAIR can be cut back substantially to eliminate duplication of forces and of missions. Under the first option—replacing the army in Asia—the 25 fighter/attack air squadrons in the corps could be reduced up to half their present strength, keeping only the marine helicopters and some close support aircraft. Air force and navy TACAIR would supply the additional capabilities needed. Savings under this alternative would range up to $1 billion annually.

Orienting the marines to Europe would require little in the way of TACAIR—as few as eight marine squadrons of utility aircraft. A major cost would come in refitting marine ground divisions for heavier "general purpose" force requirements, and their higher annual operating costs would partially offset the savings in marine air wings. Nonetheless, upwards of $500 million per year could come out of the Marine Corps budget. A combination approach orienting the corps to both Europe and the Pacific would accrue savings somewhere between the first two alternatives, depending on the emphasis chosen.

Whatever the future orientation of the Marine Corps, its separate tactical air force is an expensive luxury that does not always serve its own interests. At one time the navy foisted four squadrons of F-14s on the marines, not because they needed them but because it was one way of holding down navy costs. Until that decision was reversed recently, the marines spent $6.1 million for unnecessary pilot training in the F-14. The corps now says it will stick with F-4s until something better comes along.

The marines can make a reasonable case for keeping their helicopter assets, and probably the attack capability of the V/STOL AV-8s if the corps remains in the Pacific. Anything beyond these, particularly in Europe where substantial TACAIR is already available, is unnecessary.

FLY ARMY

The largest—if not the fastest—air force in the West belongs to the U.S. Army. It has more aircraft than any other service. It runs its own flying schools, its own mobility airlift, its own close air support, and its plans on increasing the size of its tactical air force by some 600 helicopter gunships designed for close-in aerial "fire support" of ground forces. The army also proposed to spend $3.1 billion for 481 Advanced Attack Helicopters (AAH) equipped to fire the TOW missile.[26]

There are strong doubts about gunship survivability in the European or other heavy air defense environments, and especially about the basic need for the AAH. On the first score, the army pins its hopes on "pop-up" and experimental "nap-of-the-earth" flying to minimize the vulnerability of the AAH and other gunships, but these have neither the evasive speed nor maneuverability of fixed-wing fighters, and are very vulnerable to ground fire.

The need for more gunships, and the AAH is particular, has not been shown. With the A-10, the air force can increase its number of daily close air support sorties by one-third, and other fighters provide an all-weather capability not built into helicopters—an important consideration in Europe. Substantial additional close air support sorties would be mounted by NATO allies, and even assuming reasonable gunship survivability the incremental firepower it would bring to a European battlefield is too small to matter. In fact, the 16 TOW missiles carried by an AAH cost six times as much as an average A-10 payload, but provide only one-sixtieth the firepower.

Like the marines, the army has a case for battlefield mobility and other support aviation of its own. It can justify the helicopter gunship in low-threat environments like Southeast Asia, but even there the army lost 2,282 helicopters to small arms fire.[27] The AAH will not help it elsewhere.

AIR FORCE GAMBLES

Unlike the navy, the air force is fortunate in having reasonably coherent missions that can be translated into flying hardware. And as the Director of Defense Research and Engineering, Malcolm R. Currie, confirms: "The environment for which we design our [weapons] systems is Central Europe;" not only is it "the most demanding, it is also the most vital."[28]

With 733 close air support A-10 fighters on order in mid-1975, the air force is clearly getting back into the business of supporting ground forces with a special-purpose aircraft. But by splitting its A-10s and A-7s between the active and reserve forces, there could be too few of these close support fighters in Europe at the beginning of a conventional conflict, when the demand for them would be greatest.

This would leave ground forces without adequate air support at a time when it will be most needed—in the initial "blitzkrieg" thrust of enemy forces. The air force undoubtedly has to make compromises in its aircraft mix, but this one is reversed in priorities: more A-10s in the active force seems prudent, particularly if they are to support marine ground divisions in Europe, Asia, or elsewhere.

Although the air force claims its F-15 and F-16 fighters are for multipurpose use, they are clearly designed for air superiority tasks. Their ground attack capability is an expensive afterthought. Multimission aircraft sound attractive, but using a $14.6 million fighter such as the F-15 in close air support missions is not cost-effective. Nor will it or the F-16 be able to generate high sortie rates for sustained periods in the manner of the A-10. The F-15 will be operational in Europe by 1977, the F-16 in the early 1980s. Whether the air force intends to deploy A-10s there is unclear, but from its congressional testimony it will obviously put the weight of its NATO effort into air superiority fighters.

The Airborne Warning and Control System (AWACS) remains the much heralded, but unproven star of air force hopes. Congress approved the F-15 program without fully understanding that this fighter's vaunted advantage over Soviet aircraft was partly dependent on the controversial AWACS.[29] The air force was slow to tell Congress that without AWACS, the F-15's long-range radar and Sparrow missiles would be wasted—they cannot discriminate between friend and foe without the help of air controllers and force the F-15 into visual range engagements. For close-in visual-range combat, the air force acknowledges, the F-16 will be the better fighter. Consequently, there is a high risk factor in the AWACS and F-15 programs, or to put it another way, a $15 billion gamble.

In the air force's F-16 program—one of the major "design to cost" ventures—the opportunity to prove that quality fighters can be built at reasonable costs may be slipping away. Recent service experience is not promising. The navy ran up a 27 percent cost growth on its F-14 before the first production aircraft was delivered, inflation not included.[30] The Air Force's F-15 program unit cost is over one-third higher than first planned, mostly because of adding more and more capability into the aircraft. The F-16 seems destined for the same dismal record. The 1972 goal was a $3 million "flyaway"*

---

* Unlike the program unit cost, "flyaway" cost does not include a share of R&D expenditures, initial spare parts or associated ground equipment. It is simply the recurring contractor price of the aircraft as it comes out of the factory, and therefore only a portion of the actual cost to the services.

cost, but to remake the aircraft into a fighter-bomber has jumped present estimates 47 percent to $4.4 million.[31]

Secretary Schlesinger has told Congress that he considers a $6 million "flyaway" cost the approximate dividing line between fighters in his "high-low" mix.[32] The air force's F-16 is nearly there. Keeping it to its "design-to-cost" limits is a far more important issue than commonly recognized, and one largely obscured by the smoke from the navy's F-18 selection. But advertising the F-16 as a high-performance, low-cost fighter can be misleading. Any procurement cost growth beyond 20 percent—say, to $5.5 billion for 650 aircraft—means that the equivalent number of additional F-15s could be bought and operated for 15 years at the same cost as the F-16s. This is not a desirable alternative, but hopes for turning away from the trend line on aircraft costs will be defeated if 650 F-16s wind up more expensive than the F-15 luxury models.

Something of the same applies to the air force's A-10 program, where upward slippage would wipe out the incremental advantages of the aircraft over the A-7, which is still in production. In addition to everything else, such persistent escalation in these programs bodes ill for air force designs on expanding to 26 tactical wings. As Assistant Secretary Sullivan has noted, "these real cost increases will result in either program stretch-outs, reduced quantities procured, or reductions in other important programs."[33] Both Congress and the Pentagon need to heed the warning.

NEW U.S. TACTICAL AIRCRAFT, 1976

- AAH:
    Now in prototype development, the Advanced Attack Helicopter gunship is intended for close support of ground forces and an anti-tank role. Each aircraft would cost over $6.4 million. The army wants 481 AAHs in a $3.1 billion procurement program.
    AAH cruising speed is 180 mph with a maximum range of 365 miles.
    Armament: One 30mm chain gun, 1450 lbs maximum expendable ordnance, including 16 TOW missiles.
- A-10:
    The twin-engine air force A-10 is a single-purpose fighter designed for close air support of ground forces. Costing $4.3 million apiece, 733 A-10s will require a $3.1 billion expenditure.
    The aircraft's maximum speed is 460 mph. Average range will be 290 miles plus two hours of loitering time while carrying 9,500 lbs of ordnance.

Armament: One 30mm seven-barrel cannon; up to 16,000 lbs of ordnance including conventional and guided bombs, additional gun pods and Maverick missiles.

- F-15:

With speeds above Mach 2.5, the twin-engine F-15 is optimized for the air superiority mission. It is also capable of flying deep interdiction or close air support missions.

The first of 749 aircraft were delivered to the air force in 1974. Total program cost is $10.9 billion, each F-15 running at $14.6 million, plus weapons.

Armament: One internal 20mm Gatling gun; nine external stations for Sparrow and Sidewinder missiles, general-purpose or guided bombs, electronic warfare pods, and combinations of other ordnance.

- F-16:

This aircraft evolved from the air force Light Weight Fighter prototype into a multipurpose airplane. It can operate as either an air superiority or an attack fighter.

Six hundred fifty F-16s will be procured for $5.1 billion, with first deliveries about 1980. Program unit price is $7.8 million expected to rise, despite cost-saving use of the same engine powering the F-15.

The F-16 flies in the Mach 2 range and has a slightly larger radius of action than the F-15.

Armament: One nose-mounted 20mm multibarrel cannon; four Sidewinder missiles and five external stations for combinations of weapons. Maximum weapons load is 18,000 lbs.

- E-3A (AWACS):

The air force's Airborne Warning and Control System is a modified Boeing 707-320B transport packed with an extensive complement of radars, computers, communications and navigation systems. It is intended for all-weather, long-range surveillance of all air vehicles over land or water. AWACS can support a variety of tactical or air defense missions by tracking hostile targets and providing air control of friendly forces. The aircraft is unarmed, carries a crew of 17, and has a five-hour endurance on station 1150 miles from base. Unit cost is $118.8 million. Air force is asking for 34 E-3As for a total program cost of $4.1 billion. Over half of this expenditure will go for R&D, Test and Evaluation.

- F-18:

The navy projects this aircraft in two versions—the F-18 air superiority fighter and the A-18 attack fighter not yet designed. Performance characteristics and costs are speculative since development has not started and congressional approval has not been given. Eight hundred F-18s and A-18s are forecast by the navy for a total program cost of $7.8 billion. The unit cost of the F-18 version is estimated at $9.7 million.

The F-18 version is a twin-engine, Mach 2 fighter optimized for fleet defense and counterair operations. Its A-18 variant would be "stretched" to carry more fuel and heavy external ordnance.

Armament: A multibarrel cannon in both versions, Sparrow and Sidewinder missiles on the F-18, and unspecified weights of external ordnance on the A-18.

F-14:

The only navy fighter to carry the 100-mile range Phoenix missile, the F-14 is designed primarily for fleet defense. Due to be reengined in the near future to better its below-goal performance, the F-14 has a maximum speed of over Mach 2 and a flight endurance of two hours at subsonic speeds. Its radar and fire control systems can track multiple targets at extreme ranges and fire six Phoenix stand-off missiles simultaneously. Unit cost is $23.5 million for the aircraft and its complement of Phoenix missiles. Only 390 F-14s will be procured for a total program cost of $8.1 billion. The separate Phoenix missile program entails an additional $1.2 billion.

Other armament: One internally mounted 20mm cannon and external stations for Sparrow and Sidewinder missiles.

CONCLUSIONS

At stake in our TACAIR programs is not just their high costs, but what these are buying in the way of adequate forces. Fundamental to that question are the service doctrines that place such high premiums on independent air operations and on aircraft designed for missions they are not likely to fly, or to survive. Since doctrine is the conceptual yardstick by which TACAIR requirements and force goals are measured, it warrants a high place in the secretary of defense's priorities. We need an air doctrine that looks to the 1990s and not to the 1940s.

The record does not support service claims of improved management in their aircraft procurement. Long-standing problems remain unchecked, and corrosive dollar increases continue to afflict all major acquisition programs. The secretary of defense's "design-to-cost" directive to the services has failed, and their lack of cost discipline means higher military budgets in the future. Most seriously affected will be the TACAIR force structure itself, which may have neither the right kinds of tactical fighters needed nor a good balance among them.

The congressional role is hampered by a plane-by-plane approach that is long on technological explanations but short on matching Defense Department goals with equipment needs. Congress and the secretary of defense urgently need to look at TACAIR on a mission basis. Equally vital, they should withhold funding for programs that do not promise to contribute significantly to an adequate military force, whose costs are disproportionate to the capability needed, or where management controls are grossly unsatisfactory.

To single out one dubious program by hindsight, both the navy and the country would likely be better off today had the F-14 been terminated, and the Phoenix missile transferred to another fighter. Foresight would apply the same stringent cutoff to current development projects. The army's AAH program is a prime candidate; ending it now would save $8-10 billion in procurement and operating costs in the years ahead. The F-18 and other proposed navy aircraft need far more convincing explanations and costing before any approval is given. The reasons for continued cost-growth in the air force F-16 program should be aired promptly, and tighter controls insisted upon. The secretary of defense must exercise more authoritity in forcing change where it is needed.

Most importantly, decision makers should not be stampeded into authorizing aircraft programs by service arguments that delay will be costly or will somehow damage the country. Neither is necessarily true, and both the secretary of defense and Congress need to call for better alternatives than have been offered.

NOTES

1. James R. Schlesinger, U.S. Congress, Senate, Appropriations Committee, Department of Defense Appropriations, FY 1975, 93rd Cong., 2d sess. (Washington, D.C.: Government Printing Office, 1974), Part 1, p. 121.

2. Ibid., p. 163.

3. David Packard, U.S. Congress, House, Appropriations Committee, Department of Defense Appropriations, FY 1973, 92nd Cong., 1st sess. (Washington, D.C.: Government Printing Office, 1972), Part 3, p. 211.

4. See chapter 4, "The Cost Evolution of U.S. Tactical Airplanes," in William D. White, U.S. Tactical Air Power (Washington, D.C.: Brookings Institution, 1974), pp. 42-60.

5. Comparisons are adjusted to 1975 dollars. Cost of World War II fighters is derived from ibid., p. 47.

6. Robert E. Donahue, Jr., taken from a June 23, 1975 address before the National Security Industrial Association, Adsecon, New Jersey.

7. Jane's All the World's Aircraft 1971-72 (New York: McGraw-Hill, 1971), pp. 370-72.

8. Dr. George H. Heilmeier, taken from a July 15, 1975 address before the Tri-Service Radar Symposium, Monterey, California.

9. Leonard Sullivan, memorandum to Deputy Secretary of Defense, April 10, 1975.

10. Ibid.

11. Comptroller General Elmer B. Staats, quoted in Katherine Johnsen, "Broad Weapons Policy Shift Set," Aviation Week and Space Technology, September 15, 1975, p. 15.

12. Ibid., pp. 14-15.

13. Senator Barry Goldwater, U.S. Congress, Senate, Armed Services Committee, Nomination of James R. Schlesinger to be Secretary of Defense, 93rd Cong., 1st sess. (Washington, D.C.: Government Printing Office, 1973), pp. 49-50.

14. Author's estimates from unpublished sources. See also Stockholm International Peace Research Institute, SIPRI Yearbook 1974 (Cambridge, Mass.: Massachusetts Institute of Technology Press, 1974), pp. 5-8, 149-52.

15. White, op. cit., pp. 66-70.

16. Steven L. Canby, "Damping Nuclear Counterforce Incentives: Correcting NATO's Inferiority in Conventional Military Strength," Orbis, Spring 1975, p. 42.

17. General John W. Vogt, Jr., quoted in "Allied Air Power in Europe: The View from the Top," International Defense Review, February 1975, p. 46.

18. James R. Schlesinger, Annual Defense Department Report, FY 1976 and 197T (Washington, D.C.: Department of Defense, February 5, 1975), p. III-19.

19. Senate, Armed Services Committee, Tactical Air Power, 94th Cong., 1st sess. (Washington, D.C.: Government Printing Office, 1975), Part 9, p. 4742.

20. House, Appropriations Committee, Department of Defense Appropriations, FY 1976, 94th Cong., 1st sess. (Washington, D.C.: Government Printing Office, 1975), Part 9, pp. 323-24.

21. Duplicate language was used in Admiral Holloway's letter to Senator John C. Stennis, Chairman of the Senate Armed Services Committee. See Congressional Record, July 24, 1975, p. S13568.

22. Senate, Appropriations Committee, Lightweight Fighter Aircraft Program, 94th Cong., 1st sess. (Washington, D.C.: Government Printing Office, 1975), p. 40.

23. Admiral William P. Houser, quoted in Aerospace Daily, August 5, 1975, p. 193.

24. General George S. Brown, quoted in Edgar Ulsamer, "General Brown Looks at U.S. Defense Needs," Air Force, August 1975, pp. 36–37.

25. General Louis H. Wilson, quoted in John W. Finney, "Marines Face New Role as a Reserve for Europe," New York Times, June 30, 1975.

26. Senate, Armed Services Committee, Tactical Air Power, op. cit., Part 8, pp. 4430–59.

27. Official figures from Public Affairs Office, Department of Defense.

28. Dr. Malcolm E. Currie, Program of Research, Development, Test and Evaluation, FY 1976 (Washington, D.C.: Department of Defense, February 24, 1975), p. VI-4.

29. The AWACS controversy centers on technical doubts that the system would be survivable in the European environment, and that its electronics would be relatively invulnerable to enemy counter-measures. Following severe criticisms of the AWACS program by the General Accounting Office, the secretary of defense convened an ad hoc panel chaired by Dr. Harold P. Smith to perform an independent assessment. The panel questioned whether AWACS could support offensive operations, but found that it had reasonable effectiveness in purely defensive roles. See Senate, Armed Services Committee, Tactical Air Power, op. cit., Part 8, pp. 4031-120.

30. Ibid., Part 9, pp. 4696-99. See also White, op. cit., pp. 50-55, for an analysis of cost growth in the F-14 and F-15 air-craft, and the SAR Program Acquisition Cost Summary (as of June 30, 1975), Department of Defense Fact Sheet, September 12, 1975.

31. Sullivan, op. cit.

32. James R. Schlesinger, House, Appropriations Committee, Department of Defense Appropriations for 1976, op. cit., Part 1, p. 58.

33. Sullivan, op. cit.

15

THE MILITARIZATION
OF OUTER SPACE
James Willis

In July 1975, with the dramatic Apollo-Soyuz linkup, Soviet and American astronauts greeted each other in outer space for the first time.

To the civilian television viewer, this space docking experiment illustrated a U.S. and Soviet use of space for peaceful purposes in a spirit of detente. To the military-minded observer, however, the event was additional confirmation that either spacecraft—fitted with the space weapons now being developed by both countries—could destroy the other side's military and civilian satellites.[1] In fact, an increasingly large part of the space programs of both powers is for military purposes. The space programs of Britain, France, and China also have military implications.

Military satellites were first used in warfare by the United States, which used them during the Vietnam War for communications, weather prediction for bombing raids, and navigation for naval bombardment. According to the Pentagon, the importance of satellite systems to the function of U.S. tactical forces will become paramount in the next decade.[2]

Space technology has long been an important part of U.S. strategic nuclear forces, and has been used for surveillance, navigation, and early warning since the 1960s. Now, the United States is adapting its military space program to support its strategy of "flexible response," a variation of nuclear doctrine that emphasizes nuclear war-fighting capabilities at various levels of "limited" nuclear war. Space technology is vital to this strategy by providing the capability for increased centralized operational control over nuclear forces; the capability for "damage assessment"—necessary for making appropriate "response," in an exchange of nuclear salvos; and increased accuracy for missiles and other delivery vehicles.

According to U.S. Air Force studies, an attack on our major satellite systems would come about only under conditions leading to a full-scale nuclear war. Nevertheless, the weapons capable of fighting wars in outer space are now being planned and built. On the eve of the Apollo-Soyuz flights, the Pentagon's director of research and engineering, Dr. Malcolm Currie, said there is no doubt that "over the next ten or fifteen years space is not going to remain the unmolested territory, the sanctuary, that it is today."[3]

SPACE AS A MILITARY MEDIUM

Outer space begins where the earth's atmosphere ends, or about 100 miles out. Both superpowers regard space as a medium—much like the oceans—to be used militarily. From the beginning the military uses of space have involved more than manned or unmanned spacecraft. ICBMs that by necessity pass through outer space in their trajectories have been part of the U.S. and Soviet inventories for more than a decade-and-a-half.

How Many Satellites?

Much of military space information is secret. However, using United Nations and other unclassified data, outside experts have estimated with some confidence that about 60 percent of U.S. space launchings have been conducted by the military; a slightly higher percentage is true for the Soviet Union.[4] Just how many military satellites there are in orbit is even more difficult to assess. The Pentagon says it has 21 active satellites as of June 13, 1975. Nine of these are for communication, five for navigation, three for meteorology, three for early warning of impending attack and one for research and development.[5] The list of military satellites does not include surveillance satellites, which are a major element in the military space program, and which the Defense Department may be operating for other agencies, like the Central Intelligence Agency and the National Security Agency. Because of secrecy, the total number of military and related satellites and their uses are not known to U.S. citizens.

Antisatellite Weapons

At recent hearings conducted by the Senate Aeronautical and
Space Science Committee, Currie pointed to the militarization of
space as follows: "to the extent that our satellite assets become central to our national security, central to our military capability, I
think that we must prudently look forward to the day when satellites
are very vulnerable and anticipate this."[6] Currie has also alerted
members of Congress to a "space vehicle threat."[7] This is no doubt
a reference to the Soviet Union's antisatellite satellite, which was
tested about 10 times between 1967 and 1971. This Soviet satellite
can maneuver within lethal range of its target and then explode and
destroy or neutralize the enemy spacecraft. The United States once
had a similar program known as "Saint," but apparently it was never
tested. The Pentagon is continuing its research and development of
antisatellite weapons. One project concept calls for the launching of
small interceptors from either the ground or from space in order to
knock down or severely damage an enemy satellite. Another space
weapons project involves the use of satellite-based high energy
lasers.[8]

Both the United States and the Soviet Union have also developed
land-based missiles that can be used against satellites. Such U.S.
missiles, carrying high explosive warheads, are on Johnston and
Kwajalein Islands in the mid-Pacific. In addition, nuclear-tipped
Titan II missiles, possessing powerful boosters, may well serve
the same purpose. The Soviet Galosh Antiballistic Missile, which
also carries a nuclear warhead, could be adapted to shoot down
U.S. satellites.[9]

Revolutionizing Warfare

One of the most advanced satellites in U.S. space technology is
the Navstar "global positioning system," a triservice project managed
by the air force. According to the Pentagon, Navstar "can have a
revolutionary effect on both strategic and tactical warfare."[10] Navstar will be a constellation of 24 satellites which will provide three-
dimensional positioning within 30 feet anywhere in the world to
anyone—or anything—equipped with a receiver. This prospect, says
the Pentagon, "opens up vast new opportunities for multiplying force
effectiveness manyfold."[11] One of the primary users of Navstar will
be missiles, which will thereby acquire unprecedented accuracies.

The Pentagon has already launched an experimental satellite to test the Navstar concept. The first satellites of the Navstar system will be launched in 1976 and the system will be in full operation in 1984. Navstar will cost an estimated $2.6 to $3.7 billion during the first 10 years of its life.

Increased Dependence

Increased dependence on military space systems has led the Pentagon to conclude that "we must renew our efforts to protect these space assets, to make them less vulnerable to physical and electronic attack."[12] Considerable importance is now being attached to satellite "survivability." Projects in this area include research into antijamming devices, protection against the effects of nuclear blast, the use of redundant systems and maneuverable satellites as well as space-based sensors.

One reason for the increased dependence on satellites is that some satellites are so effective and relatively inexpensive that older ground systems, such as the DEW-line radar system, are being abandoned.

Many Types of U.S. Military Satellites

Following are descriptions of types of American military satellites.[13]

Early Warning Satellites: These satellites, operating from synchronous orbits of 20,000 nautical miles, can detect either land-based or submarine missile launches almost instantaneously, using infrared sensors. There are two early warning satellites in orbit over the western hemisphere, and one over the eastern. These three satellites form part of a larger warning system that also includes over-the-horizon radar in Greenland and elsewhere. The headquarters for the U.S. early warning system is located inside Cheyenne Mountain, Colorado.

Surveillance Satellites: These satellites, also called "spy" satellites, fly in a very low, elliptical orbit, with a perigee of 100 miles or less. Sophisticated photo-reconnaissance satellites, carrying powerful cameras, can provide highly detailed ground intelligence. The 11-ton "Big Bird" satellite locates targets, monitors troop and missile deployments and watches the world's trouble spots. It can provide "live" coverage or film packs, which it ejects to be recovered by airplanes. The 125-pound Ferret electronic intelligence satellite monitors radio transmissions, radar frequencies, and probably telephone conversations. An ocean surveillance satellite is being developed to monitor the movements of the Soviet fleet.

Communications Satellites: The Defense Communications Agency operates the Defense Satellite Communications System, a general purpose system of fixed terminals which serves the Pentagon's World Wide Military Command and Control System, and special users, like the White House and the State Department. Of the 26 initial satellites launched between 1966 and 1968, about five to seven were still operational in 1975. Replacement satellites are being launched and improved versions are being developed for the 1980s. Two advanced satellites have been launched, serving 54 terminals worldwide, including NATO and the United Kingdom.

The navy is now developing the Fleet Satellite Communications System, which will provide communications between ship and mobile ground terminals. An Air Force Satellite Communications System now also under development, will use navy satellites and the Satellite Data System as host satellites.

Navigation Satellites: The navy's Transit navigation satellite, in use since the early 1960s, was designed primarily to allow missile submarines to fix their positions at sea. By 1984 this will be replaced by the global positioning system, Navstar. Former Defense Secretary Schlesinger has said Navstar will provide the highly accurate position-fixing system needed to launch ICBMs from specially built aircraft.[14] Navstar will provide high accuracy for nuclear weapons attacks. It will also be used to synchronize the automated battlefield.

Meteorological Satellites: One important function of military weather satellites is to help predict cloud cover. This information can be used not only for planning bombing raids, but also for scheduling the flights of photoreconnaissance satellites.

Research and Development Satellites: These perform a variety of tasks, sometimes simultaneously, including radar calibration, oceanographic functions for the navy, and geodetic surveys for the Defense Mapping Agency and for targeting ICBMs.

Surveillance of Space

The North American Air Defense Command (NORAD) operates the Space Detection and Tracking System. This involves monitoring the more than 3,000 man-made objects now in orbit, including spent rocket casings and other debris. More than 4,000 objects that once were in space have fallen back into the atmosphere and burned.

Careful tracking of decayed payloads and debris is necessary to avoid setting off a false alarm in the missile-attack warning system. Another reason is the United Nations' space registration agreement, which holds a country liable for the damages caused by its returning "space junk."

Surveillance of space is an increasingly important military function. In 1975, as justification for additional money for surveillance of space, the Pentagon cited "the growing Soviet utilization of space for strategic and tactical purposes."[15] Studies are being made to determine whether the space detection system can serve as a warning against satellite attacks. Such a system could also be used, it is said, as a precursor to a space traffic control system. Satellite surveillance of space is also being considered, possibly using laser sensors, in order to monitor Soviet satellites.

U.S. Space Shuttle

After Apollo, the next generation of manned spacecraft will be the space shuttle—NASA's centerpiece—scheduled for readiness in 1980. With the shuttle, the manned space program is to take over the launching, servicing and recovery of both military and civilian satellites. Carrying a crew of seven for a maximum of 30 days, a shuttle-craft, about the size and shape of a transport aircraft, will return to earth and land like an airplane after placing satellites in orbit. The rest of the shuttle system will consist of an expandable fuel tank and two reusable boosters for lifting the shuttlecraft into low earth orbit.

The shuttle project, in effect, is a joint NASA-Defense Department effort, representing a significant step towards the unification of civilian and military space operations. The Pentagon plans extensive use of the system and the air force is responsible for the development of the system's upper-stage booster for taking satellites from the shuttlecraft and placing them in higher orbit. Although NASA is paying for nearly all the $6.3 billion in initial research and development costs, the Defense Department does plan to refurbish Vandenburg Air Force Base launch facilities in California for about $800 million and to purchase its own shuttlecraft at about $300-500 million each.[16]

In addition to ferrying military and civilian satellites, the shuttle could conceivably be used for reconnaissance as well as antisatellite purposes. A Soviet "spaceplane," which will fly cosmonauts to space stations, would have the same potential.

Soviet Space Programs are Growing

The Soviet military space program is similar in nature to that of the United States. Soviet military space launchings are now three to four times as frequent as U.S. launchings, [17] a reversal of the situation of the early 1960s, when the United States was launching three or four times as frequently. The launch figures are somewhat misleading because the largest single element of the Soviet space program involves Cosmos reconnaissance satellites. These spacecraft have an operational life span of only 12 to 14 days—compared to about three to four months for similar U.S. satellites—so they require more frequent launching to provide reasonably continuous reconnaissance. However, the number of Soviet launchings is impressive and indicates a strong drive to improve their space technology.

The Soviet manned programs include the Salyut space station program, begun in 1971. The Salyut is the Soviet counterpart to NASA's Skylab. Recent Salyut flights were probably equipped with high-resolution cameras for earth reconnaissance. The Soviets lag considerably behind the United States in the technology of manned space flight. This lag may be as much as 10-15 years, according to what has been learned in the preparations for the Apollo-Soyuz project.

The Soviets have experimented with a Fractional Orbital Bombardment System (FOBS). FOBS is, in effect, an extended ICBM, designed to escape detection by flying the long way around the world at a low, partial orbit. It uses an SS-9 as a launcher and was tested about 18 times before 1971. The United States considers FOBS to be unwieldy and unreliable and has not developed one.

Militarization of Space Is Expensive

Since 1959, when the U.S. space program began, about $85 billion has been spent on space programs. The Defense Department spent at least $26 billion. This year, the Pentagon has requested $2.2 billion for its space programs, but this does not include all military space expenditures. For example, the U.S. Air Force's budget request for fiscal 1976 contains a miscellaneous amount of $670 million under "Missile Procurement." When asked by Senator Stuart Symington about such a large figure, Air Force Secretary John McLucas at first attributed the amount to a secret Central Intelligence Agency budget entry. Later, he corrected the record to show

that the $670 million is being sought for secret Defense Department
space programs.[18]

Department of Defense space budgets itemize for navigation,
communications, mapping, early warning and weather satellites, but
contain no specific request for surveillance satellites that are presumed to be carried in a secret part of the budget. Any tabulation of
the costs of the military space program must also take into account
space hardware developed by the National Aeronautics and Space
Administration for use by the military, particularly the highly expensive manned spacecraft. Although the space shuttle system development costs will reach $6-8 billion, the Pentagon is paying only
about $150 million of these costs, even though the shuttle is being
designed for both military and civilian use. The total published space
budget for fiscal 1976 is $5.5 billion. Including the space shuttle
funds approved for NASA and the secret military programs, the
military space budget this year is $3.2 billion. The total life-cycle
costs, over 10 years, of Navstar is estimated to be at least $2.7
billion.

PEACEFUL USES OF SPACE?

Legislation and Treaties

In the National Aeronautics and Space Act of 1958, which established the U.S. space program, Congress declared that "it is the
policy of the United States that activities in space should be devoted
to peaceful purposes for the benefit of all mankind."[19] The 1967
United Nations Outer Space Treaty, ratified by 69 countries including
the United States and the Soviet Union, also calls for the peaceful
exploration and use of space. Article I specifies that the exploration
and use of outer space "shall be carried out for the benefit and in the
interests of all countries . . . irrespective of their degree of economic or scientific development, and shall be the province of all
mankind."[20] Article IV specifically bans placing nuclear weapons
and other "weapons of mass destruction" into orbit.[21] However,
neither the space act nor the treaty attempts to define the word
"peaceful." This creates a real problem in determining whether the
developing military space technology is devoted to peaceful purposes.

Dual Uses

An additional difficulty in making such a determination is that
military and civilian space programs are often intertwined. Many
satellites have dual uses, at least potentially. This dual aspect is
reinforced by U.S. legislation requiring that there be minimum duplication of space programs. Coordination between NASA and the Defense
Department is especially close during research and development. A
top air force official has explained that "Sharp definition of separate
roles for military and civilian space efforts has not always been
easy. In actual fact, the two programs have worked in close and
economical cooperation, sharing specially qualified manpower, and
the ever-broadening expertise that comes with experience."[22]

The Pentagon says that Navstar, which will "revolutionize"
warfare, will also be available to civilian users. Some commercial
shipping uses the navy's Transit navigation satellites, designed for
nuclear submarines; the navy is augmenting its tactical communications by leasing from civilian satellite facilities. The Department
of Defense and the National Oceanic and Atmospheric Administration
are planning compatible weather satellite systems.

In actuality, there is only one U.S. space program: it is a
combination of military and civilian components. Although data from
the NASA earth resources satellite are widely used and accepted internationally, they have no intended military use. Earth resources, part
of NASA's civilian applications program, has run into repeated difficulties with the Office of Management and Budget, despite major support in Congress. The space shuttle program, which was questioned
on economic grounds by the General Accounting Office, would probably now have funding difficulties in Congress if the Pentagon had not
assured extensive military use of the shuttle.[23]

Pinpointing Targets

While reconnaissance and early warning satellites have been
used to verify arms control agreements, the nuclear arms race has
not been slowed. Reconnaissance satellites may be useful in reducing
tensions by providing accurate information about strategic building
programs, but they are also used for pinpointing enemy targets.
Without precise target information the current counterforce doctrine
for fighting "limited" nuclear wars would not seem practicable.

Generally, it is unrealistic to speak of the peaceful uses of
military space technology as long as the superpowers are competi-

tively engaged in arming themselves with nuclear weapons that increasingly depend on space systems for their credible use. Nearly all satellite programs now being developed will facilitate nuclear as well as conventional warfare.

Space: A New Source of Danger

Military space systems have become central to the military operations of both superpowers and are probably taking the bulk of their space resources. These systems are converting space itself into a potential battleground, thus providing a new arena for superpower confrontation. The SALT agreements stipulate that neither side is to interfere with the other's satellite verification technology, essentially military intelligence satellites performing a dual purpose. However, the Outer Space Treaty, though designed as an arms control agreement for space, does not cover any of the military space activities, including the development of space weapons, now under way or being planned.

The rapid growth of very effective space technology is an important element in the belief among military planners that nuclear war is feasible, that such wars can be fought and "won." With particular relevance, Navstar, by increasing this country's ability to destroy Soviet ICBMs, strengthens the advocates of a nuclear warfighting strategy, who maintain that the Soviets are developing their own counterforce capability. Navstar is an example of advanced military technology that is fueling the nuclear arms competition and will potentially destabilize superpower relations.

In summary, current developments in military space technology contain two serious dangers: first, the possibility of an unchecked arms race in space, unless new arms-control efforts are undertaken; and second, an undermining of restraints surrounding the use of nuclear weapons. These dangers are not widely perceived today, but they are real and need to be addressed in U.S.-Soviet arms negotiations.

NOTES

1. U.S. Congress, Senate, Aeronautical and Space Sciences Committee, NASA Authorization FY 1976 and 197T (Washington, D.C.: Government Printing Office, February-March 1975), Part I, pp. 501-02. See also Aerospace Daily, April 11, 1975; and Lawrence

Griswold, "Lasers: Harnessed Lightning," Sea Power, September 1975, p. 16.

2. U.S. Congress, Senate, Armed Services Committee, Defense Department Authorizations FY 1976 and 197T (Washington, D.C.: Government Printing Office, March 1975), Part 6, p. 2707.

3. "Importance of 'Military' Space," Air Force, June 1975, p. 28.

4. Charles S. Sheldon II, United States and Soviet Progress in Space (Washington, D.C.: Library of Congress, Congressional Research Service, January 13, 1975), p. 38 ff.

5. Major John Duemmel, information officer, Office of the Secretary of the Air Force, Department of Defense, in a June 13, 1975 interview in Washington, D.C.

6. Senate, Aeronautical and Space Sciences Committee, op. cit.

7. Dr. Malcolm Currie, Senate, Armed Services Committee, op. cit., p. 2703.

8. Philip J. Klass, "Special Report: Laser Weapons—3, Current Systems Still More Cost-Effective," Aviation Week and Space Technology, September 8, 1975; see also "Industry Observer," Aviation Week, May 19, 1975, p. 11, and August 11, 1975, p. 13.

9. Charles S. Sheldon II, "The Soviet Space Program," Air Force, March 1975, p. 56.

10. Senate, Armed Services Committee, op. cit., p. 2708.

11. Ibid.

12. Ibid., p. 2707.

13. Interviews by the author with Major John Duemmel; Charles S. Sheldon II, chief of the Library of Congress' Science Policy Research Division; Philip Klass, senior editor, Aviation Week and Space Technology; and Richard Tuttle, managing editor, Aerospace Daily. All interviews in Washington, D.C., 1975.

14. Senate, Armed Services Committee, op. cit. (February 5, 1975), Part 1, p. 59.

15. Ibid., Part 6, p. 2704.

16. Senate, Aeronautical and Space Sciences Committee, op. cit., Part 1, pp. 92-94, 194, 501. Also, interviews with Dave Garrett and Dennis Williams, public affairs office of the National Aeronautics and Space Administration.

17. Sheldon, "The Soviet Space Program," op. cit.; see also "Tyuratam Test Facilities Dated," Aviation Week and Space Technology, June 2, 1975, p. 26.

18. Senate, Armed Services Committee, op. cit., pp. 498, 524.

19. National Aeronautics and Space Act of 1958, as amended, Sec. 102(a), Title I. U.S. Congress, Senate, Aeronautical and Space Sciences Committee, National Aeronautics and Space Act of 1958, As Amended, and Related Legislation, staff report, March 11, 1975.

20. Treaty on Principles Governing the Activities of States in the Exploration and Use of Outer Space, Including the Moon and Other Celestial Bodies, reproduced from Message of the President of the United States, executive document D, 90th Cong., 1st sess., February 7, 1967, pp. 15-19.

21. Ibid.

22. Lieutenant General Kenneth W. Schultz, "USAF's Conquest of Space," Air Force, August 1974, p. 38.

23. Congressional Record, April 25, 1974, p. H3217.

AAH (advanced attack helicopter), 228, 230, 233
A-7, 226, 228, 230
A-10, 228-31
A-18, 226
ABM (see, Antiballistic Missile System)
Abshire, David, 83
accuracy of nuclear weapons, 83, 130, 131-33, 140
Advanced Research Project Agency (ARPA), 207
AEC (see, Atomic Energy Commission)
Aerospace Daily, 210-11
aircraft carriers, 90, 179; Constellation, 82; Hancock, 84; Oriskany, 84
air force: aircraft, 222; tactical wings, 217 (see also, TACAIR)
Air Force Magazine, 210, 212
air refueling tanker, 105
air-to-air missile: Phoenix, 105, 220
air-to-surface missiles: Maverick, 105, 203; TOW, 228; Walleye, 179
airlift, NATO-Warsaw Pact comparisons, 33
Alsop, Joseph, 93
Antiballistic Missile System (ABM), 123, 145
anticommunism, 7-8
antisatellite satellite, 238
antitank weapons, 32; TOW missiles, 32, 103, 125, 203; Dragon missiles, 32
Apollo-Soyuz, 237

Armed Forces Journal, 205-06
Armed Services Committee: House, 47; Senate, 20, 22
Arms Control and Disarmament Agency (ACDA), 93
army division, 216
Army magazine, 32, 204
Asia, 180; cost of U.S. forces, 45; U.S. tactical nuclear weapons, 182-83 (see also, Japan; Korea; Northeast Asia; Southeast Asia)
ASROC (Antisubmarine Rocket), 179
assured destruction, 141-43, 144
attack helicopter, 105
Atkinson, Edward, 32
atomic demolition munitions, 178
Atomic Energy Commission (AEC), 147, 198
Aviation Week, 206, 213-14
avionics, 220-21
AWACS (Airborne Warning and Control System), 20, 123-24, 229, 231

bargaining chips, 146
B-1 bomber, 119-20, 166, 174; costs of, 166, 172-74; versus B-52, 169-70
B-26 bomber, 102
B-52 bomber, 86
Backfire bomber, 171
Ball, George, 9
battlefield sensors, 204-05
Bayh, Birch, 124
Belgium, 22, 25
Bell helicopter, 106
Berman, Robert, 209

bombers, 167-69
bombing, 14
Bradford, Zeb, 46
Brehm, William, 22, 29
British Vampire, 102
Brodie, Bernard, 21
Brookings Institution, 126
Brown, George, 13, 14, 27, 67, 72, 131, 134, 226

C-5A transport, 33, 86
C-130, 223
C-141 transport, 33
Cambodia, 11
Camp Casey, Korea, 47
Canby, Steven L., 223-24
Captor, 208
Case, Clifford, 93
Central Intelligence Agency (CIA), 91-92, 109
CEP (Circular Error of Probability), 131, 132, 140
Chafee, John, 83
Chieftain tanks, 103
Chile, 8
China (see, People's Republic of China)
Chrysler Corporation, 116
Civil Reserve Air Fleet (CRAF), 33
Clements, William, 127
close air support, 222
Colby, William, 90
cold war, 5, 6, 24
Collins, Harold, 135
Commanders Digest, 205
communications satellite, 240
Conference on Security and Co-operation, 24
Constellation aircraft carrier, 82
conventional forces, 17, 18, 20; costs, 19-21 (see also, TACAIR)
Cooksey, Howard H., 32

cost: B-1 bomber, 119-20, 166, 172-74; conventional forces, 18-21; U.S. forces in Asia, 45; forces in Europe, 17, 18-20; U.S. forces in Korea, 45, 46-48; U.S. forces in Vietnam, 17 (see also, individual weapon systems; Defense, Department of, budget)
cost overruns, 220
counterforce, 122, 141-44
cruise missile, 122, 140, 208-09
Culber, John, 93
Currie, Malcolm R., 202-03, 210, 211, 228, 237, 238
Czechoslovakia, 25, 31

DD-963 destroyer, 105, 107
Davidson, Michael, 30
Defense, Department of, 11, 17, 30, 34, 82, 93, 162, 198, 236, 237, 241, 244; budget, 7, 17, 19-21, 33, 85-86, 115-27, 217
Defense Marketing Service (DMS), 205
Delta submarine, 158
Denmark, 23, 30
deterrence, 20, 21, 47, 50, 159
Diego Garcia, 82-83, 84, 85-87, 91, 103; costs, 86; functions, 85-87; U.S. policy, 93-94
Donahue, Robert, 220
Dragon antitank missile, 32

EC-135 aircraft, 86
early warning satellite, 239
Enthoven, Alain, 185
equivalent megatonnage (EMT), 135-39
escalation ladder, 186
escalation of nuclear war, 185-88
essential equivalence, 129, 141, 143, 144
Europe, 12, 23, 24, 25, 91, 92, 109, 110, 189; effects of nuclear

[Europe] war, 180–81; U.S. land
    forces, 16–21; nuclear wea-
    pons, 14, 123–26, 180–81
European Economic Community,
    23

F–4 fighter, 49, 53, 65, 103,
    107, 227
F–5 fighter, 220
F–5E fighter, 49, 106
F–14 fighter, 20, 103, 107, 126,
    227, 229, 232
F–15 fighter, 20, 126, 229–31
F–16 fighter, 22, 126, 229–31
F–18 fighter, 106, 126, 231–32
F–86 fighter, 102
F–104 Starfighter, 65
Faisal, King, 104
Ford, Gerald, 4, 11, 13, 17,
    25, 149
Fractional Orbital Bombardment
    System, 242
France, 30, 102, 110; arms
    sales, 102
Fraser, Donald, 84
Frog missile, 187
FS–T2 plane, 65

General Accounting Office (GAO),
    124–26
General Dynamics, 116
General Motors, 116
Germany: Berlin, 24; East
    Germany, 25; West Germany,
    25, 31
Goldwater, Barry, 222–23
Goodpaster, Andrew, 24, 35
Graham, William, 204
Greece, 8, 197

Halperin, Morton, 184
Hamilton, Lee, 93
Hancock aircraft carrier, 84
Harrington, Michael, 118
Harris, Louis: poll, 46–47

Hawk missile, 103, 105
Heilmeier, George, 220
helicopters, 228 (see also, AAH;
    air-to-surface missiles)
Hercules troop-transport, 105
Hirohito, Emperor, 62
Hiroshima (see, Japan)
Hiroshima equivalents, 135
Holloway, James, 88
Honest John missile, 178, 181
Houser, William P., 226
hovercraft (see, surface effect
    ships)
howitzer, 178
Hughes Aircraft, 106
Human Reliability Program, 198
Hungary, 31

ICBM (intercontinental ballistic
    missile), 121–22, 136, 137,
    159, 161, 162, 167, 209
Ikle, Fred, 121, 161
India, 89, 93, 95, 107; nuclear
    explosion of, 105
India–Pakistan War, 83
Indian Ocean, 5, 6, 86, 89, 93, 94;
    military presence, 82–85, 91–92,
    94–95; Soviet naval threat, 87–
    92
Indochina, 4, 8, 12, 14
Ingersoll, Robert, 69–70
Iran, 31, 82, 100, 103–04, 105–11;
    weapons, 105–08; Shah, 108,
    109, 110
Iraq, 89, 92, 95, 104, 105
Israel, 92, 104, 108
Italy, 8

Jackson–Nunn amendment, 21
Jane's All the World's Aircraft,
    213
Jane's Surface Skimmers, 208
Japan, 12, 42, 45–46, 91, 109;
    Air Self-Defense Force (ASDF),
    64, 68; Fourth Five-Year

Defense Plan, 68; Ground Self-
Defense Force (GSDF), 68;
Hiroshima, 177; and Korea,
66-67, 177; Maritime Self-
Defense Force (MSDF), 65;
military budget, 62, 68;
Nagasaki, 177; nuclear weapons, 69-70; U.S. relations,
62-63, 71, 75; self-defense
force (SDF), 64-65, 67
Jones, David C., 22, 27-28, 31,
32
Jordan, 105
jumbo-jet transport, 105

K (hard target killing power), 131
Kahn, Herman, 186
KC-135 tanker, 86
Kennedy, Edward, 93
Khlestov, O., 27
Kim Il Sung, 50, 67
Kissinger, Henry A., 4, 5, 6,
7, 8, 10, 12, 92, 93, 121,
131, 160-61, 162
Korea, 43, 46, 47, 51, 52 (see
also, North Korea; South
Korea)
Korean War, 72
Kuwait, 99, 103, 108, 110

Lance missile, 178, 181
La Rocque, Gene, 69
laser cannons, 203-04
Light Weight Fighter, 220 (see
also, F-16, F-18)
Lukasik, Stephen, 207, 213
Luxembourg, 25

Mack, William, 10
Mansfield, Mike, 23, 84, 93
Maneuverable Re-entry Vehicles
(MARV), 140
Mark 57, 179
Mark 101, 179
Maverick missile, 105, 203

Mayazawa, Kiichi, 66
Mayaguez incident, 4, 5, 11
MBFR (see, Mutual Balanced
Force Reduction Talks)
McCain, John, 84
McClellan, John, 19, 118
McIntyre, Thomas, 122, 123, 174
McLucas, John, 119, 126
McNamara, Robert, 141, 143
Marine Corps, 226-27
Mediterranean Sea, 89, 94
megatonnage, 135, 136, 137, 138
meteorological satellite, 240
Michael, Louis, 26
Middendorf, William J., 121
Middle East, 5, 83, 99, 103
Middle East War, 32, 82, 84,
187, 223
Mig 21 bomber, 102
Miki, Takeo, 62, 66
Miki-Ford Joint Announcement, 70
military aid, 11, 99, 102; arms
sales, 99, 102, 110-11, 116
(see also, France; Persian Gulf;
United Kingdom; United States
arms sales)
Military Airlift Command, 33
Military Review, 46
military satellite, 237
Mill, John Stuart, 12
Milton, T. R., 35
minicomputer, 135
Minuteman ICBM (see, ICBM)
MIRV (Multiple Independently
targeted Re-entry Vehicles),
135, 147, 149, 156 (see also,
ICBM)
Mishima, Yukio, 68
Moorer, Thomas, 89
Moynihan, Daniel, 93
Murphy Commission, 7
Murray, Robert, 29
Mutsu, 69
Mutual Balanced Force Reduction
Talks (MBFR), 25-26, 29, 34-
36, 189

National Aeronautics and Space
  Administration (NASA), 241,
  243-44
NASA Act of 1958, 243
National Defense magazine, 200,
  210
navigation satellite, 240
Navstar, 211-213, 238-39, 240,
  244, 245
Netherlands, 23, 25
New Frontier, 93
Newhouse, John, 131
New York Times, 8
Niedenfuhr, Francis, 206
Nike-Hercules missile, 178
Nixon, Richard M., 25
Nixon-Brezhnev agreement, 145
Nonproliferation Treaty, 70
North American Air Defense
  Command (NORAD), 240
North Atlantic Treaty Organiza-
  tion (NATO), 8, 24; GNP of,
  23; and MBFR, 25-26; supreme
  commander of, 190; U.S.
  forces, 17-22; and Warsaw
  Pact comparisons, 26-34; war
  games, 185; weapons, 23, 27,
  32, 182
Northeast Asia, 42, 45
North Korea: military balance
  with South Korea, 48-50
Northrop Corporation, 106, 220
North Vietnam, 42
North West Cape, 85
Norway, 23
nuclear accidents, 198-99
nuclear artillery, 178
nuclear forces, 130, 188; number
  of, 130-34; sea-based, 134
  (see also, strategic nuclear
  forces; tactical nuclear forces)
nuclear missile submarine, 153-
  65
nuclear sufficiency, 139
nuclear war, 186-88; scenarios,
  134

Office of Federal Procurement,
  221
Office of Management and Budget
  (OMB), 221
OPEC (Organization of Petroleum
  Exporting Countries), 110
Operation Sagebrush, 185
Oriskany aircraft carrier, 84

P-3C patrol aircraft, 65, 86, 105
Packard, David, 217
Pahlavi, Mohammed Reza, 104,
  108, 110
Pakistan, 82, 95
Park Chung Hee, 44, 56, 57
Peking, 51
People's Republic of China (PRC),
  8, 14, 24, 42, 51, 57
Pell, Claiborne, 93
Pershing missile, 178, 181
Persian Gulf, 6, 11, 82, 83, 84,
  85, 86, 91-92, 94, 109, 110,
  111; arms sales, 99, 102-04,
  110, 111; military budget, 99;
  governments, 104; weapons,
  102
Phalanx gun, 208
Philippines, 197
Phoenix air-to-air missile, 105
Polaris submarine, 85, 157
Portugal, 8, 197
Poseidon missile, 155-56, 157
Poseidon submarine, 85, 157
Precision Guided Munitions: artil-
  lery shell, 203; smart bombs,
  28, 203-04 (see also, Maverick;
  TOW)

RAND Corporation, 14
Reischauer, Edwin, 45-46, 56
REMBASS (Remotely Monitored
  Battlefield Sensor System), 205
research and development satellite,
  240
Resor, Stanley, 26

Richardson, Elliot, 31, 133
Rockwell International, 116
Rostow, Eugene, 6
Ruina, Jack, 146
Rumsfeld, Donald, 129n, 131
Russell, Richard, 84

SALT (see, Strategic Arms Limitation Talks)
Salyut, 242
satellites (see, individual satellites)
Saudi Arabia, 95, 99, 102, 104, 105, 108, 110
Schlesinger, James, 4, 6, 14, 17, 18, 20, 22, 25, 28, 30, 31, 33, 34, 35, 44, 48, 50, 62, 63, 67, 84, 86, 89, 91, 92, 93, 121, 122, 134, 141, 144, 161, 172, 184, 186, 217, 224, 230, 240
Schmidt, Helmut, 23-24
Scud missile, 187
Seapower, 85
Secretary of Defense, 221 (see also, Rumsfeld, Donald; Schlesinger, James)
Seignious, George, 21
Sergeant missile, 178, 181
Seventh Fleet, 89, 94
SIAM (Self-Initiating Antiaircraft Munition), 207-08
Sidorenko, A. A., 182
Sixth Fleet, 94
smart bombs (see, Precision Guided Munitions)
Somalia, 89, 92
SOSUS (Sound Surveillance Under Sea), 163, 205
South Korea, 43, 46, 57; military balance with North Korea, 48-50; relations with Japan, 66-67; military forces in, 43, 46, 53-55; U.S. nuclear weapons in, 43, 51, 183; and Vietnam, 56

Southeast Asia, 99
southern Africa, 83
Soviet Union, 7, 8, 42, 51, 65, 92, 102, 106, 109; arms sales, 99, 102; fighter interceptor aircraft, 171-72; Indian Ocean, 87-90; Navy, 87-90; space program, 241; tactical nuclear weapons, 182; threat, 23-24; and U.S. strategic nuclear balance, 129-30, 131, 133, 140, 141
space, 236-37; costs, 242; peaceful uses, 243-44
space program, 236
space shuttle, 241
Sparkman, John, 119
Spiers, Ronald, 83
SR-71 aircraft, 86
Staats, Elmer, 221
State, Department of, 11, 93
Stennis, John, 93-94
Stone, Jeremy, 134
Straits of Hormuz, 91, 107, 109
Strategic Arms Limitation Talks (SALT), 24, 145, 146, 147, 150; SALT I, 145; Vladivostok, 121, 133, 146, 147, 148-51, 161
strategic nuclear forces, 143, 154, 168, 177; U.S./USSR balance, 117-20, 131, 133, 136, 137, 138, 139, 140
SUBROC missile (antisubmarine rocket), 179
Suez Canal, 89-92
Sullivan, Leonard, 17-18, 26, 45, 47, 62, 220
surface-to-air missile (SAM), 187
surface-to-surface missile, 181
surveillance satellite, 239-40
Symington, Stuart, 90, 93

tactical aircraft (TACAIR), 126-27, 216, 217, 220, 222-33;

[tactical aircraft] acquisition
  costs, 218-19; life-cycle
  costs, 220
tactical nuclear forces, 176-77,
  188; in Asia, 182-83, 189; in
  Europe, 180-81, 182, 184,
  189, 190; at sea, 183-84; in
  U.S., 177-80, 184; unauthorized use of, 198; forces overseas, 196-97; U.S./USSR
  comparisons, 181-82; in
  USSR, 182
Talos missile, 179
Tang-class submarine, 105
tanks, 125; NATO-Warsaw Pact
  comparisons, 32
Terrain Contour Matching, 210
Terrier missile, 179
terrorists, 177, 195-96
theater nuclear forces (see,
  tactical nuclear forces)
Threshold Test Ban Treaty, 147
throw weight, 120, 134-35
TOW missile, 32, 103, 203
transport helicopter, 105
Treaty of Mutual Cooperation
  and Security, 63, 71
Trident submarine, 120, 158-59
Tsipis, Kosta, 209-10
Turkey, 8, 79

United Kingdom, 30, 79, 84, 102,
  103, 197; arms sales, 99, 102
United Nations outer space treaty,
  243

United Nations Security Council,
  75
United States arms sales, 6, 11,
  99, 100, 102, 103, 104, 106,
  110, 115
USSR, 90 (see, Soviet Union)

vertical proliferation, 129
Vietnam, 56; North Vietnam, 14,
  42; South Vietnam, 45, 56
Vietnam War, 22, 56, 87, 201,
  219; cost, 17; lessons of, 4-14;
  weapons, 13-14
Vladivostok (see, SALT)
Vogt, John, 224

Walleye missile, 179
War Powers Act, 10-11
Warsaw Pact, 14, 23; GNP, 23;
  MBFR, 25-27; and NATO com-
  parisons, 26-34
Watergate, 11
Westmoreland, William, 201
Weyand, Fred C., 18, 27, 32
White, Theodore, 9
Wilson, Louis H., 227
World War II, 5
World War II equivalents, 135-36

XM-I tank, 20, 125

Yemen, 89, 92
Yom Kippur War (see, Middle East
  War)

Zumwalt, Elmo, 87, 91, 94

GENE R. LA ROCQUE is director of the Center for Defense Information in Washington, D.C. A retired U.S. Navy Rear Admiral, he served on the Strategic Plans Staff of the Joint Chiefs of Staff for over two years. Admiral La Rocque commanded the Sixth Fleet's Fast Carrier Task Force Group (Mediterranean). After teaching at the Naval War College, he became director of the Inter-American Defense College. During his 31 years in the U.S. Navy, Admiral La Rocque was cited for participation in 13 major naval engagements. He holds the Legion of Merit, the Bronze Star, the Navy Commendation Medal, and other medals.

DAVID T. JOHNSON is director of research at the Center for Defense Information and has been with the CDI since its inception. He served on the staff of Congressman Michael Harrington with the House Armed Services Committee. Mr. Johnson has served as military analyst for the Friends Committee on National Legislation. He has done graduate work in Chinese and Russian studies at Harvard University.

BARRY R. SCHNEIDER is a consultant and former staff associate of the Center for Defense Information. He is currently the arms control and military affairs consultant to 175 Members of Congress for Peace through Law. Dr. Schneider, who received his Ph.D. in International Relations from Columbia University, has taught at Indiana University, the University of Maryland, Purdue University, and Wabash College.

ROBERT BERMAN is a defense analyst at the Brookings Institution. He was formerly a staff associate at the Center for Defense Information. Mr. Berman holds a degree in political science from American University and has also attended Oxford University. In 1974, he spent two months in Iran surveying the military buildup. Mr. Berman has contributed to Soviet Naval Developments (New York: Praeger Publishers, 1973) and Soviet Naval Policy (New York: Praeger Publishers, 1975).

STEFAN H. LEADER is a staff associate at the Center for Defense Information. Dr. Leader received his Ph.D. from the State University of New York at Buffalo. He has taught in the fields of

Chinese politics, revolution and revolutionary movements, international conflict, and American foreign policy. Dr. Leader was a research associate with the Peace Studies Program at Cornell University. He is a contributor to Nuclear Proliferation in the Near Nuclear Countries (Cambridge, Mass.: Ballinger, 1976). His articles have appeared in the Far East Economic Review, the Los Angeles Times, Newsday, and other publications.

PHIL STANFORD is a former staff associate at the Center for Defense Information. Mr. Stanford has been a newspaper reporter and editor, and he has had articles published in several national magazines. Before joining the CDI, he was a legislative aide to Congressman Les Aspin.

DENNIS F. VERHOFF is a staff associate at the Center for Defense Information. Dr. Verhoff received his Ph.D. in Political Science from the Ohio State University and was a Public Affairs Fellow at Stanford University. He served as a Peace Corps volunteer in Tunisia from 1965-67. Dr. Verhoff, formerly a research associate at the American Enterprise Institute for Public Policy Research, has served on the staff of Senator James Abourezk.

ROBERT W. WHITAKER is a senior consultant at the Center for Defense Information. A retired U.S. Air Force Colonel, his last assignment was as Chief of Staff, Headquarters, U.S. Air Forces in Europe. Colonel Whitaker was a member of the Policy Planning Staff of the Department of Defense, and exchange officer with the Department of State. He was also a professor of Political Science at the U.S. Air Force Academy. Duty in the Air Staff and as a political military affairs officer in Europe are among his other assignments. He holds the Legion of Merit, the Meritorious Service Medal, and both the U.S. Army and Air Force Commendation Medals. Colonel Whitaker received his Ph.D. in Political Science from the University of Colorado. He has received two other advanced degrees from the University of California.

JAMES WILLIS is a staff associate at the Center for Defense Information. Mr. Willis was a State Department foreign service officer from 1956-69, and was stationed in the Middle East and Latin America. He has taught International Relations at Fordham University and at the New York State School of Labor and Industrial Relations.

THE ECONOMICS OF PEACETIME DEFENSE
          Murray L. Weidenbaum

INTERNATIONAL TERRORISM: National, Regional,
and Global Perspectives
               edited by Yonah Alexander

MIRV AND THE ARMS RACE: An Interpretation of
Defense Strategy
               Ronald L. Tammen

THE UNITED STATES AND MILITARISM IN
CENTRAL AMERICA
               Don L. Etchison